/

Don't Push the River

(it flows by itself) 1970.

Barry (*Stevens*)

Other useful books from Real People Press:

EMBRACE TIGER, RETURN TO MOUNTAIN: the essence of T'ai Chi, by *Al Chung-liang Huang.* Huang learned T'ai Chi Chuan from many teachers—as a child in China, and later in Taiwan. In his teaching he reverses the traditional way and conveys the essence and process of T'ai Chi first, with the form (Chuan) coming in easily and naturally later. The essence of T'ai Chi is a way of living as well as a way of moving. This book is compiled from tapes of his workshops at Esalen and other growth centers and his university classes in dance. It includes some instruction in calligraphy and interpretation of the *Tao te Ching,* as well as showing how T'ai Chi can become a part of every facet of life. Illustrated. 250 pp. 1973 Cloth $7.00 Paper $3.50

PERSON TO PERSON, by *Carl Rogers and Barry Stevens.* Professional papers by Rogers and others—about therapy, experiencing and learning—are set in a matrix of personal response and the use that Barry Stevens has made of these papers in arriving at better understanding of herself, and her view of the problem of being human as she has encountered it in her life. 276 pp. 1967 Cloth $4.50 Paper $3.00

GESTALT THERAPY VERBATIM, by *Frederick S. Perls.* The originator and developer of Gestalt Therapy gives a clear explanation in simple terms of the basic ideas underlying this method, which at the same time makes a contribution to existential philosophy. This is followed by verbatim transcripts of complete therapy sessions, with explanatory comments. 280 pp. 1969 Cloth $5.00 Paper $3.50

IN AND OUT THE GARBAGE PAIL, by *Frederick S. Perls.* A novel autobiography in which he applies his theory of focusing on awareness, and writes "whatever wants to be written." Partly in poetic form, often playful, sometimes theoretical, the book is a many-faceted mosaic of memories and reflections on his life—in the past and at the moment—and on the origins and continuing development of Gestalt Therapy. Illustrated. 280 pp. 1969 Cloth $7.00 Paper $4.00

NOTES TO MYSELF, by *Hugh Prather.* Cogent and incisive short paragraphs, personal yet general, about living: feelings and experiences, behavior and relationships. These serve both as beginnings for the reader's exploration of his own experiences, and as thoughtful and insightful reminders about them. 150 pp. 1970 Cloth $4.00 Paper $2.00

AWARENESS, by *John Stevens,* Detailed instructions lead you through more than a hundred experiments in exploring your awareness of yourself, your surroundings, and your interaction with others. These experiments—based on Gestalt Therapy and developed in the classroom and in groups—give you actual experience with methods that you can use further, either as teacher, group leader, or on your own, to work through difficulties and get more in touch with your own flow of experiencing. 276 pp. 1971 Cloth $7.00 Paper $3.50

The name *Real People Press* indicates our purpose: to publish ideas and ways that a person can use independently to become more *real*—to further his own growth as a human being and to develop his relationships and communication with others.

4   5   6   7   8   9   10   printing   75   74   73

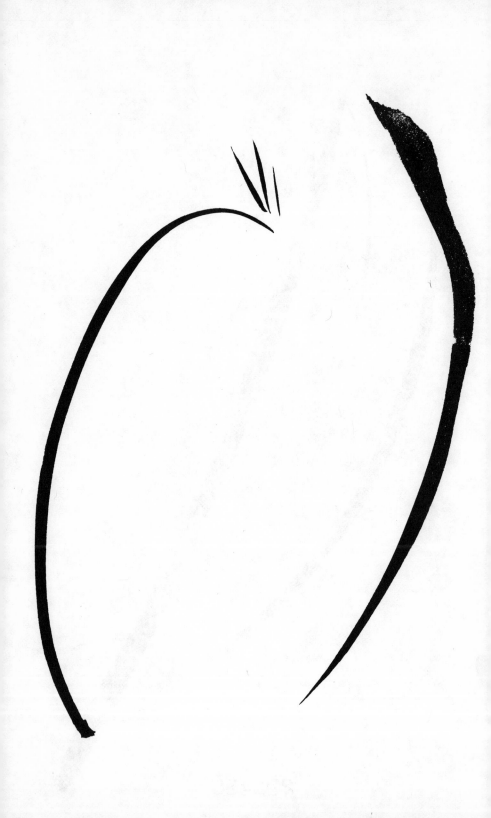

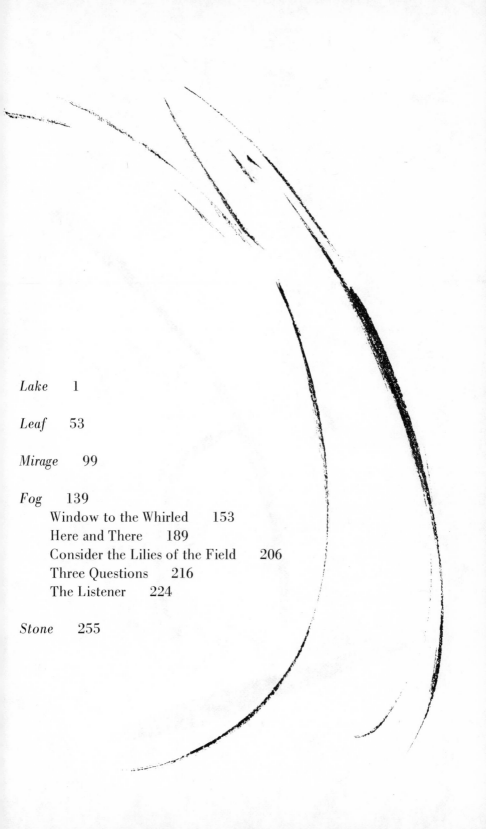

Lake

Lake Cowichan, B. C. Three months before 1970. Some spots of blue sky and light-filled clouds. Mostly heavy grey clouds about to fall into the cold rippling lake. Dry rustling maple trees on the lawns. Wheat-tasseled grasses blowing. Across the lake, all the trees look still.

A strangeness is going on in me. I don't know what I want. . . . As soon as I wrote that, I knew.

In October 1967, my son sent me an application form and a letter saying, "Sign up! You won't regret it." I signed up, for a five-day week of mornings, 9 to 12, in San Francisco, with a man named Fritz Perls, at the Gestalt Institute. I had no idea what I was getting into.

On Monday morning fifteen of us met with Fritz, in a large bare room at the Dancers' Workshop. Some other group was occupying the room at the Institute, which was the attic of Janie Rhyne's house. At the Dancers' Workshop room, some daylight came in through a door in a far corner, which opened into another room which had windows. There was a large, somewhat comfortable chair for Fritz. The rest of us sat on unfolding chairs. Fritz said, "I find it difficult to feel intimate in this room." We were a small circle of

1

people in a lot of bare space. My feet were cold. I wished I had worn wool stockings and boots instead of bare feet and sandals.

Fritz asked us each to say how we felt about the room. Everyone felt cold, one way or another. One woman wanted us all to move to her apartment. Fritz asked us how we felt about that, and we didn't want it.

That's all I feel like writing about that, now. Two years later, it seems so far, far away, and I am now at the Gestalt Institute of Canada on Lake Cowichan, B. C.

When Fritz was working with people in San Francisco, I got more and more mystified. Clearly, he knew what he was doing. Clearly, very often he got good results. But how the devil was he doing it?

Now I know, and I miss the mystification. Sometimes I get it back by doing what he did, although it comes out different because it is me. When that happens, I feel very, very good.

Once, I told Fritz why I didn't want to do what he had told each of us, in turn, to do. Then I thought, maybe there's some value in this that I don't see, and asked him, "Do you want me to do it anyway?" He said nothing. Like an Indian, he said it altogether. There wasn't one part of him anywhere that was saying anything. It was up to me.

Another time, when I was about to take the hot seat, I noticed a folder containing some of his manuscript on the chair on which I was to sit. I said, "Am I supposed to sit on it, or take it off?" He said, "You are asking me."

Both times, I had to decide for myself. I don't do so much asking now. This brings some of my power back into me.

A friend who teaches seventh and eighth grades in a school on the California desert switched from having her students say, "May I get my paper from your desk?" to "I'm coming to the desk and get my paper." The whole class livened up.

When I was small, I used to see a vision of the world, with people sticking out all over it sort of like straight-up hairs from a head, and each of the people was bowing to someone else. *All* of them. *Nobody* was doing what *he* wanted to. In such a world, *everyone* was left out. This was no world for me. Blackness shot with painful sparks and fire went on in my head. I didn't want to live in this world and I had to.

When I say "Please may I?" I may *think* that I am ladylike and superior. At the same time, I *feel* inferior, weak, pleading, at the other person's mercy. The other has my life in his hands. I lose my sense of *I*, in bowing to you. When I just *do* it (not rudely), I feel strong. My power is in me. Where else should *my* power be?

Of course, I may get thrown out.

Fritz was giving a demonstration in a high school auditorium. A fellow got up and made the usual announcement about no smoking, fire regulations, and so on. After the demonstration, a young woman asked Fritz, who had smoked all through, as usual, "What right do *you* have to go on smoking, when some of us have our tongues out for a cigarette?"

Fritz said, "I don't have the right to, and I don't have the right not to—I just do it."

Young woman: "But suppose you get thrown out?"

Fritz: "I get thrown out."

Horrors! All those people looking at me as a person being thrown out. I never fully understand introjection and projection, so I may be wrong, but it seems to me that I have introjected the notion that it is bad to be thrown out and then project this on others. For of course I don't know how many of those people might have looked at me that way, and how many might have envied me for doing what I wanted to do regardless—plus other notions which I haven't thought of. When I am centered in myself, none of them matter.

When I was young, I knew this. My Aunt Alice had a place at the beach. That beach was a magical place for me, with wind blowing, sun shining or clouds scudding, surf booming . . . booming its own rhythm through everything. White white sea shells. Golden shining sea shells. Miles of white beach. Sand dunes that shifted all the time. Sedge grass. Redwing blackbirds. Tiny puff adders. Sometimes a blue heron swaying on an elder bush. Everything was singing there. I was singing there, even when I made no sound. *Agito, ergo sum.*

One summer, I was fourteen. Aunt Alice went away and left me with a young man of twenty-six whom I didn't like. He was one of her toadies. He was also a snake-in-the-grass. He said that "Mrs. B." had told him that I would cook for him, and it seemed to me likely that she had. I wasn't going to cook for him. I told him so. All my joy would go if I cooked for him, which he could do for himself. He kept bugging me about it. I wouldn't do it. Maybe when Aunt Alice came back, she would throw me out—send me home—but if I cooked for Ruddy while hating him, and hating doing it, I would be filled with hate and not enjoy the beach *now*. I enjoyed the beach *now*, and that couldn't be taken away.

I am getting back just a little of this, now. Loving Lake Cowichan, and if I can't stay on *my* terms, I won't be loving it, and being thrown out is okay.

I have got back to feeling strange. I don't know what my terms are.

I wrote something last week in California that I feel like putting in here:

Before I sat down at the typewriter this morning, so much was going on in my head. Now I sit at the typewriter and nothing comes.

I am sitting on a porch looking through a window at the interior of the house with the garden behind me reflected in it. Where my body cuts off the reflection, I see a table—half a table. It ends where my own reflection ends, and becomes lawns and plants and trees with here and there a table leg, a counter, or a wall. I like this mixed-upness. Nothing solid. No separation of "in" and "out."

"I am so frustrated in trying to convey that Gestalt is not *rules*," Fritz said one morning in a group at Lake Cowichan.

"He's new at the job but he's doing fine." Read it, notice what you get from it. Change "but" to "and." "He's new at the job and he's doing fine." Read that, grasp it, and it's nothing. *Do* it a few times now and then, and it becomes a part of me. Do it *all* the time, like a rule, and it becomes nothing again.

Use whatever is at hand.

A young man had taken the hot seat and worked on the problem of his impotence as freely as though we were not there. Two days later, he took the hot seat again, wriggled around, said, "I'm embarrassed. All those people looking at me." Fritz got up and went into an alcove. He came back with a stack of leaflets, gave them to the person nearest him. Each person took one, and passed the rest along. Each person began reading the leaflet, which was a reprint of a Fritz paper. The young man said, "Now I'm mad at all those people reading that paper instead of looking at me!" He laughed. "Funny kind of embarrassment!"

He was made aware of something he hadn't been aware of.

"Learning is discovery."

"Even if I am right in my interpretation, if I tell him, I rob him of the opportunity to discover for himself."

In Canada, an official of the Bureau of Indian Affairs was on a ferry with Wilfred Pelletier, Indian. The government man went out on deck and as he went out the door, his hat was almost blown away by the wind. He knew that Wilfred was following, was about to warn him, and then didn't. Wilfred came out and his hat was blown away. He said, "Why didn't you tell me?" The government man said, "I was about to, but then I remembered that Indians don't tell people. They let them find out for themselves." Wilfred bent double with laughter. "You'll be an Indian yet!"

Wilfred was not Indian in letting his hat be blown away. He didn't notice. He wasn't self-reliant. He wasn't aware.

One bird is scolding, "ch-ch-ch-ch-ch." Another bird is trilling soft whistling sounds. Each is each. Neither one is trying to be the other. The mockingbird takes the songs and sounds of many birds and makes them his own, and that is *his* each.

I pause. I notice pain in my chest, light and tender and pain-full. What shall I do with it? Let what happens happen. My breathing becomes deeper, stronger. Then lighter, again. There is water in my eyes. . . . Not trying to understand it, just noticing what happens, I begin to understand in a way that is not transmissible to others. It is my own knowing.

. . . . Now I have gone into autism: thoughts, images and scenes and planning what I will do when—which is not what I will do at all. Unaware. Not noticing. No birds, no songs, no trees, no mixed-up indoors/outdoors—no nothing but what is going on in my head, no connection with reality. Not even noticing the pain where the edge of the chair and my thighs come together. Unaware of the pain in my chest and other places.

That "now" is like all nows, already gone when I begin to notice it. Already it has changed to something else.

Does anyone know the story of Epaminondas? He was a little boy who tried to be good and always made mistakes. I don't remember how he brought home the butter, but it was all melted and useless. His grandmother told him he should have put cool leaves in his hat, and cool water in it, and brought home the butter in that. Next time, it was a tiny puppy he was bringing home. He remembered his grandmother's instructions. The puppy drowned. His grandmother told him how he should have brought the puppy home, and next time he did that, but it wasn't a puppy and that didn't come out right either. And so on.

I have remembered what I got from that story for sixty years. I thought of it when a young woman took me to an airport, and was insistent that she stay until she was sure that I got off all right. She said she had taken two people to the airport with their four children and went off, "and they had to wait twelve hours!"

What did that have to do with me?

I was alone, and sometimes when everything goes wrong, wonderful things happen and I enjoy what I would have missed if everything had gone smoothly. If not, I can sleep.

I don't enjoy being treated as if I were somebody else. I feel as though I weren't there.

This sunny September noon, talking with a young woman on the lawn, Christmas came in somehow. She said she didn't like Christmas but she went along with it because she did like parts of it, like making cookies and giving them to the neighbors.

"Why hitch that to Christmas?"

"You mean, do it any time of year?" She sounded and looked excited.

("It's not the chains that bind men's bodies, but the chains that bind men's minds.")

6

One year, I sent out Christmas cards in June. Lots of people enjoyed getting Christmas cards in June. Many more than enjoy getting them at Christmas.

When I was sick and broke, someone sent me a care package of miscellaneous stuff. There was a whole box of birthday cards in it. I don't remember when anyone's birthday is and usually forget my own. I "never" send birthday cards. But I had them, so whenever I thought of someone I liked and hadn't heard from in some time, I sent a birthday card. Quite a few people wrote me of their enjoyment.

Three people remember my birthday and send me a birthday card each year. I am bored.

A bird just lighted on a branch behind me. Now he's on the lawn, and I see he is a robin. Does it matter what kind of bird he is? I like seeing him in the reflection, seeing something behind me instead of always in front of me. There is a Bates-Huxley eye-training experiment in which you close your eyes and look at a spot at the base of your skull, where it changes to neck. It's very releasing. When I do it, I realize how my eyes have been pushing forward forward forward. Reversals are a part of Gestalt. Breaking some of the chains.

The conceptual tools of Gestalt certainly are helpful. It bothers me when the tools are used without understanding, or with partial understanding, of Gestalt. Change "It." "It" puts everything out there somewhere, as if it (sic) were not a part of me. *I am bothered.*

"When the wrong man uses the right means, the right means work in the wrong way."

Quite often, good things happen when these tools are used by people of good will who don't understand them or don't completely understand them. Sometimes, someone gets knifed or clobbered inappropriately, which is damage. When a person without this good will—someone who has his own ends in mind—uses these tools, they are often damaging. So are they good tools? Should they be available? Or should we throw out the scalpel, the needle, and so on? Or restrict the use of them?

The answer lies in the person who answers. I like that "lies." It is a lie if anyone thinks he has the right answer. He has only his own answer.

My own answer, which sort of wrenches itself out of me. . . .
The answer is me, and what wrenches itself out of me is me. So what
am I saying? There is the protective part of me that wants to make
everything safe. There is the risk-taking part of me that knows that
it's up *to me* to find my own way, to make my own choices, and if I
make too many bum ones, that's it.

Where I foul up is in letting other people make choices for me.
"Respecting authority" is one of the most successful fouler-uppers—
respecting authority when this is not in accord with me, my
author-ity. I am not noticing, understanding, and acting on my own.
I *think*. I *think* this guy must be right because of his position, his
training, his age, etc. I "tell myself" that he must be right. Whatever I
tell myself is a lie for me, and I am the person I am lying to.

I had dinner with a woman whom I had known as a young
woman, when she had a lot of good rebellious spirit, and also a lot of
insecurity. At dinner, it was clear that she had given up the rebellious
spirit and had achieved that kind of security which includes a nice
house, a steady income, a steady husband, and so on. Disturbing
things were not to be talked about. It was all very nice, and I felt sad.
I told myself that it was all right, that she had chosen this way, and it
was really very nice and pleasant and comfortable. *I* was "nice" all
evening. (I think.) "Don't disturb anything" was so clearly in the air.
I breathed it like ether, putting myself to sleep.

She drove me home. When she left, I noticed that I was
humming something that I couldn't identify. I went on humming it
to the end before I knew what my organismic self was doing. Right
at the end, the words came, "Poor Butterfly." I knew my sadness,
which was real.

No one else confuses me. I do it myself.

Fritz calls it the "intermediate zone," this place where I confuse
myself. Krishnamurti calls it the "shallow mind," which can't arrive
at depth by its nature. No matter how much it thinks, it's still
thinking—thinking all kinds of things that *don't* come from me, and
yet I think of it as *I*.

Krishnamurti writes in his book *Freedom from the Known*
about driving in India with two other men and a chauffeur. The two

men were discussing awareness, and asking Krishnamurti questions. The chauffeur didn't notice a goat and ran over it. The two men didn't notice. "And with most of us it is the same. We are not aware of outward things or of inward things."

Fritz guided us in shuttling between outward things ("the outer zone") and inward things ("the inner zone") and arriving at awareness.

Just now, I feel like going back to the "conceptual tools," to the protective me and the risk-taking me. . . . My mind is blank again. What was there before, isn't present now. I notice that I feel like making a cup of tea. This is not *avoidance!* If this typewriter had a shout, my shouting would be down on paper. Sure I avoid. Lots of times I avoid. There are good and bad avoidances, and sometimes going blank is not avoidance. My shouting is because Fritz emphasizes avoidances and doesn't let people avoid what shouldn't be avoided (awareness). Many people pick up "avoidance is bad" and apply it to everything *they see as* avoidance.

Sometimes I prefer Zen even if it does take twenty years.

I'm not sure that Gestalt doesn't take twenty years to reach the same place.

I don't know any way to avoid people's mis-using anything, including Zen.

And so—I have got into the problem of mis-use anyway. Was I then avoiding the cup of tea that I didn't get? Or did my organism—the not-thinking all of me—use what was at hand, and lead me to what I want by another route?

Now I know what it is that wasn't with me for awhile. The protective part of me wants to make everything safe for everybody—no cheaters, no con men, no misleaders, no mind-distorters, no exploiters, no quacks. . . What comes next, I don't want to say because it is so idiotic—no imperfect therapy or therapists.

At the same time, my experience—my own observation—is that trying to make everything safe—like the U.S. has been doing for so long—leads to madness like the war in Vietnam, and in any case if we had a fool-proof world, only fools could live in it. That's not a world

I want. I rebel against the protectiveness of my own society.

The Indian way of relying on one's own senses makes sense to me.

Here comes in a part of Gestalt that I like. A part? It is the whole:

"Lose your mind and come to your senses."

That can be mis-understood and mis-used too.

When I came back to Lake Cowichan four days ago, I was confused, unresponsive, not *here*. I didn't know what was wrong with me. I was trying to find out. I kept finding an answer but this didn't do anything for me, and new answers kept coming in, like no end to it.

My unhappiness seemed to be about this place. June 1st, Fritz moved in here with twenty of us. He didn't know all of us. Many of us knew only one of the others. We had not previously lived together. We moved in, arranged ourselves, re-arranged the place, and the first workshop began at eight o'clock next morning. At ten o'clock we began working out things like how to feed the community. It was beautiful, watching and taking part in what was happening.

Fritz told us there would be seminars from eight to ten in the morning, followed by two hours of work in the community. Two to four in the afternoon was open for anyone who wanted to teach massage, dancing, art or whatever. Four to six was a work period. Eight to ten in the evening was seminars again, followed by community meeting. Some things switched around and were tried in other ways—and sometimes changed back again—happening as we went along. That was pretty much the way that things continued, until August 24, when Fritz went away for a month, I went away for three weeks, and many other people went away too. Teddy and Don were having a workshop during that time.

When I came back, four days ago, everything was ORGAN-IZED. Lists. Who lives where; what to do, when. Charts for the groups, like the changing of the guard—the non-organismic organization which I so much don't like, which is not *community* to me.

10

I could see no way to change this. (Never mind all the whys, and whether I could or couldn't.) I didn't want to be part of it. I wanted to stay here. (Never mind the whys of that.) I tried to decide what I would do. I saw some things that I could do that I wanted to do, and even they were unattractive. I felt somewhat nauseated. I veered from trying to laugh at it (forgetting that "Trying is lying") to trying (this is a different kind of trying) to let myself go with the nausea, and back again. I decided just to lie low until Fritz came back at the end of the week. Sneer. I didn't like that. I decided. I decided. I decided. None of them stuck. Obviously. I felt strange.

The third night, I couldn't get to sleep, which is unusual. The oil heater was making noises. I turned it off. I was cold. I got up and filled a hot water bottle. I don't remember the things going on in me, but I turned them off or made them warm too, and got into some other kind of mess. About half-past four, I went to sleep. When I woke up, I fixed some tomato soup because it seemed preferable to chicken noodle. (I haven't yet re-stocked my kitchen.) While I was stirring it, I noticed a song humming in my head. I listened, to notice what it was, and heard, "The old gray mare, she ain't what she used to be, ain't what she used to be. . . ."

What delight in my laughter! The organismic—*my* organism—*me* coming through, exactly right from-to me. Like a small sunburst, my sensing coming back, dissipating the non-sensing fog that I had been in. Then, happenings began to happen, which couldn't before, when I was un-sense-itive, and didn't respond. I and me are one.

That was yesterday. Today is a beautiful day. Cloudy skies, raining. I put on a poncho over my pajamas to go up the hill and answer a long distance telephone call. It was Neville, phoning from New York to know the dates for the October and November workshops. It was nothing, yet I was so happy, talking with him. I still am happy, as though nothing in the world could change it. Of course that isn't true—but at the same time it *is* true. Nothing in the world can change my happiness *now*.

What I shall do here has got lost. *I'm doing it.* I am out of the future, where I can't do *anything* except in fantasy, and into the present, where everything happens.

11

I have learned something.

I have recovered something, or uncovered it and re-discovered it, like Fritz is a re-discoverer of gestalt.

1948. June. I had got fired from Verde Valley School which at that time was under construction. In the bare board office shack, Ham fired me and kept saying, "I hate to do this. You're very efficient," and I kept reassuring him that it was all right. I don't like to see people suffer, even from their own mix-ups. It's only afterward that I seem ridiculous to me.

Willie, the cook, asked me, "How are you off for money, baby?"

Some of the Hopi workers invited me to come, with my son (13), to live with them in their village on the reservation.

Blackie, the manager of Sedona Lodge, came to see me with one hand behind his back. In a few minutes, his hand came around in front and he offered me a frozen chicken.

Lisbeth Eubank invited us to come and stay with her at Navajo Mountain, up north on the Arizona/Utah border.

I went in a car with a public health nurse, Josephine Scheckner, and her clerk, Grace Watanabe. Ahead of us was the very tall semi-truck carrying x-ray equipment. It had extra high springs, to protect the equipment from shocks. The truck's body swayed on the springs and looked as if it would topple over. My son rode with the driver. We lost them at Red Lake. The truck disappeared.

I pause. . . . I don't really want to write about this. That was a very insecure period of our always insecure lives, and I worried about taking care of us. I haven't forgotten that part. And still, there was so much that was vital and alive and beautiful and warm, in glorious red rock country, the sky so blue, the sun so warm. . . .

We were fairly close to Navajo Mountain when we got stuck in the sand. We all got out and dug, and put juniper branches in front of the wheels. A Navajo man appeared. He wasn't there—and then he was. He was very thin, and wore tattered pajama pants and a tattered black jacket. Navajos were desperately poor at that time. He smiled, gestured, said some words, and we hadn't a notion what he was talking about. He pointed to the sky and moved his hand like a plane circling. Then he asked, "Lady doctor?" and we thought that he meant Josephine, the nurse, though the plane didn't seem to have much to do with being stuck in the sand. Then he put his hand as though he were smoking, and asked "Cigarette?" We gave him some cigarettes.

Josephine got in the driver's seat. Grace and I got behind the two rear fenders and put our hands on the car, ready to push. We motioned to the Navajo to come and stand between us, to help us push. He put his hands on the car in the same way that we did. Josephine put the car in gear, and as it moved a little, Grace and I leaned with all our force, to push the car out of the sand. It went forward slowly, then faster—away from us. We stood up and looked back—and there was the Navajo standing there, in exactly the same position that we had motioned to him to take, as if the car were still there under his hands. He hadn't pushed at all! He laughed with the joyousness of a child.

When we got to the Mountain and told Lisbeth about the Navajo, she said, "Ohhh, that Hosteen Yazzie!" Later, when Josephine and Grace had gone, I went to a "sing" with Lisbeth at a hogan about ten miles away. When we arrived, I recognized our comedian. When he saw me, he covered his face with his hands as though he were blushing—and shook with laughter. I felt sure he had enjoyed watching the faces of the three white women as they earnestly tried to make sense out of his nonsense.

I stopped writing then, went for a walk in the damp and mist. I wanted to be there again. So much sadness was in me, remembering. All of me so sad that I *was* sadness.

My son and Robert Tallsalt dug for artifacts in the evening, after dinner. These artifacts were Anasazi—not Navajo, but people who preceded the Navajo by five hundred years or so, so Robert had no qualms about digging them up. One evening my son said to digging Robert, "There's a rattlesnake near your foot." Robert said, "He's doing me no harm," and went on digging.

Not all Navajos were that way with rattlesnakes.

A month ago a Canadian Indian medicine man told me, "What I know is just *one dot* to what my ancestors knew." He made a dot in space with his index finger. *We* think how much *more* we know than our ancestors did. . . . I think now about my parents who didn't go to school after they were twelve years old. I know so much more than they did—in one way. In another, I'm not so sure. . . . They relied much more on their own observation, their own experience, their own knowing—so much less on Professionals and Authorities. My life *is*, because of this. I was an incubator baby. The doctors in Manhattan gave me back to my father because I was dying anyway. (My mother was in the hospital for a long time, very sick.) My father didn't study books. He studied *me*, and discovered something. And here I am. (His discovery was later validated by the medical profession, when they changed their minds about how premature babies should be treated.)

Awareness. Noticing. That's Gestalt. It's also gestalt. And Indian—in the old way, only some of which survives.

Writing this, I feel good, strong, and happy. The sadness is gone.

I go back to 1948. Of course I don't go back, I *remember*, get in touch with experience in my past which is all embodied in me. That's the only place it exists. Where is "the past"? It's gone. Memory gives me the illusion (delusion?) that there is a past.

In 1948 on the Navajo reservation, the people were desperately (in our eyes) poor, hungry, sick, and they lived so much, enjoyed so much. I suffered an agony of conflict. I couldn't possibly wish anyone to be so poor, hungry and sick—and yet they were happier—enjoying happenings—than any other people I knew. I didn't know what to do with this.

In 1966 on the Navajo reservation I talked with a trader who loved Ayn Rand and hated "collectivism." He waved both arms in a gesture including the poor Navajos (not all Navajos were poor by then, perhaps not most) sitting on the ground outside his trading post and said, "You can see what collectivism does!"

One day, he told me that he has a house in Farmington, New Mexico, "but I can't live there any more. I go crazy, off the reservation." I asked him what made the difference and he said,

"That's hard to say." I asked some other questions, and he couldn't answer them—he truly couldn't. Then I said, "What is it about the Navajos that you enjoy?" and he said immediately, without a pause, "Their happiness in living!"

It's strange. At that time, I seem to have forgotten Polynesians and their happiness. They weren't so desperately poor and sick and hungry. Most of them, at the time I lived in Hawaii (1934-1945), weren't any of those at all. I don't remember remembering that on the Navajo reservation in 1948.

In 1966, a Navajo woman told me of her living in 1949, "Everybody used to be so happy, and it was kind of sad, you know, to think 'What will we eat tomorrow?' Still, we had such a good feeling. I guess it's the being and working together, that did all that, that kept each other happy. And when it comes spring, then everyone goes out to the field and plant corn, and anything they can grow, and in the fall they either eat some or store them away for the winter. . . . (sigh) Sometimes, I wonder where we went wrong."

When I became sadness, writing about that summer, I compared here with there. Now, I'm not comparing. I'm enjoying Vancouver Island again. I feel good *here*. The clouds are beautiful, scudding along the mountains. What isn't here doesn't exist, not even the warm and swimming and sunshine of three months ago, in June. I find it difficult to remember any time before this moment, and any time after it refuses to fantasize itself in my head.

An hour ago, I was wondering when the mail would come. Mail seemed important. I was hungry for something to come in. Now, it doesn't matter if it comes at all.

I would like to stay this way. There is no way that I can make myself do it. If anything, I have to *un*-make myself. I have no idea how I got *here* this time—can't even remember what I have written or what has been going on in me. I remember only vaguely that I was sad.

I'm not what I call "happy" now. I just feel good, and everything is okay. I have a vague linking of this with anesthesia, and next I remember when I was in so much trouble with my husband and myself, and got mononucleosis. The doctor gave me some drugs and I became semi-comatose. He said, "I'm sorry. I'm so sorry. It's my fault," and I said "Don't be sorry, doctor. It's *wonderful*."

My lips felt funny *then*, my speech was thick and bobbly, and I couldn't do anything. Now, I can talk all right—I just tried it. I can type. I can stop typing and do something else. My skills are available to me. I can't *make* myself smile. My face feels very strange when I try to. I would have to feel smiling for smiling to happen. Like an Indian? Have you ever tried to *make* an Indian smile?

When the Hopi Indians who worked on construction at Verde Valley school didn't feel smiling, Ham tried to "cheer them up." He sang "Come on and dance!" He was "humorous." They looked glum—to us. I envied them their holding out against him. I don't feel glum now. I just don't feel funny or laughing, and I think I would *look* glum to the white folks around here, and if they tried to cheer me up, I would *look* glummer to them although I would stay the same. Their efforts would go unrewarded. Failure. *Resistance.* Defeating them. I smiled a little when I wrote that. It's all so silly. Smiling at you to manipulate you to smile back at me so I'll feel good.

"They call it life!" came into my head then, in exactly the tones a Hopi used a few summers ago. I had gone up on Second Mesa with Barbara Bauer, looking for some of my Hopi friends. There was a dance on, a Hopi dance. After the ceremonial dance, there seemed to be comedy hour—making fun of the white folks. One of the Hopi men picked a Hopi woman from the audience and danced with her in our ballroom style and at the same time made fun of it by the way he danced. The message was clear. I didn't think it could be missed, but the Hopi made it beyond question when he turned his head and shouted over his shoulder, "They call it the dance!"

All Indian customs are not for me. All of Gestalt therapy is not for me. The places where the two come together are what I want.

I just got up to go to the toilet—and sang. My singing happened and I enjoyed it—the sound, the vibrations in my chest, neck and head especially, although they were also somewhat in my toes. *Agito, ergo sum.* Now my shoulders are in heaving, weaving motion. . . . my torso is getting into it—wider swings—a rolling motion now, like one

16

of those little celluloid dolls with round bottoms set in motion.

Now, I sit, but my sitting is altogether different—loose, free, at ease. My spine feels growing the way it often does when I have "worked" with Fritz. (We both wish we had a better word than "worked.")

I'm sixty-seven years old, remember, and not even in good shape for that mileage. Where is my stiffness, my rheumatic pains (these are few and small, but sharp) in all the rain and fog, with water drops beading the power lines. I feel so *warm*—as though I could warm everything around me. (I don't feel so sure about people!)

I have latched onto something through Gestalt, a new experience. In the past, with some people, some times, I have been ego-less—when they were, too. . . . I got up to make a cup of tea and latched onto something else, like whew! after *all* these years I understand something about me. Now, I don't know which to write first, so I'll make tea and see what happens.

Rain drips from the eaves. The stovepipe makes little ting . . . ting . . . sounds. I like the pauses, and the tings. The curtain is blowing a little, at the open window. Smoke whirls up from a cigarette in the ash tray and swirls across the typewriter. The ladder at the side of the dock looks as though it were put there for someone/something to come up from under the water. Who? What? Let each person image his own. Mine is friendly. He changes to unfriendly. I switch him back. Phony. He's neither a who nor a what—more of a which. A small tug, black hull, white superstructure, making little waves behind it and splashing white water along the cable to the log-boom filled with logs that it is towing down the lake. Suppose the log-boom started pulling the tug backwards, against its forward movement. I image it and it looks funny, struggling forward and being pulled backwards. The way that most of us live, as it seems to me. The way that *I* have lived too much. Projection? Introjection? Retroflection? Matters? Sometimes it seems to me that I introject, project the introjection, and retroflect the introjection and the projection. I don't care if that makes sense. I like the sound of it. None of it is real, anyway. It's just a way of looking at something, and those concepts are no use to me because I don't like them. Some other people do very good things with them because they like them, and some *other* people add to the nonsense in the human world by not knowing what they're doing with them and doing it anyway.

A social worker in Harry Rand's seminars spoke at length (in the guise of a question) about object-relationships and lots of other things I do not understand. It was just a lot of words, to me. When she had finished, Harry took his cigar out of his mouth and said, "This sounds like words, to me. Tell me what you mean." She couldn't.

Harry is (was?) a Boston psychiatrist, a psychoanalyst, but he made a lot of sense, and sometimes was very Fritz. A graduate student reported on a patient he was seeing in the hospital, using a stream of jargon. Harry listened till the end (unlike Fritz) and at the end said, "You mean the guy's *scared.*"

Harry had a patient who came and said nothing, and Harry couldn't get him to say anything. Harry suddenly had an image of himself as a boy when he was sent to the principal and the principal looked ten feet tall, and Harry couldn't say anything. (This is somewhat like Fritz.) Harry spoke of what was going on in him (this is like Fritz, though still not Fritz)—how he saw the patient as seeing him (Harry) ten feet tall—and the man began to talk.

I don't remember what I was going on with, earlier. Don't chase it: let it emerge. It emerges.

One evening here, Fritz asked two of the men to act as co-therapists. He didn't really ask, and he didn't really tell them, either. It's sort of like a mixture of both, or something in between. He said (*that* covers it, anyway) for them to pick one of us as patient. They were in adjacent corners of the room, and I was sitting against the middle of the wall that was opposite to them. I saw their eyes moving along as they noticed one person, passed, noticed another, and so on. Both of them arrived at me in the same moment, and each of them got a gleam in the eyes. I volunteered, feeling as though a couple of monsters I wasn't afraid of had pounced on me, and moved to the hot seat. Don and David came and sat on the couch near me, at a little distance from each other. They weren't really friendly at that time.

I am resisting going on. I don't want to go on. The reason I don't want to go on is that I'm *thinking* about it, trying to recall, to remember which came before which, to sort out what's important and what can be left out. That way, I get into trouble (in me—and then with other people, too, and sometimes with a pot or pan, or I drop things or burn my fingers or something else, or something impossible happens like throwing out a letter I wanted very much to keep, or tearing up some pages of manuscript when I haven't even read them and don't know what they say). So I'll take a walk in the rain and forget and see what comes through then.

The order doesn't matter! This introduction to what happened is just a sketch, in which any of the parts will do. (I hadn't got to the door, when that came through.)

I thought, before, that I must give explanations, so people wouldn't say "So *that's* what's going on at the Gestalt Institute of Canada." "So that's Gestalt therapy."

This time, it went this way, with *these* three people plus Fritz.

Don and David talked to each other about me. Fritz threw in a few words now and then—or perhaps it was just then. Gestalt emphasizes talking *to* people, instead of about them. I chided Don and David for gossiping. I was enjoying. Then I noticed I was shaking more than usual. I do have the shakes (*tremors*, in medical language) but I was shaking more than usual. I said so, then, "and I'm not afraid." I wasn't feeling afraid. I had begun to notice how orders and counter-orders (in me) seemed to meet and clash and produce the shakes. I looked into me, and noticed that my body wanted to get up out of the chair, and I was keeping it down. I got up and walked a few steps, then turned. David said, "I experience you as moving away from me," as if this was the reason for my moving. I noticed my body, and I noticed hesitation in moving toward David, although nothing I couldn't easily override. I did override it, easily. Then I was aware of hesitation—I became *nothing but* hesitation. Not "I am hesitating" but "I am hesitation." Even "I am" wasn't in it. Then I

19

noticed Don, legs pulled up in front of him, back up against the wall as though he were afraid of me. I said something like that to Don. Fritz said, "Yuh. Like a monkey at the edge of his cave."

Don said, "A few moments ago I had a flash (a common expression of his) that I wanted to take a walk with you."

I: Would you like to take a walk with me now?

Don said that he would, and got off the couch. Side by side we walked around the room, each with an arm about the other.

I don't remember at what point all ego left me. There was only awareness.

When we had circled the room, Don said that he felt pulled along by me. I said, "After the first three steps." Don agreed, "We started out walking together." He said something else, which I don't remember. I said, "Explanation." He said, "You want an explanation from me?" I: "No. You have given me an explanation. You said the same thing back there" (nodding toward the other end of the room).

We were facing each other. His right hand and my left hand were together. I put up my right hand, in offering, and said, "Do you care to hold this hand, too?" He put his left hand in my right.

Through all of this, there was no thinking going on in my head—no fantasies, no instructions, nothing. I was purely and simply *there*. Whatever I noticed was just noticed, without any kind of goal or any direction, and without opinion. At this point, I noticed my body and expressed it. "I have come this far. I am not coming any farther." No thinking, just expression of what I had become aware of my body doing. I noticed myself standing there as though rooted, like staying where I was.

Don said, "That's the way I want it to be."

Like Gestalt, there is no one way to tell it. There are only many ways. What came into my mind when I sat down, was the series of pictures of the ox and man in one of Suzuki's Zen books. The last one is a circle with nothing in it, and the caption "The ox and the man have departed."

Patient and *therapist* had departed. Neither one was there. Man and woman had departed. I was aware of Don and of myself—much more acutely—and at the same time, Don and I had "departed" too. I and me had departed. There were only events, happenings, each event like each moment was just there—and then it wasn't. It wasn't anywhere. Only the moment *now*. And yet, it was all recorded and available to me.

Utter ease, and no mistakes. This is perfection. "Striving for perfection" makes no sense to me unless it means striving so hard and getting in such a bind that there is an explosion. I (ego-I) have blown to bits, and the organism which is me takes over. That's a pretty strenuous way to go about it.

I've been cooking supper while writing that. Sweet potato in the oven, then carrots in a pot on top. Soon it will be steak in the frying pan, and then I'll stay with it, letting this go. Switching back and forth easily, not forgetting the one I'm not "doing"—and not remembering it either.

When Kay left, and no one offered to cook breakfast for Fritz, he said, "I shall learn to fix my own breakfast." He told me happily one day—with humility and a touch of awe—that he had boiled his eggs perfectly that morning, without a clock.

I remember when I was young and always cooked without a clock. Even if I were absorbed in a book, I noticed *smells* and when it was "time" to do something. . . . My head has suddenly got full of all our clocks and timers and other gadgets *that we don't need*. What madness. All the toil of people who work at making them, all the toil of people who earn money to buy them. All the waste of natural resources. All the *dependence*. Keeping the economy going, the people going, to keep the economy going, to keep the people going. . . .

When Alan Watts talked about the guaranteed income for everyone (and none of this monkey-business about negative income tax where you have to report + or −) he said that people want to know where the money will come from. "It doesn't come from anywhere. It never did." He explained that money is just a measure, like inches. In the 1929 Depression, suddenly a lot of people were out of work. All the brains, skills, materials were present, but no money. He said this was the same as if a man went to work as usual on a job, and the boss turned him away saying, "Sorry. No work.

We've run out of inches." All the brains, skills, materials still present, but no inches.

That's the way I feel about our "economy." Not to mention that it is an "economy" built on waste.

I like scarcity—not deprivation, but scarcity is nice.

The enlightenment that came to me some pages back was this: All my life, people told me that I could (and therefore should) take on bigger jobs than I did. I didn't want to. I liked taking a back office job where I didn't have to be so phony. Once I took a back office job which in three years became a front office job with Fortuny cloth drapes and a sunken garden outside my window. I was stuck with it and might as well go all the way, so I brought in a beautiful and appropriate lamp of mine and a Droege woodblock print. But there were still those times when the President of the place came in and kept his eyes on his shoes because I was wearing a dusty smock and my hair was all out of place, because I had been digging into something.

But there was something about my not taking on bigger jobs which I didn't understand. I just knew I didn't want them. I didn't want to be a boss. Now, this is clear to me. Wilfred Pelletier calls this "vertical organization"—the white man's system, and I don't like it either. He writes about this in an article "Some Thoughts about Organization and Leadership"—a paper given to the Manitoba Indian Brotherhood in 1969.

I went to a week-long cross-cultural conference in Saskatchewan about a month ago, "run" by Wilfred who let it run itself, with himself taking part in it. There were no programs, no schedules, and only one man lectured. I'm not sure that he was supposed to, but he went on and on and on and on and on. I went out and got some fruit and came back and passed the brown paper bags around. As usual, I didn't understand how Indians can sit looking so amiable when harangued by a white man. I found out afterward: they go fishing or hunting in their heads. Wilfred told me how "the bear went SPLASH! into the water, and the water sprayed all around." He flung his large arms high and wide. My, how he did enjoy it.

Fritz says, "When you're bored, withdraw to somewhere you feel more comfortable."

I did this in a weekend workshop with Jim Simkin. I don't know if it was boredom, but I got a headache (rare) and such pain at the back of my neck that I couldn't be interested in anything but that. I told myself (Barry lying to Barry, as she so often does) that it was *because* I hadn't got enough sleep the night before. I could have flopped on the floor (I never have learned whether "lay" or "laid" is correct, so I write "flopped") and slept. Instead, I "went away." First I went to Salmon Creek and felt the wind and the sand under my feet and heard the surf boom and curl and smelled the salt air and saw the colors in sky, surf, sand, and grass-covered dunes, and felt the springiness in my stride as I walked along the beach. Then I came back to the room of people—then back to Salmon Creek. After that, I went to a remote finger of Lake Mead at sundown, where the golden cliffs on the opposite shore were reflected in the water, and fish leaped out of the water and flipped back in again. The bushes along the edge of the lake rustled, the birds chirped, and my hands felt the smoothed beach stones. (When I told this to a friend, she said probably someone who knew me was on the beach and said, "I could have sworn I saw Barry, and then she wasn't there.")

I doubt the whole thing took more than five minutes. This kind of travel is wonderfully fast. No more headache—then, or later.

The cross-cultural conference was run (by not running it) in what Wilfred calls the "horizontal" way. "It seems to me, as I watch it, that vertical organization is resorted to as a result of a depletion or absence of communication. If you can't somehow or other have a community movement which is a spontaneous sort of urge which results in something coming about, then the only alternative you have is to build some kind of pyramid and put the toughest guy at the top, or maybe you don't put him there, he just automatically gets there. You have an organization within which there is no communication, there is simply a passing down of orders from the top to the various levels and this is no longer society—this is a machine."

Horizontal organization, as I have experienced it with Hawaiians (years age—I don't know about now), is like what Wilfred describes as the Indian way. A person arises as a leader for a particular thing at a particular time—and moves back whenever that time is over.

Communication is present. I have experienced this among white folks too, in occasional places. Trust is present, too. Here at Lake Cowichan we were working toward horizontal organization. As soon as something got out of hand a little, some people were pushing for the vertical way. But we got it back to horizontal. Now, in Fritz' absence, it has become vertical. Organization. Intellectual organization instead of organismic organization. The white man doesn't realize that his burden is the one he puts on his own back. Then he educates everyone and they put it on their backs, too.

"This is a machine." I see the big machine chomping all the people who have erected it and put it on their own backs.

At the cross-cultural conference, the man who lectured stopped talking (for a few minutes) when an Indian girl who had been sitting on the floor was suddenly lying on it, writhing, with moans and groans. He asked an Indian, "What's wrong with her?" The Indian said simply, matter-of-factly, "Her grandfather died last night."

"Oh?" said the lecturer. "And she has some illness, too?"

"I don't think so," said the Indian.

Not all white men have been through Gestalt (or some other such thing) and know the value of releasing distress organismically—throughout the whole body. But *this* man, the lecturer, was head of an Indian center in the U.S. and that's how much he knew about Indians! The one-way street. We induct you into our society. We don't bother to learn about yours.

A woman who worked in Welfare under the Bureau of Indian Affairs had worked most faithfully, climbing the mountains and trudging into the canyons, finding the people to help. When she was about to retire, she sat down at a kitchen table, put her head in her hands and said, with sadness, dismay, and puzzlement, "And after all, I still don't understand them."

In my language, out of my observation, her words meant, "No matter how I go about it, they *won't* do what I tell them to. I haven't found any way to make them become like me."

A few months earlier, I had heard her expressing indignation about the Navajo girl who worked in her office. "She said she didn't like the way we were doing things. I told her, 'That is NONE of your business.' She said, 'But these are my people.' I told her, 'That has NOTHING to do with it.' "

Vertical organization is a machine, and the people who stay in it become little machines within the big machine, and don't understand people who hold out against becoming machines.

I know. The welfare woman didn't understand me, too.

Neither did the teacher of the Hopis, who had a great time—they both had a great time commiserating with each other, the teacher and the welfare worker. I washed dishes, keeping as much of the talk as possible out of my ears. "Indians are so stupid." (How can you be a help to people you think are stupid?) "Indians are so ungrateful." On and on. When it came to "They're so rude!" "I know. They don't say 'Thank you'!" I couldn't stay out any longer. "Isn't it true," I asked (knowing perfectly well that it was true, and that B.I.A. people think that only B.I.A. people can know anything about Indians, so I put it inquiringly) "that they don't say 'Thank you' to each other?" (I love this not saying Thank you, and wish we didn't.)

The teacher of the Hopis turned to me and said, "No, they don't! They're *very* rude."

("And after all, I still don't understand them.")

After that, I went dry. I feel now as if there's no more water in the well—no more to be written. I could go back and look through what has been written and pick up some threads. I have no desire to, and also no concern. I'm curious what I'll wake up with in the morning. Right now I feel as though the morning will produce nothing because there's nothing to be produced. I can always shuttle and see what happens. Something always does.

The prisms on my window sill are alive with colors which are reflected in the window pane. Where do they all come from? A small city of lights, reflections, colors. What a world that would be to live in! I think I'd get tired of it very soon.

Next morning: Last night I dreamed that I received a letter from Bertrand Russell. He said that he had read the first six pages of

Person to Person and wanted very much to meet me. I felt hurt that he didn't remember that for three years we were very close. He said that he was coming to the United States for the first time. Then, I didn't feel quite so hurt, because he didn't remember that he had been in the United States, either. I still felt a little hurt, because our lives together, at the time they were, seemed to me more memorable than the United States. He said he was a little afraid of coming, that it was quite scary. He was always a little afraid of the U.S. At that time, I wasn't.

I am loving the rain. I have been sitting here loving it, not noticing for some time that that was what was happening. Today, the first line of hills across the lake, thick with maple trees and crested with pine trees, is visible. The mountains beyond them aren't there. Of course I *know* they're there, but for me now they aren't there. The scenery has changed. I am living in a smaller world. I feel cozy in it.

I think that I cannot work on this fragment of a dream in the Gestalt way. What I "think" is usually a lie. So then I tell myself (another lie) that I don't see how *I* can do it, so I shall have to wait until Fritz comes back and see what he can do with me and it. And, maybe, prove him wrong (a little) about Gestalt? This spitefulness in me, to prove Fritz wrong, is small, occasional, and not very strong, because I know that Fritz doesn't like his arrogance either, and along with it, he has such beautiful humility. This is the "meekness" of which Jesus spoke, which so many of us resent because even in the dictionary it means piously humble and submissive, submitting to injury, and so on. We resent *our meaning* of the word, and rightly so. But go back closer to Jesus, and to the translation of the Bible into English, and the word meant simply "soft and gentle."

We take care of our own breakfasting here, each person for himself. The exception, in the beginning, was Fritz. Kay, who was paid to do this and other things—although Fritz wanted this to be a community in which no one was hired to do anything—made breakfast for Fritz. When Kay left, I made Fritz' breakfast for two mornings, when it came easily. Next morning, I didn't. I told him that those two mornings, it was for both of us. If I had done it the third morning, it would have been for him. He expressed understanding and acceptance, without using one word. (If I weren't five hours a day in groups, plus other stuff, I mostly would enjoy fixing breakfast for both of us—delighted—and rarely disinclined.)

Fritz had said occasionally that he knew nothing about cooking, that he had never learned to cook. Later in the day when I had not-fixed his breakfast, he said, soft and gentle, "I will learn to cook my own breakfast." Soft, gentle, and *neutral*. No martyrdom, no appeal, no pride. I got him an electric percolator that would shut itself off, and stocked his refrigerator with food he likes for breakfast, plus a few foods that I thought he might like. He has taken care of his own breakfast ever since. This is his own place. He bought it. He took the risk. What all of us have got out of being here—about ninety people, so far—has been made possible through him. He is the founder of Gestalt therapy. Without the usual advertising—just a brochure, and word of mouth—his new book *Gestalt Therapy Verbatim* has sold 20,000 copies in six months. He was honored at the American Psychological Association (of which he is not a member) at the convention this year. He is seventy-six years old. He is well-known for his arrogance. He fixes his own breakfast and is happy that his eggs got boiled exactly right without a clock.

How can I Gestalt a fragment of a dream in which a letter from Bertrand Russell comes through foggily—as if in a fog—I don't really see it, and his handwriting that I know so well isn't there—although some of the message comes through clearly? This seems impossible to me. That is a lie. I *think* (that liar) that it is impossible. I *know* that it is possible. If there were *nothing* there, Fritz would say, "Be what isn't there."

I have already worked with this dream in my own way, a little. I looked at the first six pages of *Person to Person* which Bertie said he had read, and wanted to meet me. They included Carl Rogers' Preface and my Introduction. Phooey! What could I get out of that? That wasn't the meat of it—or me. If he had read the Curtain Raiser, that would have been different.

I was about to set the book aside—let my thinking set it aside—but I do trust my dreams. I read those six pages and discovered some things I had forgotten, that I need to be in touch with now. I read through quickly, but I shall go back and read those passages again. They are deeply relevant to my life here at this time.

I want to go on about this. . . I'm afraid that my ego finds it fascinating, for my organismic feeling is that I am hungry, and "going on now" is against this. Intellect/ego/I is not strong enough to resist me. I leave the typewriter and go to the refrigerator and the stove.

My hunger must have been ignored for quite awhile. I was flurried fixing simple things like eggs and toast. A feeling of hurry when there wasn't any hurry. I felt weak. I hadn't stopped in time. If an emergency had emerged, I would have boggled it. Fortunately, it didn't—and often it doesn't, of course—but to live in readiness for an emergency (without anticipation) is to live. Getting supper last night went fine. The eggs got a little too fried this morning.

How much I enjoy fresh orange juice! Savor it from my lips and mouth down whatever tube it is that food goes through, and into my stomach. I lose touch with it, there. I would rather have fresh orange juice once in a moon than the maltreated reconstituted frozen stuff every day. The only thing to do with most of our food today is swallow it and forget it, which is what most of us do. Canada isn't as bad as the U.S. yet, but she's going our way. I don't know which came first, the swallowing and forgetting or the lousy food, but we need to stop the spiral and start it heading the other way. I don't think that Laws and Programs and Planning will achieve that. Each man has to do it himself. Then, it happens. I don't need to push anyone else into doing it—just do it myself. Then I have done my part, and my part is all that I have to do. To go beyond that is fantasy, leading to exhaustion.

Bertie didn't like "America" very much. Once he said that he liked it better this time than in the past. Each time he arrived, he got into a sort of whirl in himself for several days, a kind of mixed-upness.

*In America I am
a Personage, which I loathe. But
otherwise I liked America better
this time than on former occasions.
It's a queer country.*

He loved best the Irish coast at Connemara where he experienced what we have so many names for and they all sound silly, so I won't label it. In fact, it is beyond labeling. At any rate, on that rough and stormy coast (as he described it—I've never been there) he was so much in touch with the universe that it made everything he did in his usual life seem silly—not worth doing. Like plucking an ant from a planet.

Or like me when I was an editor at the University of New Mexico Press. The professor-authors (who took years to get a 100-page manuscript written) started pushing me as soon as their manuscript had been accepted. Was I working on it yet. Had I got it to the printer yet. When would it be coming out. Push push push. A good deal of the time, I resisted—although usually not enough. But sometimes I would lose ground, and then I was pushing me even harder than they pushed me. Suddenly, explosion. I was both inside of me and outside of me at once. There at the desk was the little ant-me, knowing nothing but the manuscript I was editing and taking it all so seriously. And here was the big me, enjoying the whole goddamn glorious planet to which I was born. The absurdity of ant-me! I laughed. I went on laughing. I was so ridiculous, sitting there taking a bunch of words seriously, and taking seriously the vanity (or ego) of the men to whom it had become so important to get into print. I wanted to shake everyone in the place happily and shout "WAKE UP!" If I could BOOM it from a mountain top, that would be even better. What scabrous little fantasies I had invested my life in, thinking them *real*. The universe was me—and me, the

29

universe. (Why do we use a capital for I, and lower case m for me? It's not a question to be answered, but asking it feels good, like opening up something that had been closed, before—and no teacher telling me, "That's the way it *is*, so learn it, and stop disrupting the class.")

Light from the desk lamp is shining on my typewriter, the bluish color gleaming, fading into dull away from the lamp. The carriage handle shadow moves along this dullness, then slides away. The little square criss-crossed light which shows that the motor is running (as though I couldn't hear it—and even if I had no eyes, I feel the vibrations) is steady orange, more sturdy than the machine itself. Hands touching keys. When I notice this touching, my hands become softer than they were, more gentle, using just enough pressure to move the keys, no more, and then there is no kickback against myself. It is more like music. I feel in harmony. Even the tapping of the keys against the roller seems more soft as I soften, non-resisting. Rippling through my body and across my face is something that feels like laughter—not huge laughter—gently tickling laughter, featherlike. I am my own doing.

Walking over the moors of Cornwall, each time we came to a gate, Bertie opened the gate and while he was doing it, I skipped up and over the stile. At the fourth one, he said, "You don't really think I'm opening these gates for myself, do you?"

I felt chagrined.

But if he wasn't opening the gates for himself, why didn't he follow me over the stile?

He was an old man, then. Fifty-five years old. Now he is an old man in his nineties and I don't know how he feels about anything any more.

It seemed so important to me then to know which of the two men I loved I should marry. Thirty years later, it seemed that it wouldn't have made any difference. I can't explain that. It still seems that way. . . . Having written that I couldn't explain it, I began thinking about an explanation, trying to arrive at one. What difference would it make if I did arrive at an answer? Even a true answer. What could I do with it? Ego would be inflated a little by its cleverness, that is all. . . . Funny. It seemed that way to me, then. I had such a time deciding, and thought I *should* be able to choose. So I chose, and built up reasons for my choice.

My first husband was different. He was a mistake which I got out of. The best decision I ever unmade. I don't mean that he was "bad." He just wasn't right for me.

My dream. Hmm. I'm still resisting working on it in the Gestalt way. I don't know what this resistance is. I don't feel threatened. I do feel, "Aw, too much trouble." "For what?" I notice that it is raining harder now. My eyes are closing, as if I were sleepy. I yawn—a nice big yawn, now that I know it feels good and don't stifle it any more because that's "common."

It isn't easier to type than to work on a dream. It *is* easier, when I feel sleepy or tired, to go on with what I'm doing than to disrupt it and move to something else. Those words came through half-sleep, sleepier, sleepier. Am I hypnotizing myself? Or am I just sleepy, and the sound of the rain helping me on with it? When I yield to it, it feels good, and I don't care. Questions are disappearing. I yawn, and a sound comes with it, "Ahhhhhhhhhhhh," and that feels good too. Sometimes it seems to me that feelings are always good, and it's just thoughts about the feelings that give me trouble. When thoughts stop, feelings are okay—even painful ones. When I move into them, instead of pushing them away. Now my eyes water along with my yawning—my yawns are bigger and stronger each time, and my eyelids scrooch together. My body is swaying toward the typewriter and back. This letting things happen feels good. My yawn just now sounded like something in a zoo. My feet were under the chair. Now they're under the table, legs stretched out, heels on the floor instead of toes. Now they're going back and forth. All of me is moving backward/forward backward/forward even as I type. I feel like that old game, "My grandmother went to London. . . ." What fun that used to be. I'd like to play it here. It seems like a good gestalt game, somehow. I'm afraid I wouldn't get any enthusiasm—or even acceptance—for it here unless it were done in a group and called Gestalt therapy.

𝒮𝒟

I'm still rocking.

⟨ ⌣ ⌣

Now I can't type while I'm doing it any more, because at the same time my arms are flinging out, then in. The rhythm is like an automaton. The chair creaks. My heels tap the floor. My neck is throwing back now, in the backward movements. All of me is now involved.

Abruptly, the automaton stops. I .slump in the chair, arms hanging down at the sides, feeling rest like it comes after good exercising. I exhale deeply. Out/in—out/in. Happening by itself.

I feel all exercised, and am not sleepy any more.

All right. The dream.

I am the fog. I get between me and everything else. At the same time, I soften everything, and this softness is good. (I go back to being the fog. Limp and rested as I am, this is much easier to do.) I am a funny fog—warm. Floating. Drifting. Those words in the letter would come through much more harshly if they didn't come through me. I soften them. Not blur them. You read them right through me—well, you couldn't *see* the words through me, but you *heard* them through me. As fog, I blurred your eyes but not your ears.

"What? What sense does that make?"

Never mind *sense*, just go on sensing.

I am fog between letter and Barry. Between message and Barry. I am soft. I like my softness. I like me. Letter is harsh on one side of me. Barry is soft on other side of me. Pain from letter is not so much hurt when it goes through me.

Barry: Pain? What pain? Sure, some pain, but not so much you have to soften it. Don't make things easy for me! Get away! . . . .

32

That's better. Now the letter is closer to me, and we belong together.

As Letter, I couldn't type any more. To be/feel Letter, I had to move to another chair. I didn't know why. Now it seems that Softness was in this one. When I changed seats and was Letter, I became much more strong and firm. My hands moved down my thighs to my knees, then lifted, went back, and repeated, over and over. My exhale/inhales became much more pronounced—as though going through a tube instead of all the open space of my mouth. Eight times, ten times? About that. Then all of it stopped.

How am I now?

I sure don't feel sixty-seven any more. I still feel fat, but I don't feel old lady.

As Letter again: (a bit sharply) I told you. I read those six pages, and I want to meet you.

Barry: (also sharply) You *have* met me! You know me! You've forgotten those years.

Letter: *You've* forgotten.

Barry: I did not! I remember—you don't. You talk about *meeting* me, as if this would be the first time.

Letter: (sotto voce) Every time's the first time. (louder) I said *meeting*. We didn't really *meet* before.

(Liveliness is coming up my spine again.)

(A little dampness comes into my eyes. I start to deny "We didn't really meet before," and the wetness in my eyes is a denial of my denial.)

Barry: (with humility) You're right. We didn't really meet, before. We thought we did. (a little angrily) Have I ever met *anyone*?

Letter: Past. Looking into the past is like looking into the future.

Barry: You mean the past is like a crystal ball? You can see anything in it. All illusions.

Letter is silent, and the silence is assent.

Barry: But that *did* happen with Bertie, about the stiles. And it *did* happen that when he came to lunch at my apartment in New York, and asked if I had a paper clip, I rolled up the mattress and picked one out of the bedspring, and he asked, "Do you always keep paper clips there?"

33

Letter: So what does that do for you?

Barry: (after a pause) Makes me know that I *was* alive, once.

Letter is silent.

Barry: I was! I *was*. I WAS!

Letter is silent.

"Was" rings in my ears. *Was*.

Three little letters w a s encompassing my total past.

Whew.

All the other things I was are in it, too. I feel good about that! All those awful things are tiny little things too. All bundled up in one little was. I hold them in my fist and shake my fist, and THROW them away.

The silly thing is, this works. And it *all* came out of *me*.

The existential message that I get from this dream is not new, and is not new even to me. But my way of knowing it has changed. Right now, I feel as though every cell of me is aware of this, and that my presence will be a little more present from now on.

I'm now ready for the next step—about "Bertie's" fear of coming to the United States. Every thing and every no-thing in my dream is me. It's *my* dream, not someone else's. *My* experience and experiencing are in all the parts of it. . . . There is some light in some of the clouds now. The mountains beyond the hills are visible, and the clouds are like mountains beyond mountains, formidable and glorious both at once. Powerful. What power in all that stuff that I could put my hand through if I were there!

I feel that power in me and it *is* in me. I'm not afraid of it now.

If you try to copy my journey, you will not be following it, for that is not where my journey began. Go on your own journey, wherever it takes you.

Right now, I'm going to eat. My eating will not fill your stomach.

The lake shimmers.

I still feel good at having thrown out that whole little bag of past. I hope it stays wherever it went.

I am empty again. What will there be to write tomorrow?

No answer.

I'll know when tomorrow comes.

I hate exercises.

Experimenting, exploring, experiencing—joy. I never know what's coming next.

Sometimes in the past, experimenting with myself got me into trouble. I knew what happened. I had a goal. I pushed. Experimenting without a goal, and without trying to hold onto anything that I arrive at, has never got me into trouble. If it should, at some time in the future, still the odds are pretty high against it.

When a therapist has a goal for his patient, I think his patient is in trouble. Of course the therapist is in trouble too, but that's one of those "normal" troubles that we take for granted. The kind of trouble that a patient has when a therapist has a goal for him is a compounding of the trouble he had to begin with, which made him go to a therapist.

"I try as far as possible not to think."—Fritz, of himself as a therapist. When I am at my best, there is no therapist. I don't know anything and don't know what I'm doing. At such times, I am "amazing" to others, "have my own style" and I am delighted with what happens.

"To assign a fixed norm to a changing species is to shoot point-blank at a flying bird."

This morning, I have made lots of typing mistakes, have got stuck, have not enjoyed what I'm doing. What is my goal?

I want to get this book done. Which came first, I don't know. The more I don't enjoy doing it, the more I want to get it done. The more I want to get it done, the more I don't enjoy doing it.

What's going on in my body? I make this split deliberately, now. Or do I simply notice what is? At any rate, when *I* notice *my body*, clearly I am not whole. But I am a step on the way to getting out of the split in which I override my body as though it is a thing belonging to me. *I* make *it* do things, the way that so many people ride a horse or drive a car, or push a broom for that matter.

35

When I noticed my body yesterday and let "it" do whatever it wanted to, let "it" take over (against all the prohibitions in my society) in the submission of "myself" (phony self) to "it," I became *me*. This morning, I am split again. I *know* there are pains in my shoulders, but I am not aware of them, not responding to them. Like I can *know* that another person is with me and not be responding to him. When I know that someone is with me and I shut him out, I am not aware of him. When I let him in, I become aware of him.

I am not saying that shutting out is "bad." Shutting out my body is something else.

"Accepting my body" in the sense of nudity or sex is not accepting *my body*. It is accepting an *idea*, an abstraction.

> The Arch-Fiend in his universe may be summed
> up in the word abstraction, meaning any idea
> to which a man subscribes as if it were
> more living than himself—
>
> (leaving a perfectly distinct unhe;
> a ticking phantom by prodigious time's
> mere brain contrived: a spook of stop and go)
>
> e. e. cummings

In a world in which everything must be "instant," quick, requiring no effort, no observation, no investment of myself in what I do, and painless, people scoop up (or abstract) some bits of a man's theory, a few of his conceptual tools, and pass these along to others as "salvation." This is quackery.

It took us a long time to debunk the whole Freudian crap, and now we are entering a new and more dangerous phase. We are entering the phase of the turner-onners: turn on to instant cure, instant joy, instant sensory-awareness. We are entering the phase of the quacks and the con-men, who think if you get some break-through, you are cured—disregarding any growth requirements, disregarding any of the real potential, the inborn genius in all of you.

Fritz, in *Gestalt Therapy Verbatim*.

Our view of the therapist is that he is similar to what the chemist calls a catalyst, an ingredient which precipitates a reaction which might not otherwise occur. It does not prescribe the form of the reaction, which depends upon the intrinsic reactive properties of the materials present, nor does it enter as a part into whatever compound it helps to form. What it does is to start a process, and there are some processes which, when once started, are self-maintaining or autocatalytic. This we hold to be the case in therapy. What the doctor sets in motion, the patient continues on his own. The "successful case," upon discharge, is not a "cure" in the sense of being a finished product, but a person who now has tools and equipment to deal with problems as they may arise. He has gained some elbow room in which to work, unencumbered by the cluttered odds and ends of transactions started but unfinished.

In cases handled under such a formulation, the criteria of therapeutic progress cease to be a matter of debate. It is not a question of increased "social acceptability" or improved "interpersonal relations," as viewed through the eyes of some extraneous, self-constituted authority, but the patient's own awareness of heightened vitality and more effective functioning. Though others, to be sure, may also notice the change, *their* favorable opinion on what has happened is *not* the test of therapy.

("To be free of *their* opinion." When I was learning to paint, a few years ago, my son joshed me about my paintings. I went on painting. When an artist wanted to frame several of them, I told her, "I know they would *look* better, but the faults I see in them would still be there." I went on painting, not thrown off *my* course, my own development, my observation, my knowing, either by being kidded or by being praised. I am not that way about everything, but I'm getting stronger.)

Such therapy is flexible and itself an adventure in living. The job is not in line with widespread misconception, for the doctor to "find out" what is wrong with the patient and then "tell him." People have been "telling him" all his life and, to the extent that he has accepted what they say, he has been "telling" himself. More of this, even if it comes with the doctor's authority, is not going to turn the trick. What is essential is not that the therapist learn something about the patient and then teach it to him, but that the therapist teach the patient *how* to learn about himself. This involves his becoming directly aware of *how*, as a living organism, he does indeed function. This comes about on the basis of experiences which are in themselves nonverbal.

Fritz—in *Gestalt Therapy*

38

A Cup of Tea*

Nan-in, a Japanese master, received a university professor who came to inquire about Zen.

Nan-in served tea. He poured his visitor's cup full, and then kept on pouring.

The professor watched the overflow until he no longer could restrain himself. "It is overfull. No more will go in!"

"Like this cup," Nan-in said, "you are full—of opinions and speculations. How can I show you Zen unless you first empty your cup?"

I am and do and be my best—both in practical skills and in relations with people—when I have no thoughts *about*.

Break with psychological memory, Krishnamurti says. Get rid of convictions and interpretations—all self-hypnosis. I fumble around with grammar, trying to find some way to express what happens when I do that. I give up the impossible struggle.

Clear. Do you know what *clear* is? I don't. I only remember it, now.

Fritz: If you want to be helpful, you are doomed.

"You are trying to be helpful" is one of Fritz' most critical criticisms of us as therapists. When a person in the hot seat says to Fritz, "I know you want to help me," Fritz says "No." Sometimes he adds something of what is going on in him, which has nothing to do with being helpful.

When I try to be helpful, I have the idea of helping. I start with a concept, have an opinion, a conviction, some notion of what is "helpful," and I have a goal. All of this is in my "thinking." The free-flowing process which is me has no goals, and cannot function when I have them—or when I'm thinking.

*From *Zen Flesh, Zen Bones* by Paul Reps. Charles E. Tuttle Co., Inc., Tokyo.

Krishnamurti is sometimes quite rough on people who go around helping people. A questioner asked, "How about you?"

Krishnamurti: But I don't do it on purpose, do you see? That's the difference.

Krishnamurti: A religious man is a man who is alone—not lonely—with no dogmas, no opinion, no background—free of conditioning and alone, and enjoying it.

"Observation/understanding/action!" he said in Berkeley last year, leaving no room between the words for thinking.

I've heard him say several times in the past five years or so, that gradualism is no good, that we (I) must make a radical change, and that this radical change must be made *now—right now*. Each time, I thought, "Fine. Great. I'm willing. I want to. But *how* can I do it *now*?" This seemed to me an utter impossibility.

Now, I know that *now* is the only time that I can do it.

Then stillness comes. Completely still. And at the same time, all is dancing.

Without the stillness with no center, the dancing is *mine*, and is fictitious.

Sometimes I have been bothered by something Fritz has said or written, without being clear what my bother was. I tried once to talk with him about some of these things in his autobiography, *In and Out the Garbage Pail*, which was then in manuscript. I didn't get anywhere. I felt blocked by him. But then I realized that as I was not clear, I couldn't make myself clear to him. He said that I was trying to pick his brains. Me? Why, I knew more than he did about these particular bits. That's why I wanted him to change them. He should pick mine! Then I saw that I wanted to use him to arrive at clarity in myself, and he was declining to be used that way. Well, I let others use me only in ways I want to be used.

Now, I am clear that (in my view) Fritz has not made the mistake of pushing Zen as quick salvation: he has made the mistake of dismissing the Zendo without having invested himself in it. I think that Zen will survive.

For three months here, I thought that some aspects of Gestalt therapy I simply was not getting the hang of—some lack of brightness in me. I wasn't bothered by that: I just thought it was so. The aspects of Gestalt that appealed to me, I really learned, and I was busy with that. The rest could come later. I went away for three weeks, and thought that I would come back and get the hang of the rest of it. On the way back, I realized that those other aspects don't appeal to me. I don't *want* to learn them, and so I will not learn them—same as I never learned *about* adjectives and adverbs and predicate nominatives. They didn't appeal to me. But I can use them.

⊂⟨⟨

Coming to this training center was funny because it was the first time in my life I had been trained for anything. I came to Canada to look for a ranch or farm, for a community, a kibbutz. That doesn't die in me even though the cost of land and the scarcity of suitable places has so far made it impossible. I came to Vancouver without pre-planning beyond making a plane reservation and getting on the plane. I wanted to find out if I could still arrive in a strange city alone and find my way. There were two people I could call, one of them Fritz, but I wasn't going to call them until I was sure that I could do without them.

I hadn't thought, until now, that this is a way of going about things by awareness. I did recognize that I would be meeting Canadians and Canada in a different way than if I were introduced, escorted, directed, pointed to the most congenial places, supported by friends.

I didn't call Fritz until after I had reached a point of despair, got in a jam, couldn't see any way out of it, panicked, got unpanicked, and found my way out. Then I knew I could still do it, and called Fritz. One day in his apartment in Vancouver I met some of the people who were coming here in a couple of weeks. I wanted to come and see this place and find out what it was, but didn't otherwise see myself as part of it.

I came back from a farm-hunt two nights before they were all coming here. I was feeling stuck about finding a farm in Canada, and

41

thought I would come over with them, see the place, and go back to California by way of Victoria and Seattle.

I went to the coffee shop for a late supper, feeling unfriendly. I was feeling clumsy, too. The only place to sit was on a stool. I took one with an empty stool on one side, and wished there were an empty stool on the other. Then a man came and sat on the empty one. Why couldn't he have gone somewhere else?

I was also somewhat paranoid. Gordon had brought my suitcase into the hotel—long hair, shirt-sleeves torn off above the elbows. It wasn't that kind of hotel. I thought they didn't want me. I also had a plastic breadbag with toothbrush, toothpaste, and brush and comb in it, which I put on the desk while I registered. It wasn't that sort of hotel, either. When I left the desk to go to my room with the elegant little man who carried my suitcase, he said "Oh!" and went back to the desk and retrieved my plastic breadbag which I had left there. In the elevator, there were half a dozen people, all very prim and proper and wearing what the well-dressed person wears. The elegant little man held my plastic breadbag as though it were a jewel box. He *made it* into a jewel box. For a moment, I saw it that way myself. I was impressed. Clever people, the Chinese.

The man who came and sat on the stool next to me and whom I ignored said something to me about my beauty. This happens fairly often, and I am puzzled when I discover that they mean it. I didn't think this one did. I made some sort of acknowledgment which I hoped was cold, but suspected it was like my mother being mad at the cat and slapping it. Her slaps were so gentle that the cat purred. He began his dinner with half a grapefruit. Each time he dug into it, some of the juice hit me on my forehead or my cheek. I noticed that he waited until he was entirely through before asking me, "Have I been splashing you?"

I looked at him then, and he was so clean-skinned that he looked polished, so gray curly hair in perfect place, so white of shirt and black of jacket, unspecked, untouched by human hands, as if he had just had the plastic ripped off him, that I became even more paranoid. He knew all the waitresses. Was the management of the hotel checking up on me through him? I had only passed a wet

42

washrag over my face, brushed back my hair without re-doing it, and changed my dress before going down to dinner, because I was hungry. On the all-day trip from Kootenay Lake, we had stopped only once, at Keremeos, where I had a skimpy sandwich and a cup of tea in a friendly little shop. In Keremeos, I met a blind realtor. When I walked into his office, he stood up, held out his hand, and said, so ease-ily, "You'll have to come to me. I'm blind." He described properties better than any other realtor I've met. He said, "Prices now don't make any sense!" It was clear to both of us quite soon that he didn't have a place that I might want, and he didn't try to sell me something else.

The polished gentleman next to me asked me what I was doing here, and I didn't feel like telling him. He went on being gentlemanly. I said some things, I don't remember what. Gestalt therapy came in, and he asked me what was that. I said, "It makes people responsible for themselves." He nodded. "Free enterprise," he said.

He ate much faster than I do—practically everyone does—finished his steak, held out his cheek to me and said "Kiss me." I was eating a hot roast beef sandwich, and was very aware of gravy on my lips. Put them to that polished cheek? I asked, "With gravy lips?"

"With gravy lips," he said, his cheek still held out to me.

I kissed his cheek. He left.

Maybe that had something to do with it. Everything always has something to do with it. When I went up to my room, it wasn't long before I had committed myself to coming here. I signed up next day, and came here the day after that. Just for myself. I wasn't going to be a therapist.

When I was interviewed by the lady from the local paper, it appeared as follows:

> We asked her for a few personal comments on
> the Gestalt Workshops under the direction of
> Dr. F. Perls, psychiatrist. We quote:

I would like to call Fritz Perls a genius, but he says that people called him that all his life and for a few months he believed it and then found that he couldn't live up to it. So I'll just say that in workshops with him I have experienced more ways to approach and work through the problem of being human than I had believed possible.

It is my *own* humanness that I am chiefly concerned with. It feels good to say that, after all the years when I was told that I must "think of others." The alternative seemed to be to "think of myself," and I didn't like that. It was a beautiful moment when I discovered that it is when I *don't* think—then I am most responsive to others, most aware of what goes on around me, and function best. That sounds like idiocy. But I think that every one of us must have had the experience of doing something really well when we didn't think about it—and the experience of losing our balance or our skill when we began to think about it. There are also the times when we slip, or make mistakes, and say "I was thinking about something else." I have heard Fritz Perls say of himself as a therapist, "I try as far as possible not to think." By working on myself to get rid of what blocks me from being human, I let that much more humanness into the world, where we surely do need it.

We are told that to make mistakes is "bad." But that is a part of learning—to make mistakes and notice them. Then—if we don't fight them—they correct themselves. How else does a baby learn to walk?

44

I understand the "genius" bit better now. I am a genius when my genius is present, same as I am a cook when I am cooking, a writer when I am writing. At other times, I'm not.

In the fourth week here, Fritz had us pair up as patient/ therapist. If the laughter that came up inside me had been let by me come out, everyone would have enjoyed it. I kept it inside, and only I enjoyed it.

At the end of the week, when the notice went up of those who were accepted for further training, my name was there. I felt happy about the acceptance and glum about my future. If I stayed on now, I would have to take this training seriously, I would have to become a therapist.

My pains left me long ago. I noticed their leaving. I have been enjoying, with no thought of "book" or "getting it done." When I enjoy what I'm doing, it's silly to receive money for doing it—now or later. When I don't enjoy what I'm doing, the salary is never enough. The only way it could be enough is that it was *so* much that I could quit the job.

I'm hungry. Not too much hungry, just enough. I stopped what I was doing, and the thought (or awareness—which changes to words when I express it on the typewriter) comes in to go to Lake Cowichan today to get a few things for myself so I can make a chocolate cake that I promised Deke in June, and at the same time get some food to put in Fritz' cabin for his breakfasts when he comes back day after tomorrow, which is Sunday and the stores are closed. They're closed on Mondays too.

As I walked away from the typewriter, I noticed that I would have to change my clothes. I "can't" go to town wearing a flannel nightgown. I tell myself (the liar coming in again) that I couldn't go to Lake Cowichan wearing only a flannel nightgown because (and how often *that's* a lie-word) my doing so would be harmful to the

Institute. But if the Institute were not here would I do it? I don't have the idiocy (called blessée in France) to do that.

"Because" is a dirty word in Gestalt. Experimenting with this (it's not a *rule*), I noticed how "because" takes me farther and farther away from me and whatever I've done (good or bad), and how without that following "because" I say simply that I did it. My strength comes back to me. (In our society, "Why did you do that!" comes to us so early, and so often—an accusation, not a request for information.) Without "because," I become more Indian, living with facts, without either praise or blame—that see-saw of our existence which throws us off our center, the point of balance.

In the *Garbage Pail*, Fritz speaks of once becoming an idiot for awhile, spontaneously. I don't wonder that then he had an uncommon experience. In the groups, at times, he has someone play the village idiot as part of therapy. So far, no one has played *my* idiot.

So I changed my clothes, and while I took off this and put on that, I remembered when I was young and rainy days held so much happiness. It wasn't only that playing in the mud was good, and making rivulets, but we could wear older clothes to school. We wore *old* clothes, in any case—faded, sometimes patched—except for special school occasions when we wore our Sunday clothes. People wore old clothes to work on rainy days—even people working in Wall Street offices. It was "practical," in the days before affluence, dry cleaners, and pavement everywhere. My Aunt Alice (who was such joy to me as well as at other times a crumb) loved going to work on rainy days, sloshing her way to the trolley and enjoying it, and besides, on rainy days she didn't mind having to work.

One of the joys of a real emergency is throwing yourself into it. Another is that non-essentials get dumped.

How much is essential? *Really* essential. Our biological needs are few.

Marcia asked to hide out here. I was putting away the food I'd got and washing dishes. I said okay. I didn't know then that I'd want to write again. When I came back from Cowichan and saw the typewriter, I felt no attraction at all. When the food was put away, I did. Now, I find that I am slowed down, sluggish, pause quite often—no feeling that it's going well. I feel Marcia in my shoulders although she's lying on the couch. She isn't bothering me. She hasn't even said anything. *I* am bothering me. I want to work my way through that. . . . Well, that's out. Marcia has just left. Twice, before she left, she got up and did something or other, went to the bathroom, opened a kitchen cabinet door, and I felt irked. What was she doing? What did she want? Would the village idiot *care*?

"I don't know Marcia very well."

That's a because, a lie.

I am now not liking me very well.

I feel cross and cranky and tired, and thinking about it doesn't help. If I switch to "good thoughts," I may feel better, or think I do, but I'm still in the same slot—the separation of I and me.

Shuttle. See what happens.

A small tug is heading down the lake without any logs behind it. A tiny speedboat slashes the water, going the other way. The lake is ripples all over, sort of like moire. Within the lagoon, the water is more nearly still. Raindrops puncture the lake. My head is shaking No, No, No. Let me close my eyes and get the feeling of it, while I continue to shake my head. No no no no no no. Oh no. Ohh no. I say it aloud. My voice is somewhat deep, firm and sure, and at the same time soft. It feels congruent with the movement of my head, in rhythm with it, in tune. I open my eyes and at first glance the lake seems upside down, more like a heaving sky. I become interested. My head stops saying No. Halfway across the lake there is a sharp division. The part near me looks blackish—the distant part is like heavy frost. In the lagoon, nearest to me, the hills on the other side are reflected in the water. I switch off the typewriter, and suddenly—stillness. . . . I see my tapping, skipping fingers reflected in the window pane. Beyond the window, the waves are getting wavier. Heaving, becoming sky again. I feel heaving with the same slow swells, like breathing. The part that looked blackish now has a pattern of black and silver, like black and silver lines—thin lines—shifting, moving. There is no end to change.

My *No* now seems to be a No to stuckness, to being stuck in the past of x-many minutes ago where nothing can happen but 'round and 'round.

All fantasy. All illusion. Wake up! Wake up!

"The Creator has made the world. Come and see it."
—Pima Indian prayer.

Get with it!

I function now. My typing is much better—and is not work, or does not seem to be. What is "work" anyway? We're so mixed up about it, I let the question go.

On the Navajo reservation, Beulah, the cook in the dormitory, one morning gave the children fried eggs by putting the fried eggs in their hands. They carried them into the dining room, sat at the table, and ate them out of their hands.

HORRORS!

This was talked about over a hundred miles of reservation for two weeks—by the white folks.

When I went to work at Verde Valley School, we lived in tents. The school was being built. A dozen or so Hopis worked there, and I had no idea what they thought of me. They were stand-offish. The cooking/eating room was a small one-room red sandstone house which was on the place when the land was bought. New floor-boards were put in, and a bare wood table—no finish. One evening when floor and table had been scrubbed hard and were really clean, a small Hopi boy knocked over his glass of milk. (I got "too much into" writing. My awareness slipped. Just now, I noticed smoke, and turned off what shouldn't have been turned on. I should have noticed the smell before there was smoke. I didn't do the spontaneous shuttling which is awareness.)

The milk spilled on the table was flowing fast to the edge of the table, where it would spill on the floor. I pushed the small boy's head toward the milk on the table, saying "Quick! Lap it up!" He lapped happily, turning his head a bit so that one eye looked up at me.

His mother, Mona Lee, sat back comfortably in her chair and said, "You are not like other white women. They say you must get the mop. By the time you get the mop, the milk is on the floor."

Later that evening, I went to the cookhouse. Mona Lee was sitting, with her back toward me, talking with a new Hopi man who had just arrived. As I came near the door, he stopped talking. Mona Lee threw her head back toward me and said, "She's okay." They went on talking.

Within my own society—

My living *there* felt so much more vital, and I so much more spontaneous and alive.

We're killing the Indians.

America needs Indians.

We're killing ourselves.

Indians think we need them too.

"Indian" is not skin-color. It is a way of living which does not lead to Vietnam.

"Indian" is a Navajo woman who told me that when she was in school, the white woman physical education instructor taught her how to cheat, how to stumble so that it would throw off another player and seem to be an accident, how to *win*. "And now," she said, "I have to work *so hard* to get that out of me."

Some of us here are working so hard at that too. Some others of us are just now discovering the games we play, and that what we're out for is to win. Even husbands and wives and parents and children and children and parents and children and children.

At the cross-cultural conference in Saskatchewan, a white man suggested that a way to help the Indians would be to educate them about our legal system and procedures. Indians, everyone agreed, are disadvantaged with our police and in our courts because they tell the truth.

Who should switch, the Indians or us?

Which world would you prefer to live in?

⟨flourish⟩

I got a set of measuring spoons today. All I wanted was one of those ringed-together sets with stubby handles. I had to get square-bowled ones with long handles with a rack to hang them on which gets screwed into a wall. I remembered Donald Stewart's success story, and how he got to the top. "When a man wanted a *two*-cent stamp, I sold him a *ten*-cent stamp. When a man wanted to go to the sixth floor, I took him to the twelfth!"

They're not ringed together and the handles are so long, I decided I might as well hang them on a wall around a corner of a cabinet. I didn't get the bar straight. For a moment I thought, "That's bad." Then I noticed that the spoons don't come out even at the bottom anyway—they're graduated by handles as well as by the size of the bowl. It was nice, looking at the bar sloping down to the left, and the bottoms of the spoons sloping up to the left. Just then, I saw something about me that bothered my husband that I never understood before. He got quite dotty when things weren't *straight*, and *even*, and as they were *supposed to be*. I understand now because I have got so much that way myself—not enough so to have satisfied my husband, but enough so to distress me. I am annoyed to be bothered—to use any of my life being bothered because things aren't the way they're supposed to be. That's how I was more alive in my paperclip-in-the-bedspring days. I was more that way too when I was at Deep Springs twenty years later. I was wearing a British wool suit that I had got in Canada. It was most beautiful wool and a most beautiful suit. I didn't expect ever to have another suit like that. In the kitchen, I sat on a high stool. The cook's big mournful Church-of-Christ husband said, "That stool is wet." I'd noticed that, after I sat down. The cook's husband said with mournful appreciation, "Nothing seems to bother you much." I was too happy to be bothered. Cruelty to people, stifling of people—things like that bothered me very much but not much else.

I'm not *that* happy now, not that alive. My perspectacles fall off

50

my nose too often. I have not that environment any more, suitable to me. Through Gestalt, I am working to arrive at the happiness *where I am*. Not pretending. Not looking for the silver lining. Being in touch, the way that I am with ease in an environment which releases me. I am working to release myself. Here is a good place to do it. Mostly the people are not very spontaneous, and mostly neither am I. At the same time, Gestalt and Fritz work to release me to spontaneity. I feel that in this community, I am living in the concentrated pressures of my society, and at the same time the place is working to free me. I haven't made it yet, but I feel spontaneity closer to the surface than it was. This is exciting.

In the Co-op store today there were cauliflowers. Some of them were small enough for me to eat one in two days. Others were immense. I looked up at the price card and they were 39¢ each. All the same price. Ridiculous! That's what I thought.

Then I noticed that the small ones were young and very white and tender, and the leaves were the way they are when they have the most delicious flavor. And *then* I remembered in Hawaii what a time I had trying to get the Japanese farmers to pick some beans or carrots for me when they were young, even though I assured them that I would pay the price of the full-grown ones so they wouldn't lose.

I bought a small one. I haven't had cauliflower that tasted like cauliflower for so long, I'd forgotten how good it is. I thought I didn't like cauliflower any more. My stomach felt easy with it too—no indigestion. How much less I need to eat when it tastes really good. I feel satisfied. I feel as though I've had dessert. Some people were eating ice cream at the House up the hill, while watching TV. (It's Friday night, and no groups again until Sunday evening.) I like ice cream very much. I didn't want it.

So much went on in me last night while I was sleeping. This has been happening often, since August. As if the language of dreams were no longer necessary, and I am being spoken to directly. No. It is like therapy going on, taking place in me, all the time that I am asleep. Fritz said that's the end of therapy—the organism taking over.

I am in trouble. This book was going to say a lot about Gestalt. The more that I know Gestalt, the less there is that I can say.

When I went to Hawaii, I was enchanted and wanted to write a book. Three years later, I still wanted to write a book and realized what a very different book it would be, out of having experienced Hawaii more deeply. This kept happening, and when I had been there for ten years, I realized that I no longer could write a book about Hawaii.

"Would you like me to carry your suitcase?"
The Gestalt change is to: "I would like to carry your suitcase."
The next step has no words.

The Ex-Poet*
by Malcolm Lowry

Timber floats in the water. The trees
Arch over, it is green there, the shadow.
A child is walking on the meadow.
There is a sawmill, through the window.
I knew a poet once who came to this:
Love has not gone, only the words of love,
He said. The words have gone
Which would have painted that ship
Colors red lead never took
In sunsets livid at the Cape.
I said it was a good thing too.
He smiled and said: Someday
I shall have left this place as words left me.

*Copyright 1962 Saturday Review, Inc.

52

Leaf

"Two" came into my mind, conventionally, to identify this section. I noticed the conventionality. That's all. Then "Leaf" came in. It stays. It won't be replaced by anything.

I don't understand what is going on in me. Some kind of alternation is going on. I am swept through by pain and weakness, overwhelmed. There is no part of me that isn't that. Then there is quietness and strength. The duration is never the same. . . . Right now, it is pain I feel, and as if I have no strength at all. . . .

I have not been pursuing any idea. The problem of responsibility arises. I see it two ways at once and am confused. I let it go. . . . Pain is sweeping over me again. I am reminded in so many ways of when I was sick. Just now, it was the doctor asking me, in the hospital, "Well, *where* do you feel *normal?*" Right now, I don't feel normal anywhere. I don't even know what normal is. I didn't ask the question, but an answer came, "Normal is like the weather which rains or shines, blows, is still, and like the day which is followed by night which is followed by day, it is the growing and the dying."

This morning Fritz said, "You were not here for the three-week workshop." A statement. I answered, "No, I was not here." That was all that said itself. It was not a program. I didn't "make myself" stop at that. The "explanation" stuff just didn't follow. Parents require explanations. Teachers require explanations. Parents and teachers are so much of my life when I am small. Then, "friends" and bosses, spouses. . . .

Last night, Fritz said of himself in the group at Esalen from which he had just returned, "For the first time in my life, I was perfect." He said that he had seen *maya* or illusion clearly. I saw this illusion clearly for an instant. What does it matter what happens to me or to anyone else when it's all illusion, like the man who falls down dead in a play?

Then that slipped a little. "Responsibility" tore into it, ripped it up, shattered it. Some things *are* bad, and therapists "*shouldn't*"—

Fritz lets some things go on that he "shouldn't." He doesn't do anything about them.

Fritz also lets me go on in ways I "shouldn't." He doesn't do anything about them.

It's all part of the same play.

I start pursuing that, and find that I can't. My mind is not a blank. What "I" wanted to pursue, or thought I "should," just isn't in it. Neither is anything else. And still I am not "blank."

I have not written anything for two days, until this morning. (The perfection of being here at this time overwhelms me. All the parts have to be seen, to know the perfection. I cannot describe it. Can you describe, please, the world?) I baked a chocolate cake for Deke that I promised him in June. I hadn't made a cake for more than a decade, and that was before I got the shakes. Measuring out quantities, especially small ones, was so difficult that it became absurd. I made so many mistakes, and as far as possible corrected them. The cake was in the oven when I noticed that I had forgotten the vanilla. I poured some on the top of each layer and mixed it in with a fork.

I was a little sad. It wasn't the cake that I had promised Deke.

Everyone who likes chocolate cake, including Deke, thought it was great. They hadn't been expecting something else.

When it was done, I felt sleepy/tired and went to bed. (Another way of dodging that "laid" or "lay" that I never learned. It's time that I got over that.) I laid down. If it's the wrong word, still it's perfectly clear to everyone what I did. I didn't sleep. Time passed. It must have. It always does. Then I noticed that I was enjoying—real delight—noticing the movement of the leaves in the woodsiness outside my window, the slender brown stems, the many different shapes of leaves, the subtle differences in color. Not *thinking* them. No words. No analysis. No opinion. Just enjoying.

I went on enjoying, knowing that this was something that I used to do often. When I was a child, a grown-up or my sister would intrude with some stupid question or demand, and when I was cross at being interrupted I would be told, "But you weren't *doing* anything."

At the cross-cultural conference, so much was going on among us. A man from Indian Affairs came in. I liked him, *and* he felt like a storm, blowing in and breaking up everything that had been going on. He pounded out his questions which were based on his answers. Most of us became very unhappy. Perhaps all of us, but I don't know about some.

Next day, when this man had gone, a white priest asked an Indian, "Is that what it's like when we (white) come into a community (Indian)?" An Indian said, with a burst of joy, "If you've learned that, it's worth the whole conference!"

Nausea. I felt it then. I got into bed and began to shudder. Chills. Then sobbing. Eyes only lightly damp. Very little sound. Huge sobbing felt through all my body, hips sobbing, chest sobbing, arms sobbing, even a little feeling of sobbing in my feet. Going in waves, like vomiting, when it is "over" and then starts up again.

Later, a small sigh. Then big sighs, quick, sharp, deep.

Now, I feel loose rather than shaky, with some strength in my looseness. I let it be. For how many decades did I pull myself together?

That noticing of leaves. So full. Complete. Nothing to be added, nothing to be taken away. No wish to change anything. Enjoyment. Joy. Not forever and ever lying in bed, a life this way, but to dip into it again is good. One of the holes in my experiencing is not an emptiness any more.

Last evening I went to David's group. Everything looked so bright. The colors delighted me. Each person was so utterly, uniquely himself. There was brightness "out there" and in my being.

"For the first time in my life, I was perfect." It seems to me that we know this possibility of perfection, and strive for it in all the ways that don't take us there, that take us *away* from it, like paddling forward to reach a place behind us.

After my sobbing a while ago, I "saw" something which formed into the words, "The problem of good and evil is that we set up good and evil, and that creates the problem."

ઠ/ ௐ

I remember when I saw very dimly that we set up all sorts of difficulties for ourselves like a barricade, haul ourselves over them, then pat ourselves on the back for our accomplishment. I saw that by noticing myself and others doing it.

"Thinking is rehearsing."

That's obvious. I can notice my own thinking, any time, and there it is. Until I notice, it is not obvious.

One of the Gestalt experiments is for people to pair up and take turns saying "It is obvious to me that. . . ." and being careful not to interpret. It doesn't sound illuminating, hearing people say "It is obvious to me that you are smiling," "It is obvious to me that you have your hand on your knee," and so on. But when "It is obvious to me that you are smiling" and "It is obvious to me that your voice is shaking" get together, something else has become obvious. Holding myself to the obvious eliminates the devious, and I become less devious, more directly in touch. After noticing the obvious in the other person, when I switch to *me*, "It is obvious to me that I am. . . . " I notice all sorts of things about myself that I hadn't before, and am much more aware of me, and what I'm doing. This is definitely *not* instant joy. A kind of labor comes first.

It's *really* crazy that we call illusion "reality" and reality "illusion."

Fritz said, "You were not here during the three-week workshop."
I said, "No, I was not here."
We both were Indian.

"Fantasy!" says the man who reads Facts to the man who reads Fiction, unknowing that the facts are fantasy, or even if they weren't when written, they are by the time they're read.

This place is nice. With all the rain, there's nothing for the gardening crew to do. Most of them have now switched to a baking crew, which we didn't have before. The kitchen seems to run now with horizontal organizaiton, for the first time. With vertical organization, everyone who wasn't working in the kitchen had to stay out. With horizontal organization, we can drift in and have tea or coffee and enjoy ourselves and each other, and get better acquainted.

I am experimenting with baking in my cabin. First, the chocolate cake with all its mishaps and corrections. That came out fine. There must be something to do with millet meal, but I haven't yet found out what. I got a "millet loaf" in Victoria. Deke and I ate it on the way back, and shared it with some people we picked up. I was sorry I had got only one millet loaf. In the Co-op I saw millet meal and got a bag. On the bag was a recipe for making porridge. I tried that, and it tasted very strange. Even with sugar and cream, the strange came through. So I thought I would try baking with it. What I remembered of that millet loaf tasted like cake, so I made a cake recipe, substituting millet flour for white flour, and brown sugar for white sugar. The batter tasted awful. I keep trying to think of something that will take the taste out of my mouth. Maybe if I ate something else that tasted just as bad, this would neutralize it. . . . I just looked in the oven. The stuff isn't rising much. All that I have learned so far is how not to cook millet.

Good heavens, they are beautiful! I made them in muffin pans. They came out *perfectly* for looks. Light, fine-grained, and a golden color that I don't have a name for. . . . They taste good, too. A little sandy, which I suppose is the millet meal. I'm letting the taste settle in to see what the aftertaste is, before offering them to anyone.

. . . . What I haven't said is that *first* I read recipes in two cookbooks, sort of tasting them, before I decided which one to use for the millet. . . . Now I've got that millet taste in my mouth again, in spite of brown sugar and vanilla.

Today, I've been getting into "projection." I think it began yesterday. Instead of simply doing what I want to do here, I've been thinking (sic) that other people think I should be doing more. I have not had one clue that this is so, so even if it is true, it's projection. The truth seems to be that I *want* to do more, or be in more. So it's the old have-to/want-to mix-up, that I got worked out so thoroughly a year ago. It seems to be time to house-clean again. When I look over the "have to's," I find so many that I *don't* have to. Then, all the others turn out to be "want to's." When I take on too many "shoulds," I feel so burdened, so bilious, that I don't even want to do what I like to do, and *all* of them feel like "have to's." I'm "nothing but" a slave, pushed and harried, and life isn't worth living. It is this "not life" that isn't worth living.

Fritz suggested an industry for the community—putting out *mis*fortune cookies, like, "All your catastrophic expectations will come true."

58

When I came out of sleep this morning, I heard the rain. . . .

I am stuck. Trapped by language. I was about to write "I opened my eyes," and that looked ridiculous. How did I do this doing to myself? With my fingers? I changed to "My eyes opened" and that looked silly too. *My* eyes. They belong to me?

I am seeing something in *haiku* that I did not notice before. I like the fresh feeling I get from *haiku*, the directness and unclutteredness. I noticed that many American attempts at haiku were sentimental, not *haiku*. I did not notice what I notice now in memory. Is my memory right? I don't know. It doesn't matter. I am on to something.

Suppose I. . . . There I go again. Unnecessary words.

Ears open

Rain.

Eyes open

Sun.

That was my experience this morning.

The afternoon when I arrived at the cross-cultural conference in Regina, as I entered the room Wilfred was saying that Indians say simply "rain." They don't understand our language. Wilfred: "*It* is raining. Where is this *it*?"

I received a letter from a professor at the University of Chicago two years ago. Few letters I keep. I kept this one to remind me of some things I know.

> So much of the time you seemed to be saying exactly what I have found myself saying the last few years—not that my saying it means that I don't need to learn it. I think I need to be reminded of things I already know more than I need to be told things I don't.

> In any honest autobiography, the commonest phrase would be "I got confused." I say that and know it to be true of myself, but the

compliments I get on my teaching, writing, and miscellaneous conversation always use words like "lucid" or phrases like "You make things so clear." I'm glad, but I'm not sure I understand. Whatever clarity I achieve is refined out of so much confusion that I am often more aware of the muddle than anything else.

Not sure where I'm headed. Increasingly, I want to interrupt students and colleagues by saying, "Those are the wrong questions, the wrong words, the wrong categories, the wrong assumptions. You can't even think in that vocabulary. It can only lead you deeper into confusion and irrelevance." And sometimes I do. But I don't even really want to interrupt them, because then I just get sucked into an argument which uses the same damned vocabulary. And I want to get away from it and into a language I can think in.

If the student responses mean anything, I seem to be a good teacher. But I have begun to bore myself. I'm tired of repeating things which seem to me self-evident truisms. And when I discover that they are radical new insights to the students, I don't know whether to be glad or depressed. Example: I point out to a very bright senior doing an honors paper that she has evaded the obvious problem in her paper. She agrees and says that she had to evade it because she didn't have an answer for it. I say she doesn't have to have an answer because there aren't any, anyway, and that the problems she can't answer are exactly the problems she ought to explore, that if she can just clarify a real question or two she will have performed an enormously useful and comparatively rare function. She comes back a week later and tells me that what I said was an overwhelming revelation to her, that it was the first time she had ever realized that you don't have to have answers. And she says, "How did I ever get this far without realizing that?" Well, we all know the answer to that one.

I think it's useful for me to go on saying such things, but I'm tired of it. I want to go on to what I don't know. At Deep Springs I discovered that I really *was* what I had been *pretending* to be, and I'm still trying to integrate the implications of that.

My book (ex-dissertation) will be out in a month or two, and I'll send you a copy. In part because of its subject, its tone is mostly pessimistic or satirical, but I think it touches on a few things you would find relevant. I'm tired of that book, too. The damned things go through so many proof readings that you would have to be fatuously narcissistic not to get tired of them. Want to go on to something else.

I'm not really as gloomy as I sound. But I have all this junk clinging to me, bits and pieces of worn-out selves, and it often seems as if the world insisted on patching it back together instead of encouraging me to throw it away. And being a professor exposes me to more than the usual quota of that.

With what is called "English," I proceed.

I woke up this morning feeling cross. What does that mean, this "cross"? We all know, and nobody knows. I change to "irritated." I felt irritated. I felt nyahnyahnyah. I did again what I wasn't going to do. (So I must have made a resolution that I wasn't aware of until now.) Last night, I talked too much, too loud—real stupid talk. I feel as though it vomited from me for hours and hours. That can't be true. I left my cabin at quarter to eleven and was back at half-past eleven, and I didn't talk *all* the time. It still feels like hours, like all night, like engulfed in a cloud of upchuck as big as the night.

I don't want this. It is one of my troubles in my own society. My own society is here, and I am struggling to find some way to live in it, here, where there is also support which I do not have in most other places.

It wasn't *all* waste. It was 95% waste.

I answered questions, utterly senseless questions like what does my son do, what does my daughter do. This woman I talked to knows she doesn't want to do that. I am not responsible for her. I was unhelpful to both of us by not being responsive to myself. *Once*, I noticed what I was doing—and let it go. Mostly, I enjoyed this woman's face—a mixture of ravaged and smiles moving in and out like changing, overlapping colors. This is something that I learned to do when I was bored and didn't know what, otherwise, to do with it. That not-knowing time is past. I still go on doing it. An obsolete behavior pattern.

A while ago, I thought, "Well, there goes another theory—that what I notice takes care of itself. I have noticed this stupidity of mine for a long time and it hasn't gone away.

But this noticing is *after*, and I make a *resolution* not to do it again. That way, I'm bound to lose.

And, in the first place, I went up to the house last night because I thought (sic) that I "should," not because I wanted to. That way, I'm bound to lose.

Earlier in the evening, when I wasn't tired, I was much better with this woman, although not perfect.

I like this woman. If I don't pay more attention to *me*, I'll begin to dislike *her*, maybe even hate *her*, and avoid *her*. I'll feel that I'm keeping myself intact, and I will be—including my avoidance of *me*. *This* avoidance is not deliberate. Now that I know more of what I am, this process, I *want* to be "with it" still more. Any other "with it" is illusion.

I have been writing as it comes. Just now, I slipped out of that. I wrote a paragraph three times before I realized that I am not attracted to going on now, that I am *trying* to say something. Then, it becomes "work." I have been *thinking about* which is as . . . . Well, like *talking about*.

In the Gestalt groups (here I am feeling interested again, alert, curious what is coming next) the person in the hot seat is sometimes requested not to "gossip." Speak directly *to* the person. Whether what you are saying is "good" or "bad" or "negative" or "positive" is irrelevant. Don't say to another person, "He. . ." but turn to the person you're talking about and say "You. . ." If the person being talked about is not present, put him (that is, fantasy him) in the empty stool opposite you and talk to him.

This request not to gossip is made within a concrete situation. The person switches. When he does this, there is so much noticed beyond what could possibly be said, and all of this becomes a part of him by his experiencing of it.

I, as a member of the group, have not had *his* experience, but I have had *my* experience of what happened, and I can do this at other times myself, either within the group or outside of it: do it directly, or to an empty chair or whatever.

If I make a *rule* of it, which is *not gestalt*, then I am in trouble.

In the kitchen, a man expressed his feeling cheated by a therapist who wasn't doing a good job. A girl (she is old enough to be a woman but she hasn't grown that much) said, "Well, he's been having a rough time" and added a few words about the man's personal life (the "because" that wipes out *what is happening*). Then she shuddered, looked over her shoulder. "I feel there's someone standing behind me. I'm gossiping." "Don't gossip" has become a rule, a prohibition, another monkey on her back, when monkeys already there have got in the way of her growing.

That is neither gestalt nor Gestalt.

Suppression isn't *any* kind of therapy.

"I feel frustrated in conveying that Gestalt is not *rules*."

This is the hazard: looking for rules and finding them. If you find *rules*, you have not latched onto Gestalt. You haven't latched onto Client-centered therapy, either. Or Jesus or Buddha or John Dewey or Maria Montessori or A. S. Neill. You may learn from the Master, but then you have to dump him and take off on your own. It's sort of like what Szent-Gyorgi wrote to a young man in London who had asked, "How do you do research?" Szent-Gyorgi's reply was, "You do it according to your own personality, if any."

Fritz: "Michelangelo would have been a sculptor even if he had no chisel."

"I only asked if you are aware of what you are doing. I didn't say you shouldn't do it."

A book is odd. Between those two paragraphs, I made gravy. Life is odd, too, in somewhat the same way.

In the mornings, Teddy, Don, and David have the people in small groups, about ten in each. In the evenings, Fritz meets with all of us for two hours or more. He seems to think he should give some lectures. The first one didn't go on very long. The second was even shorter. He said he was having trouble about what to say, that he doesn't like to repeat himself and of course he has said it all before. After that, some people took the hot seat, and he "worked" with them. He is softer, more gentle, while just as keen and just as firm. I didn't detect any bitterness or spite, and there was more compassion. He seems easy-er, all around. "There must be something to my method. I am still learning."

I didn't complete the "no gossiping" part. By *noticing* the no gossiping—what happens—I have noticed many other things too. How simple it is when I stay with what *I know*, which is *all* I know. How uncluttered I am when I eliminate what I have heard, which I don't know, but only believe or do not believe.

Often, an Indian says, "I don't know" and white people are sure the Indian is lying because he *must* know (what happened at Chilchinbito last night)—his *brother* was *there*.

Wilfred Pelletier says of Indians, which includes himself, "He will only answer the one question at a time." I like this. How often have I been given too many "answers" which weren't answers to my *one question*. "Have you seen Hal recently?" "No," would be an answer to that. Or, "two months ago" would have been an answer. In that case, they couldn't know about Hal what I want to know. All the "information" I get, about where they saw Hal when, and what went on before and what went afterward, and where he had been before they met him where he was. This may all be fascinating to *them*. It has no interest for me. It has nothing to do with my question.

Do I do that? I'm sure I'll notice, now, when I do.

How I loved Alex, a small boy who was visiting his friend in the house where I was living. A woman asked him, "Do you have any brothers or sisters?"

"One," said Alex.

Fritz came in today and said, "About the letter from John. . . ." I didn't know anything about a letter from John. Fritz mentioned "the introduction," "paperback," and "brochure." Everything became clear for me, as we went along, and when he left, I wrote the letter that he wanted me to write, although he hadn't said so.

I like this way. It is slow, giving only what information is necessary, with spaces between for my thought-pictures to collect in and complete the picture. When Fritz left, my picture was complete. I had no questions.

Wilf Pelletier writes: "The Indian language does not paint a picture in the same way the English language does. That is, in English most people tend to talk of details, also about the obvious. In Indian, that is, the dialects I know, do not talk of the obvious. They do not say good morning if it is obvious that it is a good morning, nor do they speak of the condition of the road if it is obvious to the one they are speaking to that he also knows this. I may be to some degree overemphasizing this, but it is only to get across my point. When I talk of a picture language, I mean that you form your own pictures of what might have occurred, as most Indian people tell you only the beginning, then the end. You then form your own pictures as to what happened as you relate to it, and not as it might be told to you in English with all the words inserted. . . . These important differences relate to organizations in many ways. When a group of Indian persons came together to form an organization, they didn't talk about organizing or forming the organization. Instead they talked about their relationship to it. There was no need to talk about the organization as that's why they came together in the first place."*

This is the same as my experience of the Koolaupoko Improvement Club on Oahu, which formed itself because so many Hawaiians were interested in keeping unwanted improvements *out* of Koolaupoko. I became a Member of the Board. I wasn't voted in or appointed to—it just happened or came about when this was a good place for me to be. It was only later that I realized how powerful our non-organized organization was, when a member of the Big Five (the five corporations which controlled the Islands at that time) came to

*"Two Articles" by Wilfred Pelletier, booklet, available for $1.00 from the Institute for Indian Studies, Rochdale College, 341 Bloor Street West, Toronto 181, Ontario, Canada.

break us up, and had to play an underhand trick to do it—and didn't succeed. They had only the *appearance* of breaking us up. It took the Japanese attack on Pearl Harbor and the aftermath of unions and Henry Kaiser to do it really. That trio broke up the whole way of life in Hawaii.

The Indian way has almost gone too—not entirely, but we have almost wiped it out, and what a mess *we* are in now, I don't hear anyone denying, except officially or diplomatically.

When I finished *Person to Person*, I had got so much out of doing it that I didn't care if it got published or not. Now, Kolman tells me that he went to New York before he came here, and a friend gave him *Person to Person*. He expresses the strength it gave him to continue on his *own* way—only recently chosen. I feel good that my son took the risk of going into the publishing business—a new endeavor, without prior experience of publishing and with everyone saying that he would fail because he couldn't get distribution—so the book would be available to people. He kept the costs as low as possible too, for that reason, including any profits to himself. This is not The American Way. I like it. Not many people appreciate that my own lack of money is my chosen way—not that that would make much difference to those who don't. I would be crazy instead of stupid, that's all, to *choose* this way. I like money as much as anyone else does. I would like to have scads of it. I just can't put money *first*, except in an emergency. There are very few real emergencies. I felt bad about those few until I read in the *Panchatantra* "Indulge in no excessive greed (a little helps, in time of need)." Some other lines I liked are:

> One makes, in following the professions,
> Too many wearisome concessions
> To teachers.
> Scholarship is less than sense
> Therefore seek intelligence.

It seems strange that three thousand years ago there was this same problem, that we are just now beginning to deal with.

I wish that everyone who believes it important to be sophisticated would look up in the Oxford Concise Dictionary what it means. The meaning hasn't got adulterated there. Or look up the derivation of the word in Webster's. Notice when you're feeling sophisticated, and the discovery is there without a dictionary.

In the beginning, when we are young, we know this of ourselves. We "put it on." We don't realize that's what everyone else does, too, and if they're older, most likely they've forgotten.

One of my friends has a daughter who has been blind since she was a few days old. She was born prematurely and was given too much oxygen. Her eyes shriveled up like dried peas. She isn't just blind. She hasn't any eyes. In her teens, she says, "Ugh! I don't like him. He's *ugly*." "I hate the color of that dress!" These are things her sisters say. How many things do *I* say, of which I have no experience, only "knowledge"?

There is Walden, and there is Walden Two. Here feels like Walden Five to me, in its potentiality. Kolman is delighted that on the farm he found for us—although we don't know yet if we'll have it—one part of the scenery is called Skinner's Bluff, and nearby there is Walden.

He showed us maps last night and pointed out that this farm is in "a very strategic area—Indian lands on both sides." We will be protected by the Indians from invasion by other white men.

Each new workshop, I think the same thing: "We seem not to be having Jews this time." Then people begin referring to their Jewishness in one way or another, or I say something like, "Ilana looks and seems Irish to me," and someone says, after first being astonished, "All I can say is, that's a goy's view." By the end of four weeks, I know that lots of us are Jewish. Then we get a new bunch of goys.

Fritz. . . . I was about to write something about Fritz. I threw out the first word that came to mind, then the next, then the next.

All of them have been used so squanderously that they seemed belittling. I start over.

Tonight, I told Fritz what I had noticed about his work since his return. Rather, I told him *that* I had noticed, and my pleasure in the noticing. He said—without pride or boasting, simply as a fact—"Finally I am perfect. I have arrived. I can't do any better." I have this same sensing of what he does now—or how he is. Now that he is perfect in this way, how long will it interest him to go on with it?

Outside of groups, he has not been courting or demanding approval. He has let the people take over the community more and more, leaving them to run it, trusting them. This includes the financial affairs of Cowichan Lodge. This is a trust in people—for the people change and the Lodge continues.

I asked him about a sequel to his autobiography, out of my feeling that Fritz-now is not very much in the *Garbage Pail*. He said he is no longer ambitious. In the sense of autobiography, no doubt he was being honest. He still is eager to see the *Garbage Pail* in book form. To me, that is a part of ambition. His eagerness had no urgency in it, as it has had before, so perhaps that too is on the wane.

I don't have ambition in this respect. It's what *I* get out of this writing that interests me. If no one reads it, okay.

So what is my ambition? People often complained of me that I didn't have it. Van Dusen said that was not true, that I was spiritually ambitious—by which he meant ambitious to have more mystic experiences, I think. I don't have that, now. I do have wanting to disconnect all the junk in my head. There's not nearly as much junk as there was. I don't want *any*.

Tonight, David suggested breaking up into smaller groups and using more people as therapists. Fritz seemed to have this in mind. He will make the change Sunday evening—announce whatever therapists he has in mind. I want to do this, for what *I* would get out of doing it. I would have to do more of what I am doing anyway. I am afraid of doing it—expectations—because I am (now) comparing myself with Fritz and David here, and with Bob Hall in Mill Valley, Larry Bloomberg in San Francisco, Frank Rubenfeld in New York.

This is some of the junk I would like to get rid of. Usually, I don't compare myself with someone else. In *this* situation, I certainly am doing that and I don't like it. The fantasy of it shows in my even doing it, when I don't even know if Fritz will include me. . . . Something else comes in. *Me* be leader of a group which includes *therapists*? I am back in the same boat with Kolman, which I thought I had got out of years ago—lack of confidence in my ability because I haven't had years of "training" behind me. I *know* better, and this does me not one bit of good—a very typical neurotic situation. I want to work on myself to get rid of this, and at the same time it seems too much for me, such a wall of difficulty—all built up by me, so I *can* break through it—that I feel it's too much for me. "I need help." I *don't* need help. I can do it myself. I can do it.

I don't have a plan.

I did it.

Incestuous.

A compounded crazy-house.

That's what this place is to me this morning.

Is this *me*?

Compressed. That's me. I feel that way.

Last night I got out of fantasying and into this, which feels different. My head is mostly empty. These thoughts come in. I'm not rehearsing. I'm not responding to the lake, the wild duck on the lake, or—to me. I am a little angry.

I'm not responsive. I'm putting off. At some level, still, arguing myself out of something. Just now, I noticed the duck again and the reflection of the duck in the water—now he's dived. There is only a circle of ripples. Where will he come up? Now, he's up, with something in his mouth—he's dived again. He doesn't argue himself out of something. He *knows*.

So what do I know?

I know I want to take a shower.

I'm leaving here.

While blowing my nose, I thought, "How much will my money in Canada go down to when I go back to the U.S.?" That's leaving. Decision already made without my deciding it. The time to leave hasn't filled itself in yet. I feel strong.

I went out on the dock. It was beautiful there, with the bright-colored shore houses reflected in the water, the air so fresh and clean.

"Back to the U.S.? What will I do there, with the same fragmentation of life that I don't like here, and the smog. . . ."

No answer. I felt like coming back to my cabin and packing, throwing out, getting rid of excess baggage. On the way back, I heard the shouts from the group room, the yells, and knew that everyone else was in something like that, in the other two rooms that are being used for groups. I felt like the keeper of a crazy house as I walked across the lawn. I started to argue myself out of that, "Of course it's not that way." Whether it "is" or "isn't" has nothing to do with me. This *is* the way I feel about it, and that *does* have to do with me—and with no one else.

What I have got here will go with me, and I feel very good about that.

Thank you!
You were just what I needed.
I'll love you forever!
Goodbye!

My "loving you forever" will change if I stay, when you are no longer what I need.

I think of packing and it seems ridiculous. What am I packing for? I don't know where I'm going. Maybe this is just a fantasy, and I'll be unpacking again. "Stupid, what's the hurry?"

There is no hurry. I don't feel hurried. I just feel like packing, and packing feels good even though I hate packing. I like throwing out.

71

I have got so much out of being here. That feels good. I know something that I didn't, and correct a mistake before I have made it, and *that* feels good. I thought it would be okay to have a training center on a kibbutz. Now, I know that I don't want one on *my* kibbutz.

I feel that I have so much stuff. Uggh.

"A letter from my son." (My ex-son. He's on his own now.)

Last weekend was the workshop with Ralston's group. It went *very* well! At first, Friday evening, I was somewhat uncertain (my "little boy" thing), did the stump-cabin-stream fantasy trip as a starter. One gal really got into her cabin and started crying, so I worked with that. That evening and Saturday morning I wasn't *really* there, though some worthwhile work happened.

Then Saturday afternoon, after lunch, the sky-rockets started. One person triggered the next and some beautiful things happened. I was all there and it (I) was great. One gal had a 13-months-old baby with a bad heart; they decided on an operation which was not successful. She's been blaming herself for 16 years, but this time she really got through. She'd worked on it a few years ago. The grief alone didn't do it. But when she played the baby and told her that she (baby) *also* wanted the operation for a chance at a full life, *then* she could let go, and say goodbye.

After her, a woman really went crazy, and I mean *crazy*. *Playing* crazy, really. Slumping, twitching, schizo switches, out of touch, crying, screaming, etc. I just noticed my own indifference to her antics, and after she ignored a couple of instructions, I just relaxed and waited for her to run down. Then I just asked her what all the performance was for. She stopped dead, paused, and then went off on another tangent. Finally, I got her to relax (back in touch with her body and us) and settled for that. I was calm throughout, bemused and not rejecting—just vaguely interested. Most of the people there were taken in by the show and silently dropped their teeth when I casually asked her what all the performance was for. It was really a new thing for me. GAD! People sure are different— though I can see major patterns, the variety is fantastic. And do I have plenty yet to learn! I think I'll just have to do it for 10-15 years and pile up a host of experience to half-way know what is likely to happen. Fun.

My classes are going very well—really swinging. A thirty-year-old gal in one class came out of a fantasy trip sobbing on Friday. Today she came in looking like a lighthouse. She got in touch on Friday and worked on it over the weekend and got through something.

"I just noticed my own indifference. . . ."

That's all there is to it. What hassles I have just been through to notice that I want to leave here. Not a decision that ego-I made. All I had to do was notice. That's all I did do, in the end.

If pride or shame or good or bad or *any* opinion is present, I'm not "all there."

If anyone at this point thinks that I've been leading my son into Gestalt, go back to the beginning. He's not leading me around, either. When he applied for CO status when he was eighteen, there was the usual FBI investigation and the FBI sent him a resumé. No people were named. Places were. Some of what people had said was quoted. About half of them said that I had him under my thumb. The other half said that he had me hooked around his little finger. People on each side saw one aspect of what was happening, which in fact is a moving back and forth. When he was twenty-three, my son said, "Let's face it. You're a therapist to me and I'm a therapist to you."

It was he who brought me a paper by Carl Rogers, which led eventually to *Person to Person*. He didn't follow up on that. He was reading, over and over, Schachtel's *Metamorphosis* which I read once and dumped, except for one chapter.

We saw each other only about two weeks in a year at the time that I got interested in psychology in Albuquerque and he got interested in psychology in Pasadena. My interest arose out of discoveries when I was sick. His interest arose out of being at Caltech where "I see so many many people who aren't living up to their potentiality." He was studying chemistry at the time. Chemistry has never interested me. He wanted to study viruses and genetics. I am not interested in viruses and genetics. Before that, he wanted to go to agricultural college and learn about farming in a way that doesn't interest me. People told me that I was ruining him when I let him go along with that. "He has such a good mind." (As though a good mind can't be used on *anything*.) Before that, I was ruining him by letting him be in one-room schoolhouses, and by letting him miss a lot of school. "He'll never be able to go to college." I spent so much energy fending off all that—from him and from myself. Then, when he applied to Caltech and UC Berkeley and was accepted in both places, the same people said, "You can't keep a good mind down."

Here at Lake Cowichan, quite a few people have dropped in or been here in the workshops and told me of their enthusiasm for *Person to Person*. Real enthusiasm is appreciation. Phony enthusiasm—I get that, too—is depreciation. These people arrived here. I arrived here.

Happens.

I am much less spontaneous here than I am in many places. Many professional people here find the place fantastically free—which for a psychotherapy institute it is. I am learning ways to release people to (true) spontaneity. When I go, I take that with me.

I am people, too.

After three evenings of perfect functioning as a Gestalt therapist, last evening Fritz was not so good. "Three steps forward and two steps backward"? Fritz says that sometimes, of the way people move in therapy. That's the way it has always seemed to me that children grow. Sometimes, for awhile, it seems like five steps backward, then six steps forward.

Anyway, last night he started off haring down a false trail. He went by a system instead of noticing himself. He followed up with that for quite awhile, when it was clearly getting nowhere, before calling it off, saying, "Come back here. We are in a *cul de sac*." He gave a diagnosis to one man, a prescription to another. At the end of two hours, he said, "I am sluggish tonight."

In the *Garbage Pail*, he says that most of his life has been spent in confusion, but finally he learned to let the confusion be.

That's what I finally learned, when I was sick, about chaos. When I tried to sort it out, put pieces together into a pattern, I exhausted myself and got nowhere. When I learned to let it do itself, I came out of chaos.

I thought (sic) that I would go on with the finishing of unfinished business, which is a part of unhurried packing. This morning, I didn't give that a thought when I began to type. Now, it emerges, and I go on with it. It isn't important, just convenient. Last night I re-did the neck of a quite new dress which was coming apart because it hadn't been done properly. Now, I can wear the dress, instead of carrying it around. When I get through this kind of unfinished situation (sometimes by getting rid of, by throwing out) a lot clears up in my head. Fritz says we have to learn to "wipe our own ass." To me, this is part of it. I am not burdened now, and no one is burdened if I die. I don't do this daily or by any schedule. It's more like letting dust accumulate to a point which is still easy to clean up, and then doing it before it gets too much. I fall short of this kind of timing at times—like when I was transcribing the tapes to be edited for *Verbatim* for so many months, and let correspondence get behind—but mostly not that much accumulates.

Fritz' cabin is full of unfinished business. When I had a house and family, I went through the house twice a year and anything that hadn't been used or enjoyed for six months wasn't earning its keep. We are so afraid we might need something in the future. Glenn, who has worked with big corporations, says that lots of things get thrown out, including important papers, and all you do is say, "It isn't here." The world doesn't end. . . . I remember my husband's horror when I threw out my marriage certificate soon after we were married. He said I might *need* it sometime.

We clutter our lives and neurotically moan or groan about our burdens. Like the white man's burden to louse up the world instead of letting it be. Now we're cluttering up the stratosphere and the moon. Don't give me that stuff about "You can't stop progress." All we have to do is stop calling it progress.

Now I am empty again, and the other unfinished business comes in again.

I leave the typewriter, with a light wondering of interest what on earth will come in and fill up the rest of this page when I come back to it. . . . Just now, I thought of something else. It doesn't matter. Either it will come back later, or something else will come in. With all the millions of things to say and all the millions of ways of saying them, what does it matter which one comes in, or what comes next? Some will like one better than another, some will like another better than one. Some kind of inner order comes through on its own, in time.

Simplify. Who are you trying to impress?

I showered, dressed, ate, washed dishes and a few clothes. Now, I am drawn very strongly to the typewriter to write down what I have discovered.

A few weeks before we came here from Vancouver (and before I knew that I was coming) I told Fritz that I wanted to start a ranch or farm with a nucleus of people, and when we had got things worked out together, others could come in. He said, "Ah!" and I thought he was agreeing with me—that we saw the same thing. We came here, and soon it seemed to me that he was overriding the idea of a nucleus by bringing so many new people in, for whatever his reasons were—to make more money, or to spread Gestalt, were two I thought of. But if he saw "nucleus" in a different way from me. . . .

My own way of seeing it, expanded through my experience here, and clarified, is this:

Some of us who live more in the gestalt way would start the place, the way that we moved in here—people willing to take a risk, who don't have to have "all" the information beforehand (which in any case isn't possible). I was one of those who expected to sleep on the ground because although the two-bedroom House would be vacant on the day of occupancy, the tenants were reluctant to give up the cabins. I bought a down sleeping bag which could be opened out like a quilt, and a ground cloth designed so that it could also be used as a poncho. I didn't have to sleep on the ground. I have used the quilt all summer and the poncho when it rained. I haven't slept on the ground yet, but I didn't *know* that.

Yesterday a psychiatrist Air Force colonel arrived with his wife and their six children. They had met Fritz at Esalen for the first time last weekend. (Today is Friday.) In between, they decided to come here, came with their six children, and rented a house in Lake Cowichan before they arrived at this place. They took care of themselves. They wanted to come. They came. They didn't bother to get "all the details."

Wild ducks are flying, sometimes coming down on the lake.

Fritz came in and asked if I would like to be a leader for a week—when in fantasy I am moving into Okanagan. (I had decided to go back there and look for a ranch again—got really interested in going.) I didn't like to "give that up." Now, I know I am scared to lead a group again, so I'd better do it or I'll carry the scared with me forever until I do it. I'll even be some scared about exploring in the Okanagan. I wish the group began now, not next week. I don't want to plunge into writing and "forget" it. The more that I live now, in touch with me now and everything else now, and notice any rehearsing that starts, the better I'll make it. Right now my now is that I'm scared and my chest hurts and I want to cry a little. I'd like to yell, too, and I *don't* want to do this in a group. So let happen.

By letting the pain/fear take me over—express itself in sound and movement—I'm now not taken over by the pain and fear. And oh! the world does look so bright and polished!

Fritz mentioned that one of the psychiatrists in training here now has sixty people under him in a hospital, and he is going to change the way things are done there, and has invited Fritz to come and do something. Fritz doesn't bother with the details, and I don't want to be bothered with them. Indian talk. You make your own picture, and when it's made *in this way* you (i) live with it easy and don't get distressed, the way that you (i) (people) do when they get all the information, are sure (expect) it's the way they think it is, and then it isn't.

This psychiatrist said to me, "You don't want a job, do you?" I surely don't.

For eight years, at the insistence of my husband and because of my wish to keep him happy (not knowing then that only he could do that, and it was a silly idea anyway) I went (with him) to all the documentary movies of Hawaii. I found a distributor who kept me posted, and we would go to Brooklyn, Queens, uptown, downtown, anywhere to see them. I read about Hawaii. I learned so much that one evening at dinner when I sat next to a young man who had been in Hawaii, I talked so easily about the islands, as though I'd been there ("Do you know that little beach Lumahai, just beyond Hanalei" and so on) that he finally said, "I don't know. I was only there for six months." The words did fine, but when I got there, what I'd had in mind as Hawaii wasn't like the islands at all, or not very much.

Fritz said, "I have been so happy here, since I came back." I believe him. Feeling "sluggish" doesn't *have to be* unhappy. It's only when I think I "should be" something else that I am unhappy, and try to change it. Sluggish is. Pain is. Sadness is.

Happiness is letting all the happenings happen.

I see, too (with so few words from him) that *his* nucleus is right for him. Mine is right for me. So, I go on with mine.

This nucleus of people will arrive at good functioning in the Gestalt way—not perfect. That would *really* be a fantasy. But having somehow got the hang of it. People will hear about the place. . . . So far, that's okay. That surely will happen. If I go beyond that, as I was about to, I'll louse up the whole thing. Intellects will latch onto what I say and that will louse up everything. So that's the end of that couple of pages that I was "going to" write.

I'm still glad I started "packing," started moving in that direction. It feels right.

I've sure learned a lot here, I said this morning to Fritz. I surely have. I've sometimes thought "I don't want this place." That's the future coming in. I've stayed here. I went away and came back. As long as I stay here, it's because I want to. Even if I think (as I haven't for years, but years ago, I did) I am staying because there isn't anywhere else to go, I'm *not*. There is *always* somewhere else to go. I have chosen this place because I preferred it to other alternatives. My choice may have been good or lousy, but still it is my choice, and there's no sense in saying that I was "pushed into it." "I couldn't do anything else." The world is full of elses. It's got nothing else but elses.

When I "couldn't do anything else" is organismic, it always comes out right. When Mimi told me that she wasn't pregnant after all, that she had begun menstruating, so she wouldn't be going with her husband and me to town—ninety miles over dirt roads—I had no "information" but that. I didn't like Mimi and thought it would be better if she didn't have a baby. Organismic me somehow added things up, independent of my "thinking," and I told Mimi she had

79

better go to the doctor. No explanations, no bunch of unnecessary words. The ones I said came through clear and firm, definite without pushing. Mimi went—and stayed in town for two months on instructions from the doctor. She was pregnant, and if she had not had medical care at that time she would have lost the baby. I felt good. If I had overridden my organismic knowing, I would have felt bad. And I would have been. This is the only "bad" to me—a mis-take, a choosing of the wrong one. If I grieve about it, I hang onto it; that mis-take is still with me. Better to find some way to let it go. Otherwise, I am still making the old mis-take.

What happened with me/Mimi was awareness: I was aware. Then, I don't know how I get the answer.

I've come upon a page torn from *What Is Life* by Irwin Schroedinger which I've carried around for years. It must be 15 years since I last read it.

A blue jay is walking on the lawn. What a handsome black helmet he wears from crest to chest.

Schroedinger quotes Theodore Gomperz (whoever he is):

> Nearly our entire intellectual education originates from the Greeks. . . . You need not know of the doctrines and writings of the great masters of antiquity, of Plato and Aristotle, you need never have heard their names, none the less you are under the spell of their authority. Not only has their influence been passed on by those who took over from them in ancient and in modern times; our creative thinking, the logical categories in which it moves, the linquistic patterns it uses (being therefore dominated by them)—all this is in no small degree an artifact and is, in the main, the product of the thinkers of antiquity. We must investigate the process of becoming in all thoroughness, lest we mistake for primitive what is the result of growth and development, and for natural what is actually artificial.

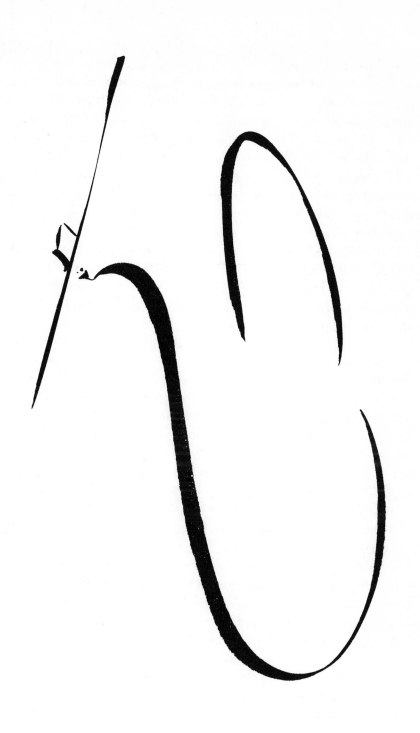

What is "therapy"?

Not psychotherapy or physiotherapy. Therapy. It makes no difference to me if I get it in the bathtub or in the group. I once worked myself into acute frustration, when I was sick, trying (sic) to write a paragraph. It kept coming out three pages. Finally, I dropped that madness and got into a tub of hot water. Zing! I was back when I was twelve years old, lived through three connected scenes (with different geography) and I fully (not intellectually) understood something that had puzzled me for forty years, and learned something about how "me" functions. Most of that is not specially relevant here, but one scene was myself walking on the dirt sidewalks of the village where I lived (I had forgotten those dirt sidewalks), going up one block and down another, my total concentration on saying over and over "I don't care. I don't care. I don't care. I don't care"—until I didn't hurt any more. I had made my own decision. It wasn't forced on me. All my mother said was "Ohh," and what I heard in her voice made me, out of my love for her (response-ability), let go of a possibility for me that I wanted very very much, so that I ached all over—first with my wanting of it, then with my giving it up. My decision was all right. At twelve, I had become too adult to go into the woods and let fly with rocks and sticks, "thrash it out" in the outside world, and *this* was wrong—was not right. Now, we have groups to do that in. We are at least beginning to make sense, even though a lot of non-sensing is going along with it in most places, where the idea is picked up without understanding. Then, there is relief without being released to growing: I am relieved enough so that I can go on living the way I have been: I can always go back for another dose. Maybe I'll try a different group. I'll meet more new people that way. "We group people know where it's at." The social whirl moved into another whirl is still the whirl. Spin, baby, spin, ain't it great?

"They call it the dance."·

Fritz is happy with the "beautiful example of the Gestalt formation" which he has discovered. The black and white picture of a woman with her hair piled high, in evening gown, sitting at a dressing table, looking into the big round mirror where her image is reflected. If you see it at a little distance, it is a skull. Her dark hair and the reflection in the mirror are eye-sockets. I forget the other details. Which one is "the picture"?

Teddy is cleaning Fritz' cabin. All sorts of thoughts can come in around that—good thoughts—mean ones. I can think (feel) good about it. I can think (feel) bad about it. The feeling follows my thinking. I can let them mix up and become very confused.

So "think good thoughts."

Not good. Illusion.

State them all, and they cancel out. No thoughts. Teddy is cleaning Fritz' cabin. That is real. All the rest is fantasy.

I am writing.

How is it going?

It is going. *How* I don't know. I have no thoughts about it.

I am writing.

I am a writer?

No.

My insistence on never becoming a something (career) makes sense to me now. Sometimes it seemed like an oddiocy. If I did, I would think of myself as that something, fashion myself to that something, become that something which is an illusion.

Just now, I went to the bathroom. I thought, "I must tell Fritz that my answer is Yes." No fear came with it. No images or thoughts of "what I will do." Just Yes.

All my "whys" of not wanting to lead a group here now were perfectly good ones. The only trouble is, they were fantasies. Until the moment came, I couldn't know what I felt. I could only *imagine* what it *would be*. When Fritz asked me, I didn't feel the way I *thought* I would; I felt the way I *did*. I had to come back from the Okanagan fantasy to feel it.

If all that seems too complicated, it surely is. Best not to think. I have set down my own foolishness as it happened so you can see the process. Emerson said he was an architect who built a house and forgot to put in the stairs. I show you some of my stairs.

Be honest, dammit! shouts in my head. I shout it. Writing it down makes it more clear and inescapable to me. That it then becomes available to you just happens.

And if it happens, that comes about through someone else, not me. This manuscript is not going to reach many people if someone else doesn't take a hand.

Navajo Mountain. The kitchen is a cozy place, with thick stone walls. Snow outside. Ken, who is part-Cherokee, Kee who is Navajo, and I are enjoying ourselves and each other, releasing our pent-up misery about lack of humanity in the Indian service. Ken says, "Anyway, I have my ranch to go back to, so I don't get ulcers." I say, "I don't have a ranch, but I can always hit the road." Kee says, "Me, too!" We each have our fantasy, a place to go and escape. We each know this is illusion. We express our joy in the freedom of it and feel good—just great. How we laugh and enjoy. The setting is different from the same scene played in many other places—homes, bars, wherever. What comes next is different, too.

A young Navajo, poorly dressed, comes in the door and stands quietly, then says he wants a ride to Inscription House. Ken says, "We're not going back that way." The Navajo stands. Kee sits. Sometimes one of them says something, then the other. Then nobody is speaking. I wonder if I am listening in on what should be private conversation, if I should go on talking with Ken and leave Kee and the young man to themselves. I have nothing to contribute. Kee and Ken know the whole country and the people in a way that I do not.

I look at Ken, to pick up a cue. He has crossed his legs and is looking at the ceiling. He not only isn't talking, he seems to have withdrawn. Why doesn't he say something to the young man, at least *try* to be helpful, instead of practically turning his back on him?

I pick up the cue. I become very quiet myself. All my thinking washes away. My mind is blank, empty. I am doing nothing. This continues for quite awhile. Then a piece of information comes in, and I say, "The dispatch didn't come today (the regular day). It will come tomorrow."

Kee and the young man say a few words in Navajo. The young man leaves. He will go to Inscription House by the dispatch tomorrow.

Kee, Ken and I move together with friendliness to look at some Franz Marc paintings. Our mood has changed.

Where, in our society, does everyone stop when a stranger comes looking for a ride?

Awareness.

Without that, I would not have realized that I did have something to contribute. I would have gone on thinking, and my thinking would have continued the way it began—like, "Surely Kee knows that. I'll be the white woman butting in."

There was no "butting in" when the information from me came from the silence in myself.

This silence is where my best functioning has come from when I have been therapist. "The ox and the man have departed."

This silence is what I'm afraid I won't have when I lead a group next week. If I knew that I would have just that, I wouldn't need anything more. Noticing and responding, without any thinking getting in my way. Then, everything happens and something has happened which produces change. Analysis is impossible, even after the event.

Did you notice what was in the hamburgers tonight, Kolman asked. He made them.

With all this noise, I said, I can't taste anything very well. I thought that I was making up an excuse for not having noticed. Then, still eating the hamburger, I noticed that it was true. With twenty people and wine making noises like Saturday night in a family-size kitchen, I couldn't really taste anything at all, unless it was strong like the garlic on the bread.

I should have known that what I said was true. Anything so ridiculous as noise wiping out taste I couldn't "think up," and when I'd said it, I was surprised, and thought I hadn't made sense.

When my feeler says "Yes" and my thinker says "No," here is confusion. What I think brings feelings with it, adding to confusion. On top of that, my feeler says things like "With all this noise, I can't taste anything very well," which *seems to be* thinking.

The absurdity of rehearsing! I've been noticing my fantasies about leading a group next week—not just noticing that I have them: noticing what goes on in them. This morning, there was a group of six people in my head, three of them indistinct. The other three were Peter, Marcia, and Charlotte. They moved and talked and I talked with them. No, I talked with Peter. I mimicked some of the movements of Charlotte and Marcia. Apart from the fact that I don't know what *they'll* do, there are thirty trainees, maybe more by now, who will be split up in groups of a size I don't know—maybe six, maybe ten—and there is no way for me to know which people will be in my group on Monday, or if these three will be in the same group, even. These three people, like all people, are real in my world when they are physically in my world. When they are in my head, they are not real. They do not even have a life of their own. They move, talk, do what I image them doing, and nothing more.

The lake now is light and dark lines moving rapidly from right to left. My right. My left. Now the lines are gone. Dark circles with light centers are. . . . they're not doing it any more.

In me, there are all these changes going on too. "How are you?"

I don't know. By the time I've noticed, I am already gone.

Now the lake is soft silvery ripples all over, everywhere I can see, moving from left to right.

How can Gestalt therapy use fantasies to negate a traumatic experience?

It doesn't.

It uses a fantasy to negate a fantasy.

I was in a hospital for a month in 1953. When I went to the

hospital, I had expectations. One of them was this: I had been going into something I didn't understand. Toward evening, sometimes, suddenly I became very cold. My son would fix a hot water bottle and build up a fire, while I went under as many blankets as possible. I would lie there, feeling that I was being sucked through a tunnel, with all sorts of strange things going on. I tried to notice them and remember them, so I could tell the doctor. I never could remember any of them—not one. I worried about this. I didn't understand what went on, and was afraid it might get worse. What was I moving into?

When I was going to the hospital in a few days, the doctor said that if this happened while I was there, to call him, and he would come immediately. The clinic where he worked was right next door. At this phase, I was mostly immersed in the medical view, and thought that he could check my body and discover something. If he were there, maybe I could tell him something of what went on while it was happening, and this would provide a clue. When I got into the hospital bed, this was one of my comforts.

Each time that I felt this strangeness coming on, I phoned. I didn't get the doctor. I left a message. He didn't come. Each time, on his next visit, he apologized, and told me what had happened. I knew what his life was like. I believed him. I didn't want to torture him; I tortured myself. That began when he didn't come: First hope, and a feeling of relief all over. Then, pain and despair when he didn't come and I went through all that strangeness alone again, with fear. I was angry that he didn't come. I was not angry *with him*. I was angry.

None of this was expressed—the pain, the despair, the anger. I didn't even think of doing this, and a hospital does not encourage it. ("And she has an illness, too?") I bound it all up tight inside me, held it in with my nerves and muscles (and wondered why I didn't get well in the hospital, now that I was "resting").

After two years spent mostly in bed, I arrived at knowing that I had to let myself be as sick as I was, not try to get well, not try to act being better than I was. "Gestalt tries to be in harmony with what *is*." "We cannot deliberately bring about changes in ourselves and others." "The organism does not *make decisions*. Decision is a man-made institution. The organism works always on the basis of *preference*."

Just then, I was first trying to remember (which of course failed) and then looked, in some notes I made for something else, for a statement by Fritz that I wanted to use here. In this instance, I wanted to use his words, not mine. Fritz came in while I was looking. Crrrrazy me. It was only when he was about to leave, and I thought about picking up my notes again (which I had already explored without finding what I wanted) that I thought "The guy's right here!" (The old gray mare, she ain't what she used to be.)

I asked him for his words. He gave them: "Any attempt to change is bound to lead to failure." I started to type and wrote "Any attempt to fail. . ." Fritz completed it ". . . is bound to lead to success."

(In the advanced training group, Fritz once told us to try to be the world's worst therapists.)

"Any attempt to change is bound to lead to failure. A counterforce is created. Like when you stare at red and then close the eyes, you see the green that comes afterwards."

Crazy. Mad. Mad, mad, mad. What I'm looking for walks up to me and I don't see it. Where am I?

In Arizona when my son was twelve, one Sunday he wanted to go hunting rabbits. Children were not permitted to go hunting alone, on this ranch. I went with him. We walked and walked through the brush. No rabbits. He wanted to go to the little lake, where (he was sure) there would be lots and lots of rabbits. I said no, that we must get back for Sunday dinner. (Never mind "why." A lot of explanation. A pack of lies.) He went on talking about the rabbits at the little lake. Probably, he imaged them there, lots and lots of rabbits.

A rabbit hopped out of the brush about fifteen feet ahead of us, and stopped. The rabbit squatted there. We walked another five steps before my son saw him, his eyes attracted by the movement as the rabbit hopped away. Too late.

Two years after I was in the hospital, something that I noticed in a different way was my exhaustion. I began noticing what exhausted me, as it happened, and getting rid of that, one way or another, whatever it was. Then I noticed that what had happened in the hospital was still exhausting me. I didn't see it then the way that I have written (see) it now, but still, I saw it. How the devil could I get rid of something that happened two years ago?

Asking the question, I got the answer. ("The way to develop our own intelligence is by changing every question into a statement. If you change your question into a statement, the background out of which the question arose opens up, and the possibilities are found by the questioner himself.")

I still wanted what I didn't get. I provided it myself. I put myself back in the hospital bed, and called the doctor. He came running over from the clinic next door. I liked that. I sent him back to the clinic and made him run *faster* to my bedside. I felt better. I sent him back and made him run *even faster* to my bed. I enjoyed that, and sent him back again. How I enjoyed controlling him instead of me!

Still, there was something missing. The doctor knew a lot about my body that I didn't, but he sure didn't know any more than I did about the crazy stuff going on in my mind. Who could help me on that? Aldous Huxley. So I brought him in, standing on the other side of the bed. I didn't have to make him run—he hadn't tortured me. So I just put him there. Then I noticed something else I didn't like—the hospital room. It wasn't cozy. So I removed all of us to a room in Huxley's house in California. On the left side of the bed was the doctor, who knew more about my body than I did. On the right side of the bed was Huxley, who knew more about my mind than I did. I didn't have to do anything—just leave it to them. I let go—and went into writhing and moaning and shaking and jumping (hips and shoulders). All this went on, with "me" comfortably inside, unconcerned. Something else began to happen after that. I don't remember what it was. I repeated this fantasy several times, on different days, each time stopping in the same place. I was tempted to go on. I stopped. When I told the doctor about this (mystified, as I am not now) he said, "It sounds good, but take it easy." He didn't know what was going on, either.

I wrote to Huxley and he replied,

> Deadlines are confronting me from every side and I have been, and am, indecently busy. Hence the delay in replying to your interesting letters and the inadequacy of this note to all but your remarks on the pseudo-sobbing, shaking and twitching, resulting in a sense of liberation and openness to healing. This is a phenomenon I have observed in others and experienced in myself, and seems to be one of the ways in which the entelechy, or physiological intelligence, or deeper self, rids itself of the impediments which the conscious, superficial ego puts in its way. Sometimes there is a recall of buried material, with abreactions. But by no means always. And when there is no such recall, many of its beneficent results seem to be obtained when the deeper self sets up this disturbance in the organism—a disturbance which evidently loosens many of the visceral and muscular knots, which are the results and counterparts of psychological knots. Disturbances of this kind were common among the early Friends—and led to their being called Quakers. "Quaking" is evidently a kind of somatic equivalent of confession and absolution, of recall of buried memories and abreaction to them, with dissipation of their power to go on doing harm. We should be grateful for the smallest and oddest mercies—and this quaking is evidently one of them, and by no means the smallest.

90

I asked the doctor what "abreactions" are. The dictionary didn't tell me very much. The doctor shuddered as he remembered, and he told me of being with a man who re-lived an explosion in a mine that he had been through, "going through the whole thing as he had experienced it before." The doctor told me of the terror on the man's face, and the man's yells, and his explosion with arms thrashing.

This sounded terrible—like something I didn't want to go through. I didn't check this with *my own experience*—didn't associate it with my own thrashing and moaning. Neither did the doctor. I didn't even suspect that the *man's* experience was different from the doctor's experiencing of the man. I got scared, and stopped exploring in that direction. What awfulness might come out of my past and smite me? Who knows what evil lurks in the hearts of men?

In the first place, I went to the hospital with expectations, and that is fantasy. When my fantasy didn't come through, I controlled myself, and that is pretense, which is also not real. When I worked with fantasy deliberately, I was still controlling myself two years after the event, and that's not real. What I did, although I didn't know it at the time, was undo one fantasy with another. Then they were both over with, and I was—in this area—real, released from the past and available in the present. Ploiinnng! The past was gone except in factual memory. That kind of memory is no bother to me. Neither good nor bad, it just is, like the dark outside my window now. When I thought of that time in the hospital after that, I didn't feel exhausted any more. I had let go of it.

I noticed another way that I exhausted myself. Whenever I thought of going next time to the doctor, I felt so tired. I didn't understand this. I *liked* going to this doctor. He was the only person with whom I was in real communication—as I described in *Person to Person*. Then I noticed that when I thought of being with him again, I imaged myself sitting in the chair beside his desk—where I was so weak and tired I could "hardly hold myself up." That's the way it was, each time I went to him. When I fantasied me talking to him while lying on the floor, I didn't get tired.

The first time I went to this doctor, already sick, it seemed to me that if I could just lie on the floor, I'd make better sense in what I told him. Maybe we both would have figured it out sooner, then. Go to a doctor and lie on the floor? Tchktchk. Right away he knows you are neurotic, crazy, an exhibitionist, or a sex maniac (according to *his* fantasies).

I learned something about doctors when I was nineteen. One of them told me to "undress." I whipped my dress and slip off over my head and was naked. He looked horrified. I felt bad. At the same time, inside myself I was saying, "I'm not bad! I just did what you told me to! I thought doctors were *used* to bodies." I went on feeling bad, ashamed. When I told friends about this incident, I left out that last part and made it a funny story, and *that* was phony.

After that, I was more squeamish with doctors. I asked them precisely what they meant. Then I became a little squeamish myself.

The whole damn sequence would never have taken place if I had told the doctor what was going on in me. Blooey. It's over.

By the time I was thirty, I had wiped out lots of categories by meeting and knowing people in many categories. "Curator" was one I hadn't met except very officially, when they were playing their role to the hilt.

I had got so messed up, in a bind, at the end of one two-month vacation that I went to my boss and told him that I was sorry I had misused my vacation, but I had, and that if I went back to work, I would louse him up too. I had been with my family on the vacation. He said he would give me another two weeks' pay if I would go off by myself for that time. I went to Bermuda alone, and I didn't even take anybody with me in my head. I noticed how good that felt. At the hotel, nobody *cared* if I was there or not, nobody *cared* if I ate or skipped a meal or two. I rented a bicycle. I would start out for one place, change course, and go somewhere else, and I didn't have to *report* to anyone. I didn't have to *think* of anyone else, or wonder if they would be cross or worried when I got back. I felt great—alert, interested, enjoying.

("Take responsibility for every emotion, every movement you make, every thought you have—and shed responsibility for *anybody* else.")

(What good—or bad—would it have done anyone to keep them in my head?)

I functioned beautifully, so often, without thinking. Just simple things. What else is life? I went to a bicycle place, told the man I hadn't ridden a bike for fifteen years, so could I rent one for a day and if I found I could still ride it, use that day's rent toward a week's rent, which was cheaper. I could still ride a bike.

I biked to the aquarium, which was in another town—not that anywhere in Bermuda is very far from somewhere else. I watched the fish in a large tank that began above floor level and continued up above my head. I was really enjoying those fish. (There were other times when I felt lonely, but not now.) A voice said "Good morning." I knew there was no one else in the room with me. I looked up, in the direction of the voice, and there was a head resting on the upper edge of the back wall of the tank. I enjoyed that head. The head said it was the curator of the museum. We chatted, and the head invited me to dinner, and asked if I would like to go trapping fish. I fantasied lots of wonderful fish that I'd never met before, all kinds of colors, and water sparkling all around. To this fantasy, I said yes.

Next day, when I went to the boat, I was surprised to find only the curator and a Negro boy. I had expected (fantasied) more people. As soon as we got out of Hamilton Harbor, the curator began flicking the boy with a rope. The boy flinched each time. The curator looked at me each time. I was appalled. I didn't know what to do. "Be still." I didn't know if that was right or wrong, but it seemed the only thing to do. I was still. The curator flicked the rope, the boy flinched, the curator looked at me, and the shimmering water rushed past the boat.

We sailed along the coast and into another harbor, I think this was Castle Harbor. There wasn't another boat anywhere. We sailed close to a rocky island which may have been all rock, and anchored. The curator pulled the dinghy alongside and got in. He held out his hand to me. I jumped in, feeling nothing but relief that now the boy would be left in peace (so I was, too). We climbed to the top of the rock. I enjoyed the climb, the rock, the sun, the air, and laughing with the curator who seemed happy too.

When we got to the top, very suddenly he grabbed me. I felt lost, helpless, beyond all hope. He was pushing me a little to the ground. The boy could no more help me than I had been able to help the boy. There wasn't another person anywhere, to call on.

Over the curator's right shoulder, I noticed a cloud, unlike any other cloud I'd seen before. Except that it was a cloud, nothing was the same. I shot my left hand out over his shoulder (I take responsibility now for what at the time seemed to be done by something not-me. "It happened," which is the way. . . . Just now I am seeing "taking responsibility for every action". . . .)

I made a sandwich and took it out on the dock. My feet were hanging over the dock edge, into the water. The movement of the water moved my feet up and down.

I said to Peter, "It feels as though it's playing with me." I didn't think the water felt that way, but still, when I changed that to "*I* feel that it's playing with my feet," something happened. A very little something, but like a mite more of me added to myself.

"Take responsibility for every action." When I didn't take responsibility for that action, I was by that much less me. On the other side, if I kill someone and say "God told me to," that's no good, either. *I* did it.

The first few times that I said "Look!" there was no change in the curator. I was aware of that, but my attention to that cloud was stronger than anything else in my world. The curator turned his head and looked at the cloud. He took one of my wrists in his hand and dragged me down the steep rocks so fast that I had an image of myself bent like a bow, and my ankles scraping on the rocks. We got in the dinghy, to the sailboat, and headed out of the harbor. There was no non-sense—all sensing. He said it was a hurricane cloud. When we got back to Hamilton Harbor, the hurricane signals were up.

I didn't like to talk much about these rescues which happened every now and then. Sometimes, I'd try to figure them out. They happened. Often, my life seemed like a miracle. I couldn't believe that I had been singled out by God for special attention. What troubles I got into, I got out of so quickly, with such ease. To believe that *I* did it also seemed to put me in some special category and I didn't like that—especially when I seemed (afterwards) to have been "taken over" at such times.

I got the first glimpse of what seemed like truth to me about ten years later. My nine-year-old son and I were staying at a beach in Hawaii which we knew very well—for all of his life, in fact. He was in the water, swimming. I was on the shore. He called to me saying, "I can't get in!" I swam out to help him. Then I was there, too, unable to get back. There was no one left on shore for me to call on. He was on his back, with my right armed hooked into his. I swam and swam and got nowhere. He panicked and flipped over and landed on top of me—eighty pounds of him. I panicked some, myself, though I controlled it.

Two people emerged from the ironwood trees along the shore. Hope! I called to them, "Help! Help!" They turned their heads and looked at us, then turned away and walked along the beach. I have never felt more forlorn, abandoned by the whole human race. They dawdled, and it was a long beach. They were almost out of sight before I came to my senses.

I noticed a few small blocks and chips of wood drifting out to sea. *Out.* They should be moving in. Off to my left, I noticed there was a place where this didn't happen. The movement of the waves was in, to shore. I swam us parallel to the shore until we were in the shoreward movement of the water. Then, the water and I together moved us in. We were almost to the surf when I felt exhausted, as though I could do no more. I pushed my son with all the force I could bring together, thinking, "Well anyway, he'll make it," and I went down, down. My head was in the water, with all the rest of me. Then my toes touched sand. I pushed that sand just as hard as I could (this time, I knew it was me) and seemed to take strength from the pushing. When I reached the top, I began swimming for the surf, the shore.

95

"Heroism" phooey! I could have noticed those chips in the first place—I say *now*.

That afternoon, a young man came to see us and go for a swim. I didn't tell him. Instead, I told myself. I told myself that he was young and strong and an excellent swimmer, and that I had got into trouble because I was a weak woman, and if I said anything he'd laugh at me for making a lot out of nothing. Maybe he would have. (The *how* of my saying it then would be different from the *how* of my now.) I felt awful when he came back and said, "Whew! I almost didn't make it back." He was strong enough to swim in against the current. Suppose he hadn't made it? I felt guilty, and my guilt was not resentment.

Awareness. If we both had been aware, the whole story could have been told in "I noticed the current, swam across to where it wasn't, and came in."

When my son and I were both on the beach, we stood there with our heads down, between our knees. I don't know why we did that. Then, after awhile he said, "Now let's go back in." How I didn't want to. Like almost utterly. I felt drowning. The sea was a black monster, a horror. I was so small and puny. Eucchh. I felt like vomiting.

My son often made better sense than I did. We went back in.

It's the same as with my fear of leading a group. If I ran away, I'd still be afraid of doing that. As it is, I'm some afraid of next time, but nothing like I was before. I was neither good nor awful—just sort of mediocre. Not nearly enough aware—of them, of me. The best, it goes without saying but I'll say it anyway, was when Fritz came in when Roy was in the hot seat. Fritz—where are the words. He was all there with Roy—not phony all there. Real. Un-real Roy came through a little bit more real. What a struggle that is. How long it takes, for just a little bit. Still, it's the beginning, which has to come first—same as my leading the group this morning is the beginning.

Valerie, Fritz and I talked awhile, after the others were gone. Valerie spoke of a woman here who has been through four years of

Reichian therapy in New York. She doesn't feel helped. Fritz, "No one thing is enough. The body is not enough. The mind is not enough. The soul is not enough." Amen.

Fritz stayed for a cup of tea with rum. "I am moving more and more into encountering the person." That's what he did with Roy. He said to Roy, "Ever since you have been here, I have heard you croaking. You have no voice." He said, "You are an artifact." His voice was soft and neutral, with no tentativeness in it.

Vacation.

Vacate.

To be empty of.

When I was sick and broke and trying to get well of both, I was working on it all the time. Each Friday toward evening, people next door and across the street were throwing things in cars and going away. I felt very very sorry for me. *I* needed a vacation more than anyone else, and I couldn't take one. I *had* to go on trying to get well and trying to find some way to make some money.

I can't stand being sorry for myself.

After a few weekends, I shut up shop on Friday evening and didn't think about money or getting well until Monday morning. I had a beautiful vacation—all the good feeling of it.

When I was working on *Person to Person*, I noticed one morning that I woke up, got up, and went straight to the typewriter—like an automaton. I had been coming closer to this for several weeks, without noticing. When I did, I called off writing and noticed what I wanted to do and did it. I stretched by hooking my fingers onto the lintel of the doorway. Went from that to putting one hand on the stove, the other on the kitchen counter, and swinging my legs. Felt hungry, opened the refrigerator door. A piece of steak was what I wanted. I cooked it, at ten o'clock in the morning. Then I tossed a yam in the oven. Walked through to the living room. And so on. When I felt like going to town to get brush painting ink and brushes, I didn't tell myself anything: I walked downtown and got them. Notice—do; notice—do. Nothing else, for two days. On the evening of the second day, I went to the bathroom, sat on the toilet, and as I was sitting down, I thought with exquisite joy, "My! but I've had a beautiful vacation!"

That was the first time that I thought of it as a vacation. The way that I felt produced it.

Then, my interest in doing the book returned, and I wasn't an automaton any more.

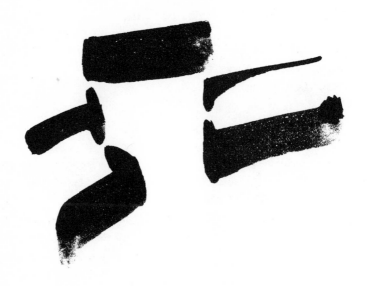

Mirage

I didn't forget everything in the group this morning. I feel good about what I did forget. I forgot that some of the people were psychiatrists or psychologists, although I know that one of them is a psychiatrist and one a psychotherapist, and I think two more do something like that. I almost totally forgot Fritz after he came in the door, while I was working with Roy. Perhaps tomorrow I shall forget even more. Vacate. Be empty.

"—and shed responsiblity for *anybody* else." At the ranch (60 square miles) and school (one-room schoolhouse) where I worked for a couple of years, one day five of the children were demanding that I give them permission to do something—I forget what it was. At this ranch, the children did things which chilled the marrow of some of the visitors. What they insisted on permission to do was *so* hazardous that I could not say yes. They jumped up and down, demanding, insisting. Out of desperation, I said, "All right, go ahead—but remember! if you do, it's *your* responsibility, not mine." They stopped jumping and yelling, and quietly, thoughtfully, went off and did something else.

Right now, I'm tired of words. If I thought of going on, even at some future time, I would feel like upchucking.

Poor Aldous Huxley and his deadlines, and his completing an article while dying—weak, sick, barely able to talk. And Laura thinking him noble.

Maya. Illusion. "World: the thing we live in."—from a *Dictionary of Five Words* composed by a seven-year-old.

I didn't lie awake last night rehearsing for today's group, either. I forgot, and went to sleep.

When Adrian van Kaam came to this country from Holland, he was appalled at the American notion that a professor should be available to everyone. In his little attic room at Brandeis we were getting into something together, working something out in a semi-but not totally intellectual way. I was feeling something happening in me, noticing something happening in him. Knock knock! That person left. Before we could get ourselves together where we had been, knock knock! Interruption. Each person entered with a demand.

In Europe, it seems, the society provides more protection, at least for professors. In my own society, I have to provide my own protection—and that is okay, as long as I *do* it.

In Saskatchewan at the cross-cultural workshop, one evening Wilfred (Indian) said, "I'm feeling strange." He asked his sister, Gracia, and me to come to his room. In his room, Wilfred was exploring his "strangeness," arriving at something. There was a knock at the door. Gracia said as she got off the bed, "That is a white man's knock!" White folks blundered in with "joy," one of them hopping onto and over the bed.

Next evening I blundered in on something, more quietly, but still it was *the same thing*. I noticed myself doing it, and I felt sad. I let a white man's non-awareness swamp me. *I* did it.

I feel like going crazy. The word is the word is the hullabaloo. I'm stuck, when I can't go any crazier than that. In fact, it looks like sense. Maybe if I went even crazier, I'd make more sense.

To try to "follow" Fritz is crazy. By the time you've done it, he isn't there any more.

When I was twenty, I laughed at a childhood fantasy when I remembered it. The sidewalks and roads in our village were all dirt. A boy I was attracted to lived on a street which was being torn up for something or other. To get to his house, you walked a block over mound after mound of dirt. In my fantasy, I walked over these mounds of earth to see him—with my hair worn piled high like a lady, and wearing a shining copper evening gown, with train. It was like a dream, in that this didn't seem ridiculous to me. I had big breasts, too. Tripping along, in my fantasy, I knew he'd *have* to notice me, and how glorious I was.

At twenty, I had other fantasies. I didn't think that *they* were silly. Notice yours before you laugh at mine. Then we can all laugh together.

Fantasies are helpful sometimes—as long as I don't get mixed up and think they are reality. When I was in so much trouble with my husband and afraid that I was insane, which I was, only not in the way he thought I was, I developed intestinal hives and mononucleosis which of course dragged me even lower. I fantasied the doctor as a radiant saint who loved me, and rested in this fantasy when I needed rest, without ever losing track of my knowing that he was just a nice guy and a good doctor and I liked him.

Spontaneous fantasies are different. A recurrent one of mine, that I haven't had lately, is of myself in a cabin in beautiful country. I am lying in bed, and whatever I need is brought to me although there are no people around. I enjoy the rest, and at the same time know, when I have this fantasy, that rest is what I need. I get the message and act on it. I drop some of the things I have been doing and this fantasy disappears.

Noticing is the first step. Awareness of what's going on in me.

101

I feel like sketching, now.

This morning's group is over. Tomorrow? Tomorrow, I get the people Don picked for his group and I don't know who *they* are. I could quite easily find out. What good would knowing do? I'm feeling good about something I used to feel bad about—not interested in knowing. During World War I, I was corresponding with a lot of young men in service—American, British, French and New Caledonian which is a kind of French but in a different place. A young Scot who was not in service was writing to me. He had got my name and address from a friend who tore it off someone else's package and never used it. This Scot did. We had a great time, corresponding. My sister asked me, "What does he *do*?" I didn't know what he did and didn't care, and felt bad (something wrong with me) because it was important to my sister. "How can you *write* to him when you don't know what he *does*!" she said, without a question in her voice. She didn't want to know. She was telling me something. I didn't know what it was. I felt a hole in me, something I should cover up. My sister was older than I, and knew so much.

I was still in the same trouble that I was as a small child, when my father carried me when we had to go any distance. Sometimes on a Sunday, we would start out from our house and go to the trolley. We took the trolley to the ferry. We went on the ferry to New York—houses and houses and houses, sometimes a whole row of them hitched together and all looking just like the others. When we got off the ferry, we took another trolley. Then we got off that trolley and took another trolley. Then we got off that trolley and went down a couple of blocks and turned and went some more blocks. We went up some stairs. My mother or my father would knock at the door or ring a bell. The door opened—and there were people whom we *knew*. How on earth had my parents found them? What clever clever people. *I* couldn't do that.

Then, when I knew the truth of me, and one or the other of them told me otherwise, there was the surge of my own knowing which was put down by my knowing their cleverness. They *must* be right. No, *I* was right. They *must* be right. No, *I* was right! They must be right. No, *I* was right. They *must* be right. No, i was right. *They* were right, and i was wrong.

I made this same mistake with my husband for a long time. He knew so much. He had spent eleven years in college, including three at Oxford and four in medical college. He had lived abroad. He knew France (and French) and Germany (and German) and geology and architecture and medicine and poetry in Latin and famous people (Julian Huxley, Henry Luce, Archibald MacLeish, Max Beerbohm and some of the Mitsuis) and India (and Burmese) and English history and literature. When he talked about people and life, I thought he must know people and life better than I did, too. It also seemed to me that he didn't, but I kept squashing that down under all that he knew.

When we went to Hawaii, he couldn't learn pidgin. He would give instructions to Sato-san, the gardener who worked for us two days a week, and when my husband had left for Honolulu, Sato-san would come to me and ask "What boss speak?" Pidgin was a breeze for me, and rollicking fun. With all his languages, my husband could neither speak nor understand it. Why was that?

Why couldn't he see how he made enemies of people who weren't enemies? There were just five people whom he trusted—four men and me. I watched three of the men become "untrustworthy" and felt this coming very close for me.

When I left Hawaii (age 43) I was "never going to learn *anything*." What was the use of knowing so much if you were so miserable with it? There was Bertie Russell too, and all his unhappiness and making no sense.

That was when I took our son, age 9, to a ranch in Arizona. From so many sides, I was told that this was wrong. A Japanese woman who worked as a maid told me that in Japan, years ago, the nobility always sent their children to live with peasants—as peasants themselves—"so they will not lose touch with their origin." That made sense to me.

Ima, who told me this, told me other things, too. During the war, she was on a bus in Honolulu. A sailor spat on her. She got mad.

Then she remembered a train in Japan, and a Japanese who was very rude to an American. "It is the same thing." That was *her* way of finishing that situation, of clearing her mind. Canceling. She had another way of dealing with Mrs. B, a daft bitch of a woman. With her, Ima explained, "Every once in awhile, you make WHOOSH! Then everything be all right for awhile."

This morning began with Fritz coming in just as Natalie took the hot seat. They worked together beautifully. I butted in once, out of my stupidity. Sometimes I am glad my butts are so mild that they can slip past unnoticed. (I didn't recognize that this was what it was until I had done it. I had been talking to me and listening to that liar who tells me.) After that, two men, in turn, took the hot seat. Peter wants help and is very determined to do everything himself. Toward the end, he spoke of his frustration. I mentioned what Fritz had said, "When I try to climb this wall, I feel impotent." Peter then tried to climb the wall. He really worked at it. Then he tried to get through by pounding it. Then he tried to undermine it. Finally he said, "I could go through the door," and he opened the door and walked out.

I imaged the Zen story of the man clinging to the bars at the window, when the door is open behind him.

I got a lot out of this morning. I give myself a direction to remember it, to dredge it up now and set it down so I won't forget. I let go of this instruction out of my knowing that it's all recorded in me. My work is to make myself available to that storage house, so that it can be available to me appropriately, as things happen. That happened a little more today than yesterday. When I *try*, this storehouse is not available to me, even if my trying is only trying to pay attention to what's going on. Then, the only thing that comes into my head is *rules*, and that is neither Gestalt nor gestalt. That kind of trying is like trying to learn a language instead of letting it sink in, come out awkwardly, and move on. It's like the difference between reading a book and stopping at every word I don't know (haven't learned yet) and reading a book guessing at the words I don't know. If I'm right, that will prove itself as the word comes up again. If I'm wrong, next time or some other time will show me—if I'm not concerned about being right.

Blunders this morning were noted at the time. (Not *later*.) They're taken care of. I don't "have to" dredge them up, work them over, beat myself on the head with them while hurting in my chest, try to correct them. Some of them I may make again. If I focus on this and berate me, I haven't noticed the "all"—that others did *not* get made again. If I cling to them, I'm *bound* to make them again. The more I try, the more I fail, because the error is in *trying*.

I'm learning. With so much less pain, less bludgeoning, now that I am willing, less torturing of me by me. Less split. A movement in the direction of being whole, of letting what *I* calls *me* take over. Then both I and me have departed.

Fritz started playing some music in his cabin next door. I heard sadness in the music. My own sadness began to rise and spread. I feel it all through me. I am sadness, and there is nothing wrong with sadness. Sadness is.

Probably nothing can be explained. George, in going through a dream, was George flapping his arms like wings, trying to fly, and sinking deeper and deeper into something. Then he was the boy in his dream, with a bug crawling across his chest. As George, he hated the bug. As the boy, when the bug had got all the way across his arm and into his armpit, the ground suddenly came up under his feet. George didn't get the message but he *felt* something. Perhaps it will get through later. Who else can get it but George? No one. It's his message.

Fritz asked Natalie this morning when she had been developing a dream and arrived at something, "Did you get the message?" She said "Yes." Fritz: "I don't know what it is."

He doesn't have to know. He didn't ask her, like in school, "What is it?" He left her with her own knowing, which need not match his, and in any case is *hers*. ("Well, if you can't tell me, you don't know." I don't know where that comes from. I hear it being said to me, at some time past, with an exclamation point at the end which said, "You are wrong!"—like "you are lying.")

"A lot of water has gone under the bridge since we last met," Liz said. "*Good* water."

105

The lake is rushing like a river. Whitecaps.

So much has flowed since yesterday. I can't remember yesterday. When I give up trying, first going to Duncan comes in. Then sitting with Fritz and Barbara and Marcia in the kitchen late last night. Then the evening group, all of us with Fritz. Then lunch comes in, and the fact of the morning group—with no details. I try to remember, and go blank.

This morning was rain again and low gray clouds. Now, sun is reflected in the water, silvery in some places, diamond-like in others. Sunshine comes through the window, warming the typewriter and my hands. I still don't recall yesterday morning's group beyond knowing that it happened, and happened here. I don't know who was in it or what they did or what I—Pat. I remember that Pat was here yesterday. Peter . . . Bruce . . . Natalie . . . the people are coming back in, now.

No orderly sequence of recall. Now I remember being in the kitchen around three-thirty with Glenn and Tom. All of it is available to me, all of it can come back. All of the past. What on earth would I do with it? Better to let it go—all of it.

This morning before the group came, I felt that if they all decided to leave, that would be just fine. They would be doing what I wanted them to do.

Now, I would not have missed this morning. I was much more in touch with my own spontaneous imagery today, and had more confidence in it. I let too many of these images go in the beginning, and it might have been a shortcut if I hadn't. Then again, it might not have. It is never possible to go back and start over. So much has changed. "We never step into the same river twice." I have a good feeling now, about tomorrow. I don't want to change today. Tomorrow is another river. I feel good with my not-knowing. Interest. No apprehension. No fantasies.

One instance of imaging. Pat was being her limp lax self on the floor, then her pounding hammer-hammer self on a bench, shuttling back and forth. I noticed that her hammer-hammer self was becoming less forceful, although she still had strength. Her limp self was not as limp. I was enjoying this happening. Then I imaged Pat standing between her bench self and her floor self, and asked her to do that. What happened then was good, and ended her working for today.

I have been discovering a mistake of mine, little by little, lately, and discovering a way to. . . . Well, skip that. I'll get all mixed up with "I" and "me" and. . . . Let that go, too. . . .

From the time I first came here, I noticed how much difficulty I had remembering people's dreams when they told them. I couldn't see how Fritz could work with a person on one part of a dream, then go back to another part like ping! I thought he must remember the whole dream as it was told. I could never do that. I'd be a lousy therapist in this area of Gestalt.

Recently, I've noticed that when I let the words go by and image the dream as it is being told, then parts of it come back to me at times, and I can trust going back to whichever part does, recalling the other person to it. Then the other person moves on with this, and I move with him.

When I don't do this, I am very hazy about the dream, and can't latch onto anything, or if I do, it is in a vague and fumbling way which the other person can't connect with.

Sometimes something strange happens with this imaging. A girl told her dream (in the first person, according to Gestalt) which began in some fields. Then she moved on, and came to a bridge. That was the end of the dream. She didn't cross the bridge. That's easily noticed and remembered. She wanted to start with the fields, and this felt right to me. After that, she wanted to go somewhere else in her dream. I asked her to go to the bridge, which I had imaged at that moment. She went there, and said it was an arched bridge. It was an arched bridge that I had imaged in the beginning. I should have asked her what color it was—just so I wouldn't wonder. Mine was red. That the bridge took her on a journey from which she got an existential message is not strange.

I have been trying to hear, trying to remember, in the groups, and getting tired—then "going away" in my head for a rest. That was all right when that was all that I could do, just as the past is all right when whatever I did was all that I could do. I couldn't do anything else.

It seems to me now that my imaging of the dream as it is told—or noticing the image which takes place, which may be the truth of it—may be opening me up to noticing the images which happen while the work is going on. Openness to images.

When Runi had completed working with Fritz, and he left, Runi said, "I'm such a coward." We were taking a break. I was putting something away at the sink counter, to make room for people to make coffee. "Scared" was my image—imaged as a word. I asked Runi, "Is the word 'scared.'" In a moment or two, she said yes. "Coward" is a judgment, a fantasy. People can say "No, you're not" and "Yes, you are," and I can become confused and fight the confusion and go on fantasying. "Scared" is a reality. I can feel it, and know it's there.

I feel like putting a poem here.

108

Pusher

Beware the seeker of disciples
the missionary
the pusher
all proselytizing men
all who claim that they have found
the path to heaven.

For the sound of their words
is the silence of their doubt.

The allegory of your conversion
sustains them through their uncertainty.

Persuading you, they struggle
to persuade themselves.

They need you
as they say you need them:
there is a symmetry they do not mention
in their sermon
or in the meeting
near the secret door.

As you suspect each one of them
be wary also of these words,
for I, dissuading you,
obtain new evidence
that there is no shortcut,
no path at all,
no destination.

          — Peter Goblen

October 1st. I am hot in the sunlight. I change to a cool dress. Earlier, the warm one felt right and was right. How absurd to think that I must be always warm to people or always cold to people, to think anything. I feel warm. I feel cold. I am warm. I am cold. I love you at this time. I don't love you at this time. Don't demand of me what I haven't got. . . . Who makes this demand? I do. I make this demand of me, there is no we in me. Yield, and there is a pseudo-we. *I* am not in it—only my pseudo-self. When I demand nothing of myself, where is the demand? I don't feel it. I can know the demand is there in someone else, but I can't feel *his* demanding. Only he can feel that.

"I can see your scratch. I cannot feel your itch."

I looked up and saw a waterfall on the most distant hill. It isn't a waterfall. It just looked like a waterfall at first glance. Was I "wrong"?

I enjoyed the waterfall. An atom of delight invaded me.

A mis-take. Hardly a mistake.

Today in the break, a woman who had been demanding a response from a man—a particular kind of response, which she didn't get—then came to me and was demanding of me. I said something. She went on as before. I said something. She went on as before. I put my hands over her ears and said "You are not listening." She said, "Well how can I with your hands over my ears?"

Today in the group, Fritz asked me to let others participate "the way they are doing in the other groups." This was going on yesterday, so I didn't have to make a change. Then he added choosing a co-therapist, and also supervising. Just when I've got in balance in one position, he switches me to another and I wobble and lose my balance. I want to be in *this* group again, and do better tomorrow—but it's good the change comes now. I might forget I'm not stepping into the same river. With new people, I'll *know* it. I'll *have* to notice. Working with a co-therapist, letting others come in too, and "supervising" *all this*?

What does "supervising" mean? . . . . Super-vision. That's even worse. I ain't got it.

This is ridiculous! I looked in the Oxford Dictionary and it isn't there. Am I spelling it wrong? "superstition" followed by *supinate*. ("Turn (hand) palm upward"). . . . . I find it in Webster's School and Office dictionary, but that's not much more than a spelling book. It says "overseer."

So I'm back to myself again. No outside authority. I have to do it myself whatever it is. I know what "it" is.

I resent feeling the tugging and pulling in my chest and back again. I sure remember *that* feeling. Over and over. Just when I had got "life" all nicely arranged so I could be reasonably comfortable in it, powie! Something else came in and broke it up.

Where was the "Powie!"?

What has "hit" me, now?

Am I doing the hitting? While thinking "Now I've got to haul myself together again and start over again."

The load doesn't seem so heavy, this time. I'm just resenting having to do it *again*.

I found "supervision" on the preceding page under "super-." I don't like that way of doing it, but I suppose it makes this edition of the Oxford Dictionary concise. The word means what I thought it did. I hoped maybe I'd find an out.

Now, I don't need one, and I haven't got any burdens on my back.

Last night at the House, where Fritz eats, the curry was mostly curry. He ate bread and milk and enjoyed it, but he resented the curry. He said so in community meeting last night. It seemed to be like my resentment of a lot of food on this continent: not *only* that it is not good for me, but it's so non-sense-ible. I *like* the taste of rice, beans, peas, carrots, lamb, beef, and so on. Most of the people I know season everything so much that I can only taste the seasoning. Another gripe I have is "casseroles," in which everything is so mixed up I can't taste any of it and what I can taste is what it's disguised with, or else something that I like for lunch but not for dinner, like canned tuna.

Mixed-up dishes are okay for left-overs, but I like *sometimes* to eat what something is left over from.

I invited Fritz to have dinner with me. No, supper. "Dinner" got taken from the fashionable people who "dined," while the rest of us ate supper. Only Sunday was dinner, around one or two o'clock. We ate dinner, but we didn't dine.

It was the nicest supper that I've had for so long, with a companion and still with so much silence, and neither of us playing roles or pretending. At least, I didn't notice Fritz' role if he had one, and I wasn't having one myself. He was to have come at five-thirty or six. Around six-thirty he wasn't here, so I looked in his cabin and he wasn't there, so I went up to the House and he was sitting in the living room reading a newspaper. "Oh! I knew there was something. . . ."

Now is nextday, after the group. I did it. I feel good that I did it by not trying to do anything, which feels like doing nothing. Noticing and happening. The aftermath is that I am now much more aware. . . . I remember feeling this way sometimes after sex, the wonderful happiness of happenings all over including me. Before sex became a part of my life, there was so much of this happening. Once I heard the clocks ticking in a clockshop window as I passed by—like hearing *each one* ticking. The shop was closed—I heard them clearly through the glass window.

Steam shovel sounds from a little way off. People sitting on the dock and reflected in the water. Man lying on springboard. In the water, springboard is lying on man. People get up and walk away. Where *are* the people? Doesn't matter. Not in my world. Tooot! a whistle blows somewhere to my left. Direction is clear. Hills are rippling in the water, dark hills, light water. Notice the light, and it becomes surface, dropping off like a cliff to the dark below. Like looking over the edge of a cloud. . . . Then I tried to *force* an image. Grrrinnnnnnnnd. Grrrrrr. I let it go. That's not noticing. It's *doing*. No, *trying* to do.

This morning when I didn't try in our sense, I got back to the original meaning of "try." If I put that in, someone would try to try that way. The *meaning* would be lost, just as it has been.

People still laugh at that old story about the man who was sorting potatoes muttering "Decisions, decisions, decisions!" Where they (individually) laugh from, I don't know. If he was sorting them from his organismic self, he wouldn't be "making decisions." So I am smiling with a corner of my mouth turned down.

I didn't make decisions this morning. I didn't have a program, for me or for anyone else. This was easier because I went to bed earlier last night. That should be all caps. THIS WAS EASIER BECAUSE I WENT TO BED EARLIER LAST NIGHT.

I have sometimes become this kind of loose out of exhaustion or despair or inability to hold on. I feel so good that now it comes easi-er. I never did like those Christian heroics of the frenzied artist coming through with something beautiful. Now we have the artists who turn loose by splashing paint from a bucket. It can be interesting. It's still paint splashed from a bucket. As such, I have no quarrel with it.

What I learned this morning from the group is so much that I would have to be nuts to try to write it. I wouldn't have time for anything else. And then, you still wouldn't have it. Besides, it's in every atom of me. I feel that my toes know it, my hands know it, my shoulders know it, my belly knows it, and my head only knows it *too*. If you cut off my hand, my hand would still know it. (I feel.) This is where my knowing belongs. If it isn't all over, it isn't *knowing*. Encyclopedias are full of "knowledge." Do they know it? No under-standing. While supping with Fritz last night, sometimes we said something. No. Sometimes he said something. Sometimes I said something. So few words. So much under-standing. As we ate slowly, savored the very lightly seasoned food, he said, "People use spice instead of saliva."

He said that sometimes he envies me, that he has nightmares about expansion. I asked him if he meant about finding more housing and so on. "*Real* nightmares. I know it is my ambition." Seeing things as they are. Not pushing me into pushing *his* ambitions. No telling me that I should be more ambitious. No damning me for

113

what I am. He lets me be. I let him be. Not intellectually: *totally*.
Like my toenail knows it, my eyeballs know it. No part of me
holding back. I am not "being reasonable." Separation and
confluence both at once. Not unreasonable, either. Just non-
reasonable. No reasoning in it. Beyond reason. Beyond understanding
and misunderstanding. Here is peace is love is everything I want and I
am not wanting.

George came to me yesterday afternoon. (He is wrong-agitated.)
"Was Pat in your group this morning?" "Yes." "She's been out there
(he points to the trees) ever since, crying. I didn't know what I
should do." I say nothing. "I thought I'd better tell you."

For a moment, *I* was wrong-agitated. "So he dumps it on *me*."
But then I knew (most markedly from my chest, although the
knowing was all over) "Let be." That evening in Fritz' group, Pat
took the hot seat. She said, "I thought I didn't have any pride. I
discovered this afternoon that isn't true." "Being helpful" is robbery.

This morning, Forrest was breathing very lightly. He said it felt
comfortable. When I misuse a part of me for a long time, I feel
comfortable that way. It's the way I'm used to. I feel pain when I try
to change it. We worked on his breathing ("we" is accurate here) and
he made some discoveries not just about his breathing but his way of
life. (None of the things we asked him to do were breathing
exercises.) My way of life (or of pseudo-life) is not out there: it's
right here in me, and what I make my body do is part of it.

Last night in the large group, Fritz lectured a little on "the
question is the hook of a demand," and on chewing. Forrest asked
Fritz if he would give some examples of changing a question into a
statement. There was a brief, slow-paced dialogue between them.
That ended when Forrest realized that in asking the question he was
being (intention) "the good student." Being *something*, instead of a

process. An artifact. I am just now realizing fully what Fritz means by "artifact." Some *thing* made by man.

I feel like writing letters, now.

This morning, "out there" is nothing with lines in it. No mountains. Lake and sky appear to be the same fog. The lines are log booms, dock poles, docks. The world (my world) ends about fifty feet away.

"No interpretation." No thinking.

Yesterday, George was working on his topdog-underdog conflict. He has done this a lot since the beginning, in June. Both his topdog and his underdog seemed tired, weak, not much fight. People in the group were expressing boredom. I thought (sic). . . . I thought (sick) "They've probably gone through this with George over and over." I thought (sick) "George is probably as tired of this as we are." At one point, when George was one of his dogs talking to the other, he said, "I'm *between* you." My eyes went to the floor between the hot seat and the empty chair, with an almost no-picture image of George standing there. I didn't tell him to do it. Larry was therapist. "Let him go along with what he's doing." (Sick thought.) I "forgot" that I was to supervise. I blanked that out.

After George, we worked with someone else, and then with someone else. After group, as George was leaving, he said—

A large crane-like bird just now flapped awkwardly down and landed on the dock. He flaps his wings—he is up on a rowboat. He flaps his wings, he is down on the dock. At the edge of the dock, his beak pounces into the water. Now he is crouched a little, looking into the water like a cat.

George said, happily, "I've been thinking (sick) of my topdog as organismic. *I'm* in between!" I saw that both his topdog and his underdog had weakened—*that's* why they were weak and tired. If I had let these sensings of mine (not-sick) express themselves while he was working, George might have got even farther, and faster. This is where Fritz' genius is.

The life-style shows in the body. Of course. How could it be otherwise? I *am* my body, my body is me. How else can I express myself? If I stay curled up in a ball and say nothing, I am expressing myself. When I wriggle my toes, I express myself. When I stiffen my shoulders, I express myself. When I "don't hear," I express myself. When I get into an habitual pattern, I express myself as an artifact, a kind of statue that moves and breathes in *artificial* ways. *I* have made *me*.

That crane-like bird didn't make himself. He is not perverted. (pervert: to turn aside from its intended use.)

All us perverts who have perverted ourselves in one way are so angry with those who have perverted themselves in another, and even more we want to wipe out those who have not perverted themselves as much. All these artifacts are fighting. The world of illusion.

What about the artifactual *me*? I blank that out. I don't want to go into it. I'm just a nice old lady. . . . I want to x out that "nice"! I know I'm not-nice too. "Nice" is relative to where I used to be: seeing more, accepting more, now, and this is *nice to me*. I look up the word in the dictionary to see what it means *there*. My goodness what a lot of meanings this word has, from "hard to please" to "friendly"—and derived from the Latin which means "ignorant"!

I look up "innocent" and select from the meanings the one that suits me here, "ignorant of evil (without implication of virtue)." I am making progress in this direction.

I don't get so angry.

I look up "anger." It comes from a word meaning "trouble." I am much less troubled. "Troubled" comes from a word that means "turbulent."

I'm not holding my turbulence in; I'm not *being* so turbulent.

Bertie Russell said of himself and jealousy, "I manage to behave very well, but I get very cross inside." This is turbulence. Held back, and roiling around inside. Break through the dam, even a little, and some of the roiling has changed to a stream. A real breaking through releases a torrent. If the torrent isn't stopped—

The fog is moving down the lake. Why is "left" *down*, with me and the lake, and "right" *up*? Hills all bobbly with maple trees, with a line of pointed pines at the top, are emerging rapidly, extending.

Blue sky, Mist moving just above the water. The second row of hills, higher hills, is emerging. Green and blue and dark and light, above and reflected in the water.

If the torrent isn't stopped, afterward is peace and joy and being in the world again. I have seen that happen. Sometimes the torrent is crying, sometimes a storm of anger. Afterward, usually, the habit of perversion takes over again, but still, the experience of something else is there, and the work of breaking up old habit patterns has begun. "Three steps forward, two steps backward," Fritz says.

Like the growth of children. I think that they have outgrown some stupidity which tortures them and me—it has disappeared—and then it appears again and has to be dealt with again by the child. Like the sewing stitch called "combination" in which you take three stitches forward, and then a backstitch. This backstitch makes strong what would otherwise be weak.

Person to Person ended with a description of myself caring for a Navajo woman who had given birth to a child. When the woman looked at me with trust, without opinion, and I let go of my thoughts about myself and her, then there was only process—everything proceeding. Boundaries gone. I no longer defined me—or her—and did not limit either of us by definition.

Spontaneous me has no thoughts *about*. Just does, with words sometimes coming in . . . or out. . . . There is no *in* and no *out*. Words, *then*, are an expression of me *now, without my thinking them*, in the same way that my smiling or not-smiling is (then) simply an expression of me. Not habit. No intention. No purpose.

Hmmm. . . . How often am I aware of my intention when I speak, aware of what I'm doing? *Aware*, not just *knowing*. I can know, "I'm trying to push him around," and let it go off over my shoulder while I move on to something else, or continue my word-pushing. Awareness is getting in touch, letting my knowing be felt all through me, before moving on. That's the difference between *knowing* that I am walking down a road, and *aware* that I am walking down a road—sensing the movement of my body, the touch of road and foot coming together.

117

In the awareness work with Fritz, the slowness of saying "Now I am aware of. . . ." "Now I am aware of. . . ." and so on, is a help in getting in touch. I can say quickly what I see or feel or think or smell and run up quite a score in quantity, without being in touch with anything at all, which is, in fact, the way that most of us live most of the time. I can see in an instant that you have your hand on your knee, but "It is obvious to me that your hand is on your knee" provides a pause in which I can get in touch. I begin to see the difference between what I usually do, and awareness. This slowness is only at the beginning, like slowing down to switch to another track.

When I make *things* outside me—whether a cabinet, a dinner, a dress, or a rock garden—with awareness, there is no separation, no distance between me and what I am doing, and no deadness. There is inter-action. I am *involved*. I don't have a plan which I carry out, step by step. I move step by step and the design takes shape, with no image of the final form.

How I shall cook potatoes may change as I peel them and discover more about *these* potatoes and their potential. Or, how I cook them may change because of some other change—the oven isn't working, or someone comes home for dinner wanting to go off again right after. This is not difficult when I am free, moving with awareness. I am not "put out" by changes. They are incorporated. Co-operation. I enjoy the changes, without making a thing of them or me, and "dull routine" is impossible. This is the way of co-operation with people, too—and the way that the warm and lively co-operative society that so many of us want can come about.

A dress that I start in one way may take another, seeming to do this on its own, although in fact my awareness is moving with the material, and material and I are intertwined.

What I am making, with wood or stone, changes form or contour or design as I get in touch with the qualities of the wood or stone. If I want a wall, the stone and I will make a wall, but many things about that wall will not be known until it is completed.

No force.

Let happen.

When I am painting, sometimes I *think* I know which color I want to use next. Thinking arises out of my conditioning, out of the past. Not present. Sometimes, I start to move the brush toward the color I think I want, but my hand moves the brush to another color—almost as if the brush moves my hand. I have just remembered Fritz saying to a painter at Esalen, "Until the brush wriggles itself, you are not painting."

Making *things* outside me in this way—that the things themselves take part in. . . . Vocabulary, grammar and concepts are against me when I try to describe this intermingling flowing. I could do better conveying it with my hands and arms. . . . I image a taffy-making machine. Yes, it is something like that—the metal arms and the taffy in constant movement, seeming to be a whole. You can't really follow what is happening.

I am not "intellectual" when I make things in this way. Intellect and the rest of the organism which is *me* are functioning together, with intellect the minor part—essential and minor. Then, to "accept" myself and life is impossible. I *am* myself and I *am* life—and those are clumsy, inaccurate statements of what is. There is no I, no me—no "myself," no "life."

When I have "come to my senses" in our fictitious world, that usually means that I have accepted the values of those around me, that I *think* the way that they do. How did the meaning of *senses* get switched around to *thinking*, and arrive at *judgment*, and *opinion*?

Sensing is pre-verbal. As an infant, I sensed my hunger, sensed the rough of my father's coarse serge suit, and the smooth of my mother's face, before I knew the words that label them. I *felt* them. Now, I mostly use the words and feel nothing. When I say that I am surprised, or that I was surprised, or that I will be surprised *if*—I'm feeling nothing, least of all "surprise."

"Voids, voids, voids—noddings!" said a German woman as she used her umbrella to jab at the books on the library shelves.

The words I write are not the words you read.

We surely do have to turn ourselves upside down, and reverse our approach to life.

The prism lights are strange today. On my window sill there is red, orange, yellow, green, and in another place, beginning also from

119

the right, is blue, white, yellow, orange. On my desk, there is a wide
stubby stripe of yellow merging into wide red—and half an inch away
from it there is a long narrow stripe of thin red, wide yellow, and
then green with an aura of purple along the edge. There is also a
bullet shape on the bottom of the window frame, red at its tip, then
a small yellow stripe, a green length, then blue, and a long purple
end. A small square of red is just beyond it. A streak of blazing red,
shining like the lake in sun, starts from inside one prism and reaches
to a sand dollar lying on the sill. Across that blaze is a spear of bright
colors, with green wider in the middle. From its beginning, where it
begins, is a blaze of yellow, then stripes moving at right angles. . . .
While I describe, everything changes. The little square spot has
become yellow on one side. The purple of the spear is—was. . . .
Before I could get it on paper, it changed from yellow to pink. Now,
the red blaze is orange along one side, and green is creeping into the
little square. On the desk, the stubby wide stripes have disappeared.
The "pole" is still there. While writing that, another blob
disappeared—then reappeared. I can't keep up with them. I was
trying to—and have got a headache. Let me rest and enjoy. I do
that. . . . The moment of doing that and the moment of writing it are
not the same. Can never be. This is a true "impossible." A law of my
being which I cannot escape, any more than I can escape the
necessity of air.

A few minutes ago, I got up and brushed my hair, put it up with
silver hairpins. I noticed, then, that I am wearing flannel pajamas and
boots. The pajamas I slept in and got up in. The boots were added
when my feet got cold. When I did that, I was innocent. My feet
were cold. I put on my boots. When I noticed, while brushing my
hair, I was not innocent. I had *thoughts about, as if* there were
someone else here. Fantasy. No one is here. My thoughts had nothing
to do with *now*, but with some possible future—like feeling shame at
not "doing right" or making a virtue of it by laughing, being
"humorous," *if* someone came. Someone came, in my fantasy. No
one is here. Except me. No, no exception. I wasn't here, either. i
wasn't here either, as i was before.

"Self-consciousness is the mildest form of paranoia." I was
paranoid. I still am, a little. I am not back to the innocence of

120

before. I feel sadness. That innocence, of being and doing (functioning) appropriately to *me*, is gone. I feel *as if*. As if I *should*. As if I should *change*. As if I should change *now*.

Along with *that* lost innocence, I am feeling a little proud about those last sentences, instead of just enjoying—which is *in fact* what I do. The pride is artifact. *I* have *done something*. Split, not whole.

I have noticed in many hippie families, or tribes, children are "left free." Partly, this is good. Children put on clothes or don't, as they please. They also climb on a woman's lap, and whether she wants the child there or not, the child stays until *he* wants to leave. I have had a feeling of sickness (in me) about this, without being clear what I saw. She "wants" the child there *in her head*. It's a *rule*. She goes on pseudo-living in her head, while talking about how tired she is. She *makes herself* be acceptant of the man who left ("to do his thing") in her words, while her voice denies this. Whatever her experience on drugs, *afterwards* she intellectualizes it. Like my friend on drugs who talked with me about what she had seen, and afterwards said, "So what we all have to do is. . . ."

Sometimes a person who has had an experience of freedom following working in the hot seat, a little later says, "So what I have to do is. . . ."

What do I "have to" do? What do "I have to do."?

Nothing. Just be aware.

Doing (without prior thought) does itself.

I place my left hand on my right wrist. My left hand is the subject, my right wrist is the object. Still holding my right wrist with my left hand, I pick up a piece of paper with my right hand. My right hand has become the subject, the paper the object. Place my hands palms together—no subject, no object. No split.

Now, I have had enough of writing. I don't want to do anything else sitting in this chair. I want to get out of it. When I do, I'll know what I want to do next.

The first thing I did was take off my boots. They felt heavy.

Already I have revealed too much about Gestalt. Now (for instance) everyone who reads this knows that George's top and under dogs were not himself. This can be misused.

But hell, *everything* can be misused. If we put "Caution: may

121

be harmful if misused" on sand, water, leaves, desks, people, sinks, paper, stairs, meat, fish, coffee, people—no exceptions—this would be a bother and a clutter, but it would be *right*.

How *words* scare me. When I was listed as one of those to continue training, I thought "therapist" and got scared. When Fritz said "leader," I got scared. When Fritz said "supervisor," I got scared. Not the words, *my concepts* of what they stand for. Fantasies.

Two-thirty. I started out the day wrong, didn't correct it, and today has gone all wrong even though everything went all right.

Next day, I slept for a long time, did something for a short time, slept for a long time, did something for a short time. The sleeping periods became shorter and the doing periods became longer, without my *making* them this way. By evening time, I felt good—awake and firm/soft and *present*.

I feel like switching to something else. I am bored.

Fritz: So go somewhere you are more comfortable.

If you are bored, you can do that too—inside your head or outside—and come back refreshed.

"What will open the door is daily awareness and attention—awareness of how we speak, what we say, how we walk, what we think"—Krishnamurti.

"The continuum of awareness is basic"—Fritz, who spent two hours a day with us in the first week, working on this—and that was only as an introduction.

Almost always, when Fritz says to someone "Are you aware of" (whatever the person is doing with his hands, his voice, his mouth, or anything else) the person immediately stops doing it. Then Fritz says, with patience and compassion, "I only asked if you were aware of it. I didn't say that you shouldn't do it."

I feel like putting in here something that doesn't belong here, so if I feel like it, it has its place. I wrote it last year. John Warkentin liked it. His Board of Editors didn't. I'll dig it out:

I remember, as a child, when I had finished drinking all the milk in the glass, being wonderfully happy spitting my saliva into the glass and drinking it back in again. I did this over and over until something else attracted me, and next time that I had milk, I did it again. This happened until I had got everything I could out of that and it didn't appeal to me any more.

When my son was about a year old, one afternoon he took a nap as usual but I didn't hear his waking-up sounds at the usual time. After awhile, I went to check. He was standing in his crib, digging down into his diapers for some golden brown stuff that had come out of him, then he plastered a bar of his crib with it, with all the absorption of a master-plasterer. He had been at it for some time. Some of the bars were already completed. His interest and his happiness were a joy to see. In his total concentration, he hadn't noticed the sound of the door opening, and didn't notice that I was there. When I spoke to him, he looked at me and gave a soft gurgling sound of happy satisfaction which had nothing to do with me except that he expressed it to me.

More recently, I was with a family of six English children, the youngest three years old. He had a runny nose. The mucous kept dripping down on his upper lip. He was very full of laughter at something he had noticed and was telling us about, and licked the mucous off his lip at both ends of every few words, one of the groups of words being "It seems very odd to me. . ." It seemed very odd to me that we have so misplaced importances that we usually don't enjoy anything very much if we have a runny nose, and that something to wipe it with comes *first*, before anything else.

About the same time, I was burning a lot of rubbish in an iron barrel in the back yard. It was a wettish spring day, a little chill. The fire was glorious. I was very happy with all the spring scents and smells and sounds and colors, and the blazing fire. My nose began to drip. I fished around in my pockets. They had nothing in them. I thought, "I must go to the house and get a piece of kleenex." Then I thought, "Why must I? I didn't when I was a child. I put off going back to the house in every way possible." I wiped my nose on my arm. It felt *good*—the nose against the arm (me touching me), the coolness, the wetness, enjoyed *within* all the rest of what I was enjoying.

I told this to one of my "free" friends. She tried hard not to look revolted.

When I was a child, how I loved to have a bowel movement in the woods that were across the street from our house. I wasn't supposed to: I was supposed to come home and use the toilet. But while the toilet had been interesting at first, there was now nothing new about it, and the bathroom didn't have all the smells of live leaves and rotting leaves, the fragrances of many things growing. I never tired of that. Lifting up my skirts and squatting, I would put my head down so that I could see what was coming out of me, enchanted by the way it came, by the plop! to the ground, by the steam that rose from it. When no more came, I stepped aside and wiped my bottom with some leaves. On future days sometimes I went back to look at this part of me that I had left there, noticing the changes. Sometimes I happened on it accidentally and thought, "Yes, I was here," and went along my way.

Urine was fascinating too. I don't remember that I ever drank it, but certainly I played with it and sometimes licked my fingers.

The grownups said these things were "bad," but I was still young enough to know my own delight, although I could not assert this against my parents in the way that my sister's child did. She had a different mother. When this little girl was three years old (1920), pediatricians were saying that bananas were bad for children: they must not eat them. My sister and I came into a room and saw the child eating a banana. My sister, going by the pediatricians, not herself, said, "Ugh! Nasty!" and held out her hand for the banana, to take it away. The child shook her head "No" to her mother's statement, at the same time smiling and rubbing her stomach. "Num-a-num!" she said, setting her mother straight.

In Samoa, a few months ago, a Samoan policeman said, "Children just don't look at things the way we do." They certainly don't. When my daughter was not yet walking, one summer at the beach she crawled around naked in the sand and sedgegrass, occupying herself for hours at a time. I happened to look out a window and saw her pounce on something which I could not see, pop it into her mouth, and chew on it, with evident satisfaction. She did this again, and again. I thought I had better look into this. As I got to her, she popped another something into her mouth. I pulled down her chin, and a grey baby toad hopped out. There were lots of them around. Clearly, she had enjoyed some of them already. I didn't blame *her*, but *I* felt unhappy about those little baby toads being eaten alive, and encouraged her to explore in other directions.

Children are explorers, testers, discoverers for themselves. How else can *I* discover *me*? A small boy (5 years old) told me, "I'm smarter than people think I am!" I asked him, "In which way?" His answer was a song, a carol, singing in the air: "I do dangerous things and don't get hurt!"

I didn't tell him that he shouldn't, nor that he should. How else can there be freedom? How else can there be joy?

This morning was a three-hour group again. Afterward, I went out. It was important to leave my cabin. I noticed that I was wanting *not* to have the group in my cabin, lousing it up, wiping out the silence and my being alone. When I came back, I wrote a letter and while writing it noticed that those people were *still here*. I knew they were not in my cabin, but I felt *as if* they were still here. I was imaging them in my head "out there"—in the places they had been. Fantasies. I could call in a witch doctor or scatter some witch powder to get rid of them, and if I believed in this they *would* be gone. They're still there now. Let me see what I can do with them. It's not enough to say "My cabin has no one in it except me." If I said it often enough, maybe I'd believe it, but that would be belief too, and I don't like *believing*.

I'm not *here*. *Here* there is only me. I am sitting on cushions in a swivel chair. A nice strong old oak swivel chair. What pride is it that makes me want you to know it isn't a pseudo-mahogany modern office chair? I am typing. I see the typewriter, and my fingers hopping around tapping the keys. As I notice that I see them, I begin to feel them, as I hadn't, before. They dance more lively now, and I am enjoying this—feel lighter as I do it. My left shoulder is aching, feels heavy and hurting. I stopped typing and went into that. Then I noticed the typewriter humming, and began typing again. This time I'll switch it off. . . .

Astonishing how that pain first moved around and then dissolved, when all that I did was pay attention to it. Now, it isn't nagging me any more. It's coming into my neck. . . . When I paid attention to it—nothing more—no attempt to *do* anything with it—it shifted up my neck and then moved over my head. I went with it. Just went along with it. It disappeared at my ear, on the other side from which it began.

Charlotte is sitting on the dock, reading. Now, she isn't reading any more. I like Charlotte. I would like to be with her. But she *would talk*. I haven't told her that. They didn't both get together until just now—my liking and my not-liking. "*But*" wiped out the liking. I didn't think, "I like Charlotte *and* she *will talk*." I've held away from my liking because of her talking, and held away from her talking because of my talking. I haven't been meeting Charlotte.

The people are still here in my cabin, but more faintly, now, and they're very still—not moving around, not talking.

The lake is ripples. Small ripples in the lagoon, larger swifter ones beyond the logboom. Within the lagoon, there are fish rings. The fish touches the surface and there a circle of ripples begins, spreading out to quite fabulous size from one little pinpoint. The circles whirl as they spread out. Three of them now are spinning—gone, three new ones, gone, now five—seven—I've just looked to the right and there are eight circles—eleven—spinning, dying, new ones starting up. I *can't* count them. I can only estimate—and then *that* changes. Across the lake, where there is one small house, the maples have turned almost all gold and orange. I put myself in that house and wander around in it, knowing it isn't like that at all, but enjoying being there alone.

I'm not yet alone, here—just knowing that I am, not feeling it, although the people from this morning are almost gone. I can't see them any more, but they're still present in some kind of presence that is not my own.

126

I lean back and look out the door. So much stillness. That's what I first notice. The docks are still. The boathouse is still. I like this stillness. I feel rest. Then I notice smoke rising on the farther shore—and the movement of the water—faintly moving, but moving. Shimmering, in places. I don't like this movement right now. I like the stillness. Drink it in, seep it in. . . .

And now my cabin is still. I feel its stillness. Chairs, walls, floor, windows—all still. And myself alive within it. My face smiles. *I* smile. All through me, I feel smiling. There is now no one here but me.

I don't need to shift the group to somewhere else. I just need to let them go completely when they leave, and be here without them.

My breathing deepens of itself. I feel good. Not judgmental good or moralistic good. Just good. Ready for whatever comes and if it doesn't come, okay.

What is Gestalt?

When I didn't know, I couldn't tell you, and now that I know, I can't tell you.

I am feeling that it's a long time since I've had any insight or outsight and it's time I wake up.

I'm even out of touch with those I've had recently. That used to bother me. Then I noticed that it's like the brass ring at the merry-go-round. It comes around again and again and again, and one of these days I'll really latch onto it. Without trying.

Right now, I just feel that I'm partly asleep and I'd like to wake up.

After group. I feel so much bigger—no, *taller*. So much higher than the typewriter than I usually am. I have felt this "taller" at other times, and still I feel new. Younger. More strength all through me, even in my head which so often gets left out. Movement.

Several of those brass rings came around again this morning. Now, they're gone. No matter. I've had another look at them and they'll be back again—provided that I don't *pursue* either them or something else.

127

No wonder my right and left sides don't match. I'm lopsided. There's a man here who is childlike and childish. I flow with (enjoy) his child*like*ness and ignore his child*ish*ness. I don't *engage* him there. Fritz did, this morning, and three hours later the man was feeling good and said, "I survived!"

Allen worked on a fragment of a dream this morning. When he took the hot seat, he expressed his frustration in trying to get together with his father. "There's nothing to do but stay away from him. I've sat patiently for *two hours* listening to him. . . ." and so on. Then he worked on the dream fragment and in perhaps half an hour realized that his father had changed, that he (Allen) wouldn't let his father change, retained the old image of him, and used this old image of his father as an excuse for the big things that he (Allen) wanted to do and didn't. Boiled down the way I have written it, the life is gone. The whole was more like the aurora borealis shimmering all across the horizon and into the sky. From anger and frustration, he changed to love and tenderness.

Most of the time, I was real, going by intuition, the spontaneous movement of myself, responding in the moment *to* the moment. This is effortless, and "working" with a person is nonsense. "Playing" is a wrong word, too. Our split language doesn't have a word for what *really* happens.

"Thank you."

"You're welcome."

Roles assigned by language. "Thank you"—beneficiary. "You're welcome"—benefactor. One down, one up.

In Hawaiian:

"Mahalo."

"Mahalo."

No distinction between giver and receiver, just awareness of flowing between. No up. No down. No roles assigned by language. Happiness is, with no thoughts about it.

When Allen was loving and tender, at the end, I was moved. I didn't let that movement show. I thought (sic) "Don't suck him in." Then, I both didn't let myself out and *didn't let him in*.

Why I did that is irrelevant. I could pursue it endlessly or arrive at an answer, and it would still be irrelevant. When I start with "why?" I go farther and farther away from *here*. "Because" goes on and on, with one because behind another, and makes as much sense as if I say that *I am* because Bismarck got mad at the Kaiser and introduced universal military training, or conscription. That did cause my grandfather to leave Germany, and at that time, without which it is unlikely that he would have met and married my grandmother who came to London at that time from Ireland. Some other bloke would have got her first. That is true. But what of all the other happenings and becauses or antecedents in the lives of my grandparents and my parents and in the world they (all) (each) lived in? And in the end, *I* wouldn't have been if my parents hadn't got together and produced me at the time they did. *I* am not my sister, who had the same grandparents, nor am I any of the other possible children who might have been.

I didn't let myself out, and didn't *let him in*. I did it. I feel sad. I notice that I am pushing back my sadness. ("Don't be emotional!") Now I feel sad that I can't feel that sadness. So let *this* sadness be. *This* sadness is here. . . . Dampness in my eyes. Pain in my chest. My legs are sad. I explore, and discover sadness all through me. My head begins moving from left to right, making a minus sign. Then up and down. Up and down draws a line through the minus and makes it plus.

Plus. Ahead of where I was.

Sadness now is changing—leaving. Coming into me is more vitality, more life. Now comes in the laughter that is a kind of smiling at the world. "God sees all and smiles."

Nothing matters.

The past is gone. The future is *not*, same as the past is *not*.

I am *here*

and

I am free.

In the moment is no mattering and I do nothing wrong. Or right.

129

I don't live a great deal with images of myself. I *do* when I see myself *as* a shaky old lady.

I still have rules. They're bound to be wrong. Rules are for playing games with. Life is not a game. Life is not serious, either. Life is not something you can say anything about. Life is.

"Gestalt is not rules." "Awareness is the ABC of Gestalt."—Fritz.

"Awareness is ABC and XYZ also. What else is there—all follows from that."—Harry Bone, psychologist and psychotherapist, the only non-psychoanalytic member of William Alanson White Institute for Psychoanalysis.

Awareness is without *any* intention. No good. No bad.

That much flowed easily. Don't push the river. That is a reminder to me. I was beginning to push, to say more. Why do I try to express what I can't?

I am wanting to make my discovery available to someone else. Wanting "to be helpful."

Trying.

When I try, I have a goal.

"Oh boy!" I said out loud, then, sounding like discovery and relief.

When a tree is falling in my direction, I run. I am not trying. I am not helping myself. I just do it. If I think about it, while I think about it I do nothing. Then, it may be already too late.

If a tree is falling in the direction of another person, I yell a warning, or push him out of the way, without thinking. I am not trying. I am not being helpful. I just do it.

"Observation, understanding, action."—Krishnamurti.

Any rule is a louse-up. "Let people be." With the rule in my head, I let other people be. I don't let *me* be. I *do* something *to me—to* let others be. Let *me* be. With that rule in my head, my self-image gets actualized, and I slaughter me and the world—even if this is done kindly—with good intentions.

I remember that twice in five years I have written Carl,

"Remember, you're people too," when it was clear to me that he was ex-cluding himself—xxxxxing himself out. ~~I was aware of the~~

Let that x-out stand, to remind me that I was beginning to explain. Hooking everything together. Instead of letting things come together in whatever way they do, in me, in you. "In you." I sneer. Who is this "you"? *I don't know who you are, if any.*

in me.

This place *is* a madhouse—a place where madness can come out into the open and begin to clear.

The "old lady" image *does* come in. Not so much in terms of what I "should be," but in terms of what I "shouldn't do." Like, I shouldn't be silly. I "should be" serious. Earnest is different. I told Glenn on Sunday when we were making a biiiig dish apple pie, about this seriousness of mine which feels wrong—I don't want it. I know how it came into my life. That didn't make it go away. How could it? I'm holding onto it *now.*

Holy smokes, am I seeing how I don't let myself be.

Somewhere, about a page back, I saw something about myself that I didn't want to expose to someone else. I am capable of working on it. I thought (yahhyahh) "I don't want to write that down for someone else. I can take care of that later, all by myself." I cut it off from you—and cut it off from me, too. Now, I don't know what it is. Pursue it, and it will go farther and farther away. It has surfaced once. Like a fish, it will surface again and when it does, I'll recognize it.

"Indians" flashed in my mind as I looked, without awareness of seeing, at the last four or five lines of that last paragraph. I haven't a notion what that means.

"Comedy time" came next, like "I want it." Relief from my own seriousness.

I feel laughing inside. Raindrops which were plopping into the water are now dancing on it. I smile. I feel laughing. What moves, like bush branches, is laughing with me. Blowing weeds are laughing with me. Boats upside down on the dock, and the dock itself, are not laughing. Stupids! Dumb things. Don't know how to laugh. Maple leaves bobbing are laughing.

"Comedy hour" has been provided by me. I don't need anything more. My eyes are dancing.

So right away, I tried to hook that into "Indians" and because I tried to, I mistrust it. A voice inside says loud and deep "Damn right!" A real friend.

In this now when I'm not mad, this place no longer is a madhouse.

I feel like lecturing. "To all you young people out there."

I always did think novels were silly. All the stupid things that people in them did, without which there wouldn't be a book.

Always?

For about six months I read novels, always ones with butlers and stuff. The heroines rang for everything they wanted, and telephoned for everyone they wanted and they came. (If any of them didn't come, I skipped that part.) I *was* those heroines (without their emotions) and had a wonderful rest while reading.

When I was nineteen and my sister was twenty-five, we got in a triangle with her husband. One evening in the kitchen, my sister and I got all worked up. I'm coming to think that homely expression is an apt one. I don't remember a lot of details. I do remember that my sister and I threw ourselves into each other's arms and bawled. Then, simultaneously, we saw ourselves as characters in those melodramas we used to laugh at and we burst out laughing, very much with each other. Then we noticed her husband standing there, and got all that he expressed without words—like feeling left out, astonishment at our being together, puzzlement about what was going on. They seemed to ripple all over him, and to be summed up in "*It shouldn't be this way!*"

That was the way to live. Into it quickly, out of it quickly, and not dragging things on to make a book. How we laughed at emoting—our own included.

Why did we both marry romantics?

I can't speak for my sister, who married young. I know that I gave up looking for the man I wanted, and settled for one who had more of what I liked and less of what I didn't like, and the what-I-didn't-like seemed easier to put up with than in the others.

Very much later. Ray began working on his dream in a state of anger and confusion. He was angry and confused a good deal of the time when he was working. He came through with clear recognition that he had continued his childhood pattern with his father *after his father had changed*, and that he *held onto* his grievance with his father and used his father as an excuse for not actualizing his own potential. At the end, he was utterly clear and loving, hugging the pillow that he had previously choked (as he had choked his father in his dream), snuggling his chin in it. "I don't want to let it go."

What *can* be said is so easily said, now. I didn't wait for the time to say it, before.

I have been looking for a paperback book. I wanted to send my son a couple of stories from it. I lent some paperbacks to several people here. When I couldn't find *this* book, I thought that someone else must have it. When I awakened from a nap this afternoon, I "saw" an envelope, and my hands putting those pages from the book into the envelope. No more looking for the book. Everything I've noticed is all here in me. When I'm not in touch with it, I'm doing *something* wrong.

After that, I noticed the bad taste in my mouth that I haven't been liking lately, and wondered what I could do about it. I imaged an apple. (Or an apple imaged itself, according to whether I identify with organismic i or with intellectual I.)

Peeling the apple, I thought of "reversing," one of the tools of Gestalt. The apple began peeling me. Euggghh. I didn't like that. I went on peeling the apple, with much more awareness and caring than I'd had before. Whether this made any change in the apple, I don't know. I liked the change in me.

Last night, Bill took the hot seat with a dream that made him anxious. No verb for anxious. Strange. I looked it up. It is derived from *angere*—choke.

Bill droned, as usual. I have trouble listening to what Bill says. Fritz said, "I am being blocked by your voice. I think we will have to go into that before we can accomplish anything else." Bill became his voice, experienced how he choked himself, and so on. Fritz said, "Now choke my wrist—I don't trust you with my neck—and talk while you are doing it." Bill did this, and his voice came deep, full and resonant. He could hear the resonance, feel the vibrations. So could we. He seemed suddenly a very different Bill, not just more powerful—more interesting—like wanting to hear more.

A small tug is moving fast through the water, like plowing it, with an upcurve of wave moving out behind. A man stood up and leaned over the back, seeming to be doing something to the wave.

After half an hour of working with his voice, Bill worked on his dream of robbing a bank. Fritz asked him to be the bank. Bill described himself as the bank—structurally and functionally. I was bored with this bank. Fritz said, "There are no people in it. I don't think that is the bank you robbed."

Notice what isn't there. When I am in an air-polluted city, I am aware that the pollution is there and that clear air is not there. But in Torrance, when I was being bothered by what was there and what wasn't in many ways, there was one not-there which was making me sad and I didn't know what it was. Finally, I noticed. "No Negroes and no Jews," came into my mind. It was easy to check on the absence of Negroes. I saw only one, sweeping out the supermarket. Jews—how could I check on those? I thought of half a dozen common Jewish names and looked in the Torrance section of the phone book. I thought of another six or seven, and looked them up. None of them were there. I looked in the neighboring sections, like Hermosa Beach, and in each one of them I found all those names many many times.

Torrance was a really strange town. In a year of living there, the only event I heard about was a W.C.T.U. meeting. I never knew so much courtesy anywhere, and felt that I was living in a graveyard of courteous ghosts. They never *noticed* me. Softly flowing they moved around me, saying "Pardon me" as though I might have been a bush or tree.

They all dressed in sort of drab light colors. Their voices were all soft. Sameness. Sameness. Sameness. One day when I had been working with Zen—Torrance really pushed me to doing that—I walked downtown and each person was unique, alive, original, brightly clad. Sparkling. I'm seeing them now, there, the way that I did then, but something is missing. I don't know if they were encountering each other, or if each one was completely in his own world and out of touch with the others. I knew *then* what was or wasn't going on.

Deke used to show Fritz' films quite often—run the projector. He's tired of that and doesn't do it any more. Two other people are doing it now. It's new to them—using the machine, and also the films are new to them. They want to see them.

Bookkeepers change. Secretaries change. Kitchen crews change. There are mix-ups sometimes. Nothing fatal. And not much chance of a very established order.

Fritz talks about "filling up the holes" in a person's personality. I don't like the sound of that—like filling them up from the outside, with something extraneous. That's not what he *does*. To me, it feels

135

more like a welling up into and flowing—releasing the flow which I had blocked.

Clara was cranky when she came in this morning. In her word, "Bitchy." Later, she cried that she was always "nourishing" people and this didn't come back to her. After she had worked, she felt warm and nourishing and nourished.

That evening in the kitchen, Fritz asked "Is this your birthday?" When I said no, he said, "You look as if it is your birthday." I didn't feel like a birth-day, and didn't know what he meant.

A little later, I said I felt ridiculous taking money for doing something I enjoyed, that when the man at the University of British Columbia said he would send me a check for the three hours I spent there with Irwin, meeting with a group there, this didn't feel right at all. I hadn't worked. It didn't feel like work to me, and I had been paid by what I got out of it. Fritz said part-joshingly that one of the rules of Gestalt is somethingorother (I forget) and the other, charging as much as possible. I listened to some of the other people present, then wandered here and there in my head. The same deep voice seeming to be in my lower chest, that I had enjoyed earlier, interrupted, saying, "I *have* been paid." Such complete assurance—and such a friendly feeling in it. There just wasn't any question about it. I felt that I had a friend in me, and didn't need a friend anywhere else. Cozy. I went to bed feeling that way.

This morning's group started with a woman I didn't want to work with. I thought, "Not again!" Two things that I got out of her working were that I wasn't afraid of her anger and her shouting and she did get some insight at the end. A woman in the group reminded her of her stepmother. She really didn't see the woman *present*, almost not at all, and hated this woman. At the end of an hour, she saw *this* woman. She reached out to touch her and said, "You feel different." She caressed the woman's head, in touch with touching, then embraced her. In a little while, she laughed. "I didn't think I'd ever be doing this!"

That's not the end, for her, but it's another step. I didn't notice many mistakes. I felt good about being stronger when this was needed.

Then Ray, who worked so well yesterday, plunged for the hot seat. I wanted more time between. I didn't say so. Several times, I noticed something—then doubted my observation. Once I noticed something, and didn't go on with it. My observation was clear—I just plain let it go. All of us wound up in confusion. I let someone else suggest something that didn't make sense to me, and even went along with it myself. Then Fritz came in. He picked up on Ray's confusion—had him describe what it was, then dance it—and then reverse the dance. Ping! Ray got the message from his dance, and it was clear to me it was the message in the dream.

Then, out of the wrong suggestion which the woman made and I picked up on, Kolman was all fired up and ready to go. He worked beautifully with Fritz.

At the end, all the rights and wrongs seemed to be all right. I had noticed many mistakes I had made, and Fritz pointed to one of them when he said always to pick up "the phenomenon" (Ray's confusion). I didn't gripe myself about them or laugh them off, or plan not to make them next time. I didn't do anything, and it was all okay. They had been noticed—along with the good that came out of making the biggest one. No sweat. No grind. No laugh-it-off. Just there.

When the people left the cabin, they were gone, and I was alone.

I don't feel like a birth-day. I feel more like a rapidly-growing fetus. Today, for awhile I felt that I was growing ears—felt this physically, as though my ears were growing, and even that channels were being opened up in them, or were opening up themselves.

For awhile, I felt as though I were being "taken over" all over, in a moving changing way. Even my neck and head were involved—like more feeling or sensation moving into them. I wanted to be taken over altogether, *right now*, and have it over with—and be re-born. That didn't happen. I have been in and out of mild agonies all day—letting them come and go. I am weary of these mild agonies, which I have been having quite a lot lately. But I don't want to get rid of them by doing something to distract me or taking something. I don't want that, for then I would lose the other.

It is so hard to simply be open to my "friend." Quite often, I ask or beg or plead or say *"Come on*, dammit!" When we are in touch, I want to *hold* that touching. Trying to direct what cannot be directed. Not letting be. Last night, though, I felt that I got in touch to the point where I knew that I was being understood, that "my friend" knew that I really want to stop this nonsense of mine, and that I'm working on it. . . . I've just remembered that today for a couple of hours I felt that I was not working, not doing anything—while I was being taken over by me.

Now I've come back to intellect eye—whoops. I thought I was writing *I*. Now, I'm feeling more like an eye than an I, and what was looking like nonsense has changed back to sense—to sensing. Eye see.

My dinner was ready, then. I got up and put a piece of chicken on a plate, a potato, and a couple of beets. While doing this, eye felt friendly—like the voice that said "Damn right!" yesterday afternoon, and "I *have* been paid" last night.

Suppose this is all nonsense?

(Eye seems to chuckle.)

Suppose it is. I like it better than the nonsense of saying who said what (whether philosophers or friends or enemies), of reading the newspapers, of *talking about* as if I knew something, of adoring or bemoaning or decrying or reprimanding or praising, blaming, superior, inferior, celebrating what isn't worth celebrating—like another year lived or lived together in waiting for the celebration—or buying things to show them (*both* thems) or hunting friends, or being angry, being sweet, being bitchy, being neat, taking pills for loneliness and grief, being hot or being cool, getting an A or F in school, playing wise or playing dumb when all you're after is. . . .

Fog

This morning, I didn't want to have a group. I didn't want to have two two-hour groups next week instead of one three-hour one. Two groups a day. That's not life. That's not my life. I'll tell Fritz. When I thought of the people who would be in *this* group, I even more didn't want to meet with them today.

Guy had just started working when Fritz came in. He worked beautifully with Fritz. It was great to hear old gravel voice (Guy is young) sing his thoughts—a most beautiful voice. I didn't know he had it.

Then Natalie took the hot seat. I had been looking forward to working with Natalie. She works so beautifully, and I enjoy her so much. Peter moved in and took over. This was okay—he was free to, if and when he wanted to, and I was free to move in. I did that sometimes, not often. I noticed Peter's acting his psychiatrist self, mixed in with what he has learned of Gestalt. I thought of pointing to the non-Gestalt. I didn't do it.

I thought I'd tell Fritz, "I'm *not* interested in *training* people. I'm *not* interested in working with psychiatrists. I don't want to. I won't." Not fighting or fierce. Simple statements are sufficient from me to him, from him to me.

When the people had gone, I thought this again. Then I remembered my fantasy this morning of the group and what it would be like (not detailed fantasy, more like a deadness) and it wasn't. I don't know anything about what tomorrow morning will be. I don't know what two two-hour groups will be. As for the training part, what got me down was thinking what I *should* do, how I must sit smart and notice and be ready to catch and point out. I don't like that.

All of a sudden, I realized it doesn't *have to be* that way. Notice, and let myself grow, develop. That's all. Now, I am fascinated to see how that works out—what happens. Let myself happen. Not try to direct me.

Today's cop-outs don't matter. They were me this morning, before I'd done it and noticed my doing it. I couldn't do otherwise than I did.

Everything is okay. I feel okay, with happiness and anticipation mixed in, not strong, but lively.

When I try to keep things in my head (like remembering to notice, remembering to point out Gestalt errors) I get a headache. That's reason enough for me not to do it—apart from that old dirty-word nasty tripper-upper shyster chiseler con-man "try." I feel good to be as free of him as I am. Notice, notice, notice. Be aware.

Each time Fritz has come in and worked with someone, when he is leaving I think "What an act to follow!" I feel as if he'd notice if one eye-lash didn't move with the others when I blink, and if they all moved together, he'd notice that.

"I try as far as possible not to think." That sure leaves a lot of room for noticing.

As soon as Fritz has left the group, he's gone. I don't try to be like him, don't feel relieved that he's gone, don't grieve because I'm not Fritz. When he leaves, he isn't in my head, and I am with the people who are here. That much of me is okay. . . I've just noticed that also I don't wonder what the people will think of *me*, after having seen Fritz work. I'm me. He's he. I let him go. If I didn't, I would be invaded.

If I don't have a goal, how can I make a mistake?

Dear Fritz. This morning's feeling of his noticing *everything*—as though he had done or did do that all the time. Just now, he came in for awhile and one of the things he said was, "That's my new thing, about the voice. Did you notice this morning with Guy? I am growing ears." Growing, growing, growing. AWARENESS.

"I am in a lethargic period, now. All I can do is the groups—nothing more."

I told him about my noticing mistakes and being unbothered, and seeing what often arises from mistakes.

Fritz, with a lift of the shoulders, "Of course. Mistakes don't matter." I saw that completely, totally, seeing all and smiling.

Ten minutes later, "What do you (I) mean 'mistakes don't matter'!" and through my head run all sorts of mistakes that do matter, of course they do.

Then I saw that they didn't matter.

Then they did.

Then they didn't.

Then they did.

And now, I am suddenly altogether *here*, with the laughter in me that I've been missing.

My husband: Doesn't *anything* matter?

Me: (modifying myself, not to be too great a shock to him) Well, not very *much*.

I wasn't with that all the time. I was with it often.

Now I "see" a small statue in the Brundage collection—Maya giving birth to Krishna. She is dancing.

I am so flexible now. . . . I felt that way, and got up to see if it is true. The lower part of my back is still stiff—I could feel it, and I could only touch my fingers to the floor, not my hands. Otherwise I am—I feel fluid and move easily. And so alive. I don't feel weightless in the chair. I feel close to that, as though my shoulders were holding up my torso, my neck holding up my shoulders, my head holding up my neck and what the devil is holding up my head, I don't know but it feels great.

I turn my head from side to side—no bother. Less than a year ago, some people thought me "regal" when all I had was a stiff neck. I turned from the shoulders. I'm sure I didn't lose it, then. That was just the last time someone remarked on it.

Maple leaves falling from the trees and floating on the breeze, sometimes going up, but in the end lighting on the water in the lagoon where they float like pond lilies.

In June, here, I worked on my concrete chest and neck and head. Where are they now?

My voice! I just now let it come.

> The string o'er stretched breaks
> —and music flies
> The string o'er slack is dumb
> —and music dies
> Tune us the sitar neither low nor high.

My voice is my sitar.

How much these two weeks of "being leader"—which I was afraid of—have done for me.

Everything rights itself. That's why it doesn't matter if I do something wrong. I got that insight while slicing beets. It's trying not to make mistakes and trying to correct them that louses me up. Trying, trying, trying, when I am so built—like birds flying.

I'm still bothered by "nothing matters." No, I'm not. I *was*. Now, while I'm still in touch with it, let me set it down. When I am in the place in me which *knows* that nothing matters, I am also caring, loving, not taking more than I need, without ambition, non-competitive. If there is only bread and butter, I feel content with bread and butter. The cold chicken breast, Harvard beets, and half a boiled potato fried, tasted like the production of the most elegant chef. I function well. Without all this, it would be the wrong "nothing matters." In the wrong "nothing matters," suddenly everything changes if my life is threatened—or even seems to be ebbing away. It's a *split* "nothing matters," a "provided that," or "tomorrow I may be sorry for what I gave away today." The perfection (all is good) of the right "nothing matters" cannot be disturbed. Maybe tomorrow I wouldn't do for you what I did today, but yesterday when I did it or gave it to you is still okay.

I'm not going to be leading a group next week while Fritz is away, and I can go to Vancouver tomorrow for Thanksgiving (Canadian—in early October) and stay three or four days or a week if I like. Until I get there, I won't know what I like.

I know that the state I am enjoying now (not high, not low) may not last. It may "go away" any moment—or tomorrow. But now, I have just finished "doing" the dishes. I didn't *do* them. They did themselves with me and I enjoyed the water, the suds, the plates, and pots, and washing the beet spots off the stove was like a miracle: they're there—they're not. Movement of body. All senses sensing.

Earlier, when I made the Harvard sauce, I noticed how easy it was to read the recipe, and the measuring out of things was no problem. My hands shook only a little, not enough to be a problem. No uncertainty in what I was doing.

After tonight's meeting, I was going to the pub in Lake Cowichan with Guy. The others had already gone. Guy's car was farther away than I usually walk with ease, but not too far. Besides, it was a little uphill at the beginning, but the longer steeper downhill was at the other end. I could make it. As I walked along, I noticed that I walked with ease. My lower back was still stiff but not troublesome. The rest of me was free.

When we got to Guy's car, the battery had run down, and we walked back. I was nearly to the top of the longer steeper hill when I realized that I was walking easily, breathing easily—and talking as I walked. . . .

Phooey on those doctors who told me fourteen years ago to accept my condition as it was, because I'd never be any better. I write that and realize that my "Phooey" is a light and easy one, sort of like pooh-pooh said in good humor. I'm not angry any more. I used to be angry, because they were defeating me. Each time I said that I was going to get better—and knew I had been making progress even if the doctors didn't—when the doctor looked at me with compassion (which I appreciated—there was at least a measure of respect) or with disgust for an old lady who wouldn't accept what was, I felt as though a lead wall twelve feet thick had got between me and getting well. I had to dissolve that wall before I could again be on my way to getting better. Now, I'm not even angry with the doctor who said he had seen "hundreds of cases" just like me. Like heck he had. (silent chuckle) They are all in the past which I am getting out of. I know that I may still slip back tomorrow, and the gains may seem to be lost, but my experience tonight feels solid. If I lose it, I can let it go. It will come back.

My eyes are damp. Not *too* damp. Just damp as though maybe this is the way they should be, and they have been dry too long, not washed properly.

I knew that if I could let up on myself ("total rest") then my shakings could let up. It certainly has taken me a whale of a long time to learn how to do that. I never did believe that diagnosis of "permanent damage to the central nervous system." Damage, yes. Permanent, no. That is, it *might* be, if I couldn't find a way out, and maybe if I don't give it enough attention, but it ain't neces*sa*rily so.

My tremors have been very mild this evening—no bother. . . . I have just remembered the doctor friend in California whom I talked with on the phone a little over a month ago. I don't remember what I said about my tremors, but he said (being helpful?) "I know they bother you, I don't know why." When they're really bad, they bother me—like when I can't sign traveller's checks. The rest of the time, I know I *can* get rid of them and I want to. It's *silly* to shake like that when I don't *have* to.

Usually, I don't notice the ganglion bump on my foot unless I think of it first, then notice it. It doesn't hurt. Tonight, I keep noticing it because I feel it tugging and pulling. I don't know what's going on, but it feels good—like a dead spot coming alive. In July I noticed a small bump on my left foot that hadn't been there before.

144

By August, it was quite large. I asked a doctor who came here about it—no, my son did. He was afraid it might be cancer. I felt certain it wasn't. Anyway, this doctor said it was a ganglion thing, and that it could be cleared up by swatting it with a textbook, or by inserting a needle and sucking the stuff out of it.

When I was in California, through *Person to Person* I met an orthopedic surgeon who doesn't operate often, and prefers to work with his patients in another way. He said the same thing about treatment, when I asked what I might be able to do about it. That wasn't what I meant. I explained that I meant what *I* could do about it. He asked me if I had ever got in touch with myself at the cellular level. I hadn't. He showed me with his fingers the kind of balloon that had formed, with a small tube coming into it from the bottom. He said that fluid came in through the tube and dehydrated, and it couldn't get back through the small tube. He said that if I could let some fluid (body fluid) get into it, then the dehydrated stuff could dissolve and go back down through the tube. I worked on it that night, imaging what he had described and at the same time being in touch directly—the way one is with feeling in a toe—with the ganglion bump. A spontaneous thought came in: It can't be exactly the same thickness all over—there must be some weaker spots. Right away, several appeared in the image, one of them larger than the others, and on top. I held that in my image—just held it. I was surprised when a tiny pool of water appeared there, shimmering like a miniscule pond. Then, through the weaker spot, a tiny glisten appeared on the *in*side of the bump.

While writing that, I suddenly remembered when my mother, my father and I started out in a Model T Ford, in 1919, to drive from New York to California. My father had never driven farther than 30 miles from home. My father and I had never been farther west than Tarrytown, my mother once had gone to Ohio on a train. At that time, not many people drove across the continent. We didn't have the nerve to tell people along the way where we were going. First we said "Niagara Falls." When we got there, we said "Cleveland." When we got to Cleveland, we were brave and said we were going to Kansas City. When we made it there, we were even more brave (or audacious) and told people we were driving to

California. When I write about what's happening with my body, and then go on to the ganglion bump which I haven't even got working on yet, I feel the way we did when we said we were going to California. We didn't believe yet that we'd get there, and certainly didn't know if we could.

I haven't worked on that bump since I got back here. There's so much to work on that I would have to be dozens of people—maybe hundreds—to tackle all of them. Luckily, when some things get resolved, others clear up with them, or at least get started. Fortunately, I am an interlocking body. I just thought: "If all the rest of me got cleared up or on its way to doing that on its own, maybe I could start seeing if I could grow teeth." That seems extreme, even to me, but I wouldn't put it beyond me—the me that isn't me and really is me, or really *is*.

Where's "my friend"? I haven't heard from him today, but right now I have a friendly feeling all through me. I still miss him. I liked his voice. I don't think "he" is masculine, but possibly the masculine component in me mixed up (but not confused) with the feminine. Relative to my voice at other times, this voice is masculine—but not masculine in itself. In our language, it's *got* to be either he or she—or it, and none of those are right for *me*.

I've noticed the Indians haven't been in this much lately. I think I've got beyond them. Then again, they may come back in. When I return from Vancouver, *anything* may get into this, and I surely don't know what it will be. I only know that if I have skidded backwards by then, it won't be permanent. What is?

I got back last night—five and a half days away. I waited in Nanaimo for two and a half hours. At the bus station, a sweet little old lady in a peagreen coat and pink hat and sweater wouldn't share her doughnut with a wasp. The wasp persisted. She spilled half a cup of coffee on her shoes in backing away from him, and wound up giving him the doughnut. He took what he wanted, which was very little, and left. She could have eaten the rest of the doughnut. She didn't.

In Duncan, I waited two hours. A young East Indian in a pale pink turban invited me to have a beer with him.

I was tired and felt good when I got back. Today, I have lost ground. In Vancouver, my flexibility continued. Marion noticed the difference in my walking. I noticed the small of my back was still concrete and got to work on that, successfully. Today, I can't get to work on anything, so I've answered letters. When I got sleepy I went to sleep and slept lousy and woke up awful. My urine burns. That hasn't been happening.

I feel wasted, today.

While writing letters, more and more I wanted to get writing this—and now that I'm doing it, nothing is happening.

I have been thinking sneerily—occasionally, when I have thought of this writing—"It's more and more like a diary." So what do I have against diaries. I used to get a leatherbound one every Christmas in one period of my childhood. Nothing got written in it, but I liked the feel of it, and the look of it. That was all of me and diaries until my husband insisted that I keep one, which I did for awhile but then I got bored. He went right on keeping a diary, year after year, but he called his a "commonplace book" which elevated it to literature. It was still a diary. Year after year after year.

I asked Marion, who is part-Indian (one grandmother), what is the most important difference between Indians and white men. She said, "Work. The Indian works and rests—enjoys. The white man says 'keep working.' He gets mad when the Indian doesn't do that."

Tired. Achey. Sluggish. Sluggish. Weary. Too weary to walk up to the House, too weak.

Madness. Madness. At that point, I gave up and lay down on a couch. For a long time, noticing my aches, pains, and tightnesses didn't seem to accomplish anything. I'm not used to that. I felt like giving up. I went on—just noticing—and at last began to heave and sigh—a little relief. From that point on, the relief was beautiful. I got up, walked up to the House without effort, enjoyed being there, felt good, and enjoyed dinner.

I could have done that this morning.
I could have done that last night.
No wonder today felt "wasted." I wasted it—wasted me.

I'm not grieving. Just, *There it is.* Right now, I'm feeling good that the world goes 'round and 'round and 'round and I have another chance at the brass ring.

C (:.

I've been feeling that Gestalt has been watered down more and more here. I didn't see it clearly enough to do something about it. Yesterday I saw clearly. Today, I did it.

We were having a large group thing going which to me was—well, I've been feeling for four or five days that suburbia had moved in. Tonight felt the same way. "Pick the person you feel would give you most support." What meaning of "support"? What kind of support? What do I want support for? Then the pairs get together with another pair and they tell each other their "strengths" and their "weaknesses." I get all mixed up about these. What is "strength"? What is "weakness"? Everyone has a lot of "fun" and maybe learns something, a little.

Fritz arrived late from San Francisco. He looked happy, handing out brochures of the *Garbage Pail*, and showing proofs of the illustrations by Russ Youngreen. I enjoyed him. Some little bits of this and that went on, like arranging the groups for tomorrow morning. Fritz said that each person should pick the therapist he most doesn't want to work with. I laughed. Fritz heard me laugh and didn't hear my laughter. "This is no joke," he said. It wasn't—and it was—for me. I took him seriously, that he meant it, and what went on in me is more than I can put in words. Partly, my laugh was surprise—the unexpectedness. Partly, I felt *good* about the challenge and was surprised that I did.

When his odds and ends seemed to have been taken care of, I told him that I would like to have something like the "continuum of awareness" week that he gave us in June. I didn't expect him to pick up on it right away. He did. He said it was the ABC of Gestalt, and that without it "you're just middle class." He asked for any of the new people who have not worked with him to come and take the hot seat. "You are always aware of something—pay attention to it."

In a way, there is nothing new to me in this: "Now I am aware of. . . ." or "Now I feel a pain in my neck" or "I see Jack's face" or whatever, and perhaps adding afterward whether the awareness is pleasant or unpleasant. It was so clear the way that the people who took the hot seat avoided as soon as they became aware of something unpleasant to them. I must check up on this in me. I think this is the part that I have been missing in my work with me—and why I got fed up with the "diary" effect. What *I* avoid when I'm *with other people*. I feel good, and strong, and excited about going into this. I'd better be aware of myself when the people who don't want to come to me as therapist come, tomorrow morning, with instructions (from Fritz tonight) to air their resentments. How many will be honest and do that? How many will cheat, and go to the one they want? I have no idea. . . . Just now, I had a fantasy of *all* the people coming to my door. The fantasy is funny, and it would be funny if it were real. My laughter *is*. I didn't *make* it. It happened. In my flashing fantasy of all the people coming, they had all kinds of different expressions on their faces, from grim to joyous. I saw their body postures. Individual body postures. . . . Just now, I thought, "Suppose they all *don't* want me, and dutifully come, and get disagreeing about what's wrong with me."

All fantasy. I haven't a notion what will happen tomorrow.

Yesterday and today, I felt like leaving here. I knew that wouldn't last, but I sure felt that way, like "Ugh." So much happyhappy funfun. That, I can get anywhere.

What I am happy with now is a violation of my love of "voluntary." So much for my love. Pfft! I kiss it goodbye.

Some people didn't get anything out of Fritz' "ABC of Gestalt." They were bored. Some people got a lot out of it, and were very interested. And so it goes. The ones who got something out of it like me for suggesting it. The ones who didn't get anything out of it probably wish I hadn't suggested it, and can add that to their grievances against me. One woman didn't get anything out of it and said it doesn't fit with her therapy (she's a therapist) at all, because she wants to make things happen—and at the same time she has enough faith in Fritz and me to want to go on with it. One man who took the hot seat and missed right down the line, told me he's sure he's not missing anything, but he sounded determined to find out what it is that he isn't missing.

Things are livelier in a different way.

I feel good that I went by the truth of me. Many people use the groups to say things they otherwise wouldn't, and I like to say them directly to the person, without the support of the group. I could easily tell Fritz what I wanted, outside the group. *More* easily than *in* the group. So, I told him in the group. It wasn't difficult, but I did *expect* some difficulty—which I didn't expect about telling just him. I didn't avoid *that*, anyway.

While the people were in the hot seat (one at a time) I got a lot out of noticing them—and Fritz with them—and at the same time, I was enjoying the difference between me in June on this awareness bit and me now (more aware) and feeling a kind of blossoming and growing again, where I had felt stuck. Not *stuck* stuck, like altogether stuck. Stuck like growing in some directions and not growing somewhere else.

I also feel good that I was bored with Fritz' lectures which he put on for the new people (I think he was, too—he gave them up) and tonight, he did this awareness instead.

I feel a little sorry that it's time to go to bed. I'm not very sleepy now, but if I don't go to bed by 1 a.m., which it nearly is, I won't be in good shape for being aware at 8 a.m. when the people arrive. Kolman won't be here—that's the only one I know about. He said he was sorry he wouldn't be in my group all week. I said, "No resentments?" and it seemed to me his answer was that he resented another therapist *more*, although his words said only that he has this big resentment to air with X and he's going to do it.

It should be an interesting morning. People who don't like me (as therapist, at least—it doesn't necessarily mean that they dislike me altogether) from 8:00 to 10:00, and from 10:00 to 11:00 we'll have the advanced training group with Fritz, which he dropped at the end of the previous series, in late August, and that was something I always got a lot out of.

Nextday.

I enjoyed the (prospect of) risk.

This morning before eight o'clock I got into some craziness. All the "resentment" stuff looked absurd—like kids getting in a scrap about something that didn't happen anywhere except in their (respective) heads. I felt like laughing and going for a walk in the rain. With the people.

But that wouldn't be doing them justice, said I. You must take them seriously.

So then I became serious, and that was a performance, an act.

So go ahead and laugh. . . I wasn't feeling laughing any more, so *that* was an act.

Anything I could think of became an act. Of course.

Trapped.

I don't want to *act* and I can't see anything to do but act. One act or another. I don't want any of them, and in five or ten minutes I'll have to. . . .

Finally, I sat down and got together with me—with what was going on in me—got in touch with myself and the world again—the light coming into the sky, and in me.

At ten minutes after eight, I thought "Is everyone being 'bad' this morning—coming late out of resentment that Fritz set the beginning time back to eight this morning, instead of nine?"

I started reading a science fiction fantasy that I wrote nine years ago. Deke mentioned last night that there is so much Gestalt in it. I didn't know anything about Gestalt when this story wrote itself. I had latched onto gestalt—after years of working to discover how I had lost my early talent for writing fiction. When I had all that information, I knew what not to do with other people and their writing. I still couldn't write fiction. So then, I went after that. Finally, "I" wrote this story and while it was happening, I remembered writing in this way when I was young, beginning when I used to lie on the floor and write stories, sometimes telling my parents and my sister what was going on now in the story as it wrote itself and I saw what it was. They enjoyed, and didn't tell me that I should be writing something else.

Reading the story now, I got very interested, and it was

151

eight-twenty before I noticed that no one had come, and thought "Maybe no one is coming."

I felt disappointed. The new people haven't been in a group with me, but there are all those "old" people who have. No resentments? I didn't believe it. . . . Just now I've noticed that what I expected them to be resentful of was lack of excitement, and slowness—the kind of thing that went on last night with Fritz when he was demonstrating the ABC of Gestalt. If that was it, for anyone, they might feel shook up about resenting this in me.

Speculation. Anything I think about it is speculation. *My* speculation. I don't know one damned thing.

How many other feelings did I have this morning when nobody came? I went on reading the story and felt good sitting here enjoying it. I let myself feel as sleepy as I was, and then didn't feel sleepy any more. Then I felt sleepy again and was annoyed that nobody came when I had got up when I could have slept. Then I realized what I had got out of the expectation of their coming—the foul-up about acting, the coming clear and knowing again that I could only go by awareness in the moment, and I wouldn't have missed it the way it was.

I feel like putting in the story "Window to the Whirled" here. I knew that everything I was working on before was related to what I'm doing now, but I hadn't thought of the story as Gestalt until Deke mentioned it. gestalt, yes, of course—even in the way it was written.

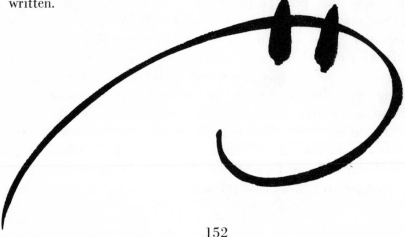

Window to the Whirled*

Anne was young and she was lovely—sweeping blonde hair, sea green eyes, ivory skin, and a body that didn't need to be changed anywhere. A girl like that, and the two things that she wanted were a treadle sewing machine and her grandmother. Why, she could have been a TV star or just about anything that most girls would give their souls to be. Anne said she'd be bored. What could be more boring, they asked her, than a sewing machine and a grandmother? That wasn't Anne's view at all.

Her grandmother had had a treadle machine and she had let Anne use it sometimes. When Anne's feet were on the treadle, one forward, one back, pedalling away, she felt that she was going somewhere. Grandmother had always had the same feeling. She wouldn't switch to an electric machine because, she said, she couldn't bear to stay in one place. Anne had never been bored when Grandma was around. They were always going somewhere together even when they sat in the living room with everyone else. Then one day Grandma disappeared, and Anne wept. But then she stopped her tears and went off to find Grandma. By the time she got to New England in search of her, she was feeling very discouraged, and when she saw an auction being held in front of a barn she stopped for diversion, unable to bear her despair.

No one knew what would be brought out of the barn next and held up for everyone to see and bid on. . . . And then there was an old treadle sewing machine. Anne started off the bidding with a quarter. Nobody else bid, and she got it for that. And suddenly she felt as though her lungs had stopped breathing. A treadle machine! Maybe *that* was the way to find Grandma.

When the men brought it to her, she got to work on it at once, looking in the little drawers, two on each side, and sure enough! There was an instruction book in one of them, tattered, but showing how to thread the machine. In another drawer there was a little wooden shelf with holes for bobbins to set in, and there was a bobbin in each one, with thread on it—blue, green, white, red,

*Reprinted from the Magazine of FANTASY AND SCIENCE FICTION, February 1962.

yellow. The colored threads were oddly luminous. She'd never be able to match them, but she couldn't bear to waste them, so she used the bobbin that had some white thread on it. There was a spool of white thread too, so she threaded the upper part with that. Then she took a handkerchief out of her pocket, folded it, and stitched the two sides together. Sunlight filtered through a big elm and dappled Anne and the sewing machine with light and shade. She used the handkerchief now for a cleaning rag. There was an oil can in one of the drawers, with oil still in it. It smelled awfully good for oil—more like perfume; in fact, more like flowers. *Why* hadn't Grandma taken Anne with her? That hurt when she thought of it, and the pain crippled her so that she couldn't do anything. So then she thought about it in another way, without emphasis, inquiring, "Why didn't Grandma take me with her?" And that way it had an answer even if she hadn't yet figured out what it was.

She began to realize that she had been too logical. Grandma wasn't. And she had been trying too hard, which Grandma had always said was bad. "You just *do* things," she had explained, "and then they come out the way you want them to—although you didn't know that's what you wanted." The way that it had happened just now, in fact. If she hadn't stopped chasing Grandma she wouldn't have noticed the auction and wouldn't have found the machine to start her thinking in the right direction. . . . If she could have listened *only* to Grandma, Anne thought. But there were all the other people telling Anne that Grandma was out of her mind.

The sewing machine was sparkling now like the shine on well-used railroad tracks, beckoning her on to. . . . When she thought about that "to" and where it might lead, she shook her head, tossed the hair back from her forehead, and went on with her sewing. Grandma said that anything you could think about was puny by comparison with what could happen if you let it, and that thinking about what you wanted narrowed things down so that only little, usual things could happen. Then people said, "Of course. That's all there is to life. What did you expect? Flying carpets?" When Anne was inside herself and Grandma, she did, but when she was inside of other people she made up her mind to be reasonable and not expect too much. She was feeling less and less reasonable now—or more reasonable in a different way.

When the sewing machine had been adjusted so that it hummed instead of clacked, Anne asked the men to put it in her car, and drove away. When she came to a fork in the road, she took the one that pleased her. In passing through a town she noticed a store and went in and bought a bedroll and a little icebox without realizing that she had changed her course from the months of sleeping in motels and eating in restaurants like everyone else. She just knew that she was strangely happy and that she wanted to get back west. But she was in no hurry about it. She stopped when she felt like it, and used the sewing machine. The things she made were more beautiful all the time. People wanted to buy them but she gave them away, saying that they were too precious to be sold because of what was sewn into them. She didn't know herself what she was talking about but she knew it was right.

People wanted her to stay, and offered her a fine place to work in, but she always sooner rather than later put her sewing machine in her car and went to another town. And another town. And another town. Until she sometimes wondered if she were making any kind of sense or just re-living a fairy tale absorbed in childhood. Sometimes it seemed to her that the fairy tale had been telling people how to live, but at other times she was doubtful about this. Then she would remember "Don't think!" and she would stop, and then she enjoyed everything around herself again.

Eventually she got to California where the weather was usually mild, and she began taking her sewing machine with her on trips to the mountains, the desert or the lakes, and there she would sit in the sun and treadle away, which wouldn't have been possible with an electric machine which tied you to a wire and a generating plant. She would leave her machine to take a swim, or to climb a mountain, and she was becoming stronger and more flexible all the time. She was also becoming more beautiful—perhaps radiant is the word—but she didn't notice that: she was too fascinated by the fact that she was learning. Things kept coming into her head. She began to understand mathematics and physics and lots of other things she hadn't bothered with because she had thought them dull. She thought of moving on to a place where there was a university, so that she could go to college, but when she spoke of this to a man who was visiting in the town, a professor from Berkeley named Stan Blanton, he said, "Heavens no! You'd lose what you have, and what you didn't lose you'd be fifty years old before you'd begin to know." This was Grandma talk, and Anne felt at ease with it—and with him. He was a nice sort of person, but somewhat sad. He was fifty years old and hadn't done half the things he wanted to, because of all the things he had "had to" do, and he wasn't sure that the ones he had done were worth doing. This made it difficult for him to keep on doing them, so he was tired all the time, which he thought was because he was growing old.

He was very conscious of his age, so although he felt younger with Anne than he had for years and she was the nicest thing that had ever happened to him, he went away.

Anne was then a little sad, for he had seemed to have possibilities that other people didn't have. She felt separated from something. But she could always get together inside herself by working things out with the sewing machine. She might use one of the attachments that she hadn't tried, she thought. She fitted one to the machine, and took a long thin strip of material to try it out on. But no matter how carefully she sewed in a straight line, and kept the two ends of the strip apart, it always wound up with the ends together, like a belt with a twist in it, so that the outside went inside or the inside went outside until you couldn't tell which was outside or inside.

She thought she would play with the threads that she had been saving, so she took the bobbin with the yellow thread and put it where bobbins go, and took the green one and put it on top where the spool should go, so that the yellow and green threads would intermingle like buttercups in a field. But when she started to treadle, the cloth slipped out from under the foot—and the green and yellow threads went on spinning themselves together. There didn't seem to be any end to it. The two bobbins were always full. And instead of threads, it was now becoming a piece of cloth. "Oh, how I should love to have a cape of this!" she thought, and went on treadling. And the material grew. But now it was growing into a piece of very special shape, and she began to see the outline of her cape, although it was a little confusing the way the inside and the outside kept changing. Then she seemed to have done the cape, or the machine had, or they both had, for she wasn't sure how much of the spinning had come out of her and how much out of the machine, and sometimes she felt that maybe she and the machine weren't two things anyway. Machinery wasn't like nature, she had always thought. Nature you could feel your way into, and know what it was to be a tree or a rock or a pool. But machines! Even treadle machines weren't something she could get *inside*. They weren't natural. But now she wasn't so sure about that. A bird's nest was natural. It was made by the bird. A beaver's dam was natural. It was made by the beaver. And machines were made by men even when they were made by machines because men made the . . . .

When the cape was done, she snipped the threads which held it to the machine, feeling that she was cutting an umbilical cord. Then she stood up, started to fling the cape over her shoulders to find out how to get into it, and it wrapped itself around her.

There was a knock on her door, and she called "Come in!" And there was Stan Blanton. "What a beautiful cape!" he said, which wasn't at all what he had come two hundred miles to say. "Isn't it?" said Anne. "But I can't decide which side is inside and which side is outside or which one I am in!" She gave the cape a little flip as she said that, and it seemed to mix up its inside and outside in a quick flashing movement, and then it was gone. So was Anne.

Stan couldn't tell what he felt first, or whether they rippled all over each other like the colors on a dying dolphin. He was astonished, dismayed, puzzled, delighted, and a number of other things that he didn't bother to sort out. But when the rippling stopped, he was bereft. It had taken a tremendous effort to overthrow the forces of convention which said that he should stay away from Anne, and to break loose and come to her. And now she was gone! He sat down on a chair with his head in his hands and his elbows on the sewing machine, and tried to figure out what had happened. The answer seemed so tantalizingly near. But suddenly he began to think of other things. Anne had disappeared. Missing young girls and elderly men were meat for scandal. He'd better go back to Berkeley in a hurry. Quickly he went down the stairs and out to his car and drove home. Maybelle wasn't there. He sat down in the living room trying to think what to say to her when she came in and asked where he had been. His head ached. What *could* he say?

When Maybelle came in he looked up and said, "Hello, dear," as usual. She said, "Hello dear," also as usual, and went upstairs as usual.

This made him mad. "After all I've been through!" he thought. And then he got even madder as he realized that he hadn't been through anything but a lot of nonsense that hadn't happened anywhere but in his head. He dashed out of the house and down the street, feeling like a fool, after all the years he had sat quietly in a chair resolving his problems in a mature way and arriving at sane conclusions. Now he suddenly saw all those years as submission to something he really didn't give a damn about, and how *mature* was that? He had felt that he was taking things into his own hands when he left Anne's place abruptly, but he had been a puppet, pushed around by all the stuff that he had no use for. He should have *stayed*, and tried to find Anne.

Anne was back in her room right after he left, actually—if by "actually" you mean according to *our* time. *She* had been gone for weeks, and found this very refreshing. After that she spent more and more time looking into other places, and her absences began to be noticed by the neighbors. Next time she disappeared, someone called the police and said she was missing and foul play was suspected. No one thought anything of the kind, but they wanted to find out about Anne, and "foul play" was a signal you used to get the police moving into other people's affairs. Stan was the only conceivable "man in the case," so they tracked him down in Berkeley. Maybelle left him, which was both satisfying and convenient.

Anne's picture appeared in the papers, along with Stan's, not that there was evidence that he had anything to do with her disappearance but it made a good story. Stan, disgusted, yelled, "It's

158

phony! *Everything's* phony!" which of course people did not wish to believe because it included themselves, so he "told all" just to show them. After that, he was permitted to stay at home but he was examined by psychiatrists. He was lying in bed one night, far from sleep, when . . . .

Anne suddenly appeared beside his bed and said, "What do you mean, talking about me that way, as if I were a curiosity!"

Stan wasted no time on words, which could come later, and were more likely to if he acted first. He reached out, grabbed the cape and whipped it over her head, saying, "Stick around for awhile."

Anne laughed. "I've been places and learned things," she said—and disappeared.

Mournfully he spread the cape on top of the bed and leaned back against the pillows. Before his eyes, it whipped off the bed and wrapped itself around Anne, who was suddenly there laughing at him again. "I can only disappear without it," she said. "I can't *go* anywhere." Now that she had the cape, she did.

Stan was coming to his senses, now that he wasn't trying to do or be or live up to anything in particular. He dressed and went to the place where Anne had lived and claimed her sewing machine. In the nearest motel, he started studying how to use it. When he got as far as the moebius strip, the rest was easy. Then he went to Anne's room "to look for something." It would be perfectly easy to find Anne. All he had to do was start from where she had been and glide down the strip to where she was. He put on his cape, and gave it a flip as Anne had done.

It was wonderful in nowhere, the place between everything. He hadn't known it would be this glorious—like being the only ship on an ocean, or the only skater on a frozen Lake Michigan. He had had dreams like this, but had dismissed them as thinkless wishing. Swooping, swerving, curving—and all on nothing, so that there was no possibility of falling off. He began to feel a zestful eagerness, a curiosity about where he might find himself when he slid off the strip and into Anne. Would she be surprised!

Zing!

He was in his own room, right at the spot where Anne had been. But Anne was not there. What a fool! He tossed his cloak on the bed and sat on it, and pulled his hair with his hands. He was so oppressed by failure that it didn't occur to him that all he had to do was take off again. Where *would* she have gone? Past and present, future too, and she could be anywhere in anywhen of them. He'd been so *sure* he had got it figured out, and all that he had done was to follow himself home. He had a sudden harrowing thought that maybe that was all he could do.

He got up from the bed and paced the floor, then went downstairs, not that it made any sense but he had to do something so that he wouldn't be so certain that he wasn't doing anything. He sat down in a chair and rubbed his eyebrows with the heels of his hands—*hard*. This time, he wasn't going to start with *any* preconceived ideas. As they arose in his mind, he wiped them out, one by one, until there was nothing left. But what help was a blank? He shook his head angrily, then thought "The hell with her. I'm going to do something *I* want to do." And he ran upstairs, swirled his cloak over his shoulders, and went skating down the strip through the clouds of nowhere to somewhere he had always wondered about. . . .

It was morning when he arrived. A bright clear beautiful morning, crisp and sharp as autumn and with the soft warmth of summer in the air. Tall buildings, towering in isolation, stood out against the sky. Around each of them were areas of low buildings, with lawns and trees. People walked the streets in clothes as soft and bright as flowers, making his own conspicuously dull. Quickly he got back on the strip and returned to the motel where he had left the sewing machine and let it weave new clothes for him. Putting them on, he replaced the cape on his shoulders and skated forward to where he had been, where he was inconspicuous now. But even so, he felt a sense of loneliness. At moments, in passing close to someone, this loneliness departed, but then it returned. He wanted to join with other people, and since some of them were going toward one building, he went there too. It seemed to be some kind of theatre or hall. There were no posters or canopy signs, so he walked a little closer to the man nearest him and asked, "What's playing today?"

The man stopped, and a smile began to play about his face. Then he said quickly, "I'm sorry, I thought you were one of us. I don't quite know the words to use to explain to you. This is a sort of playground, I suppose. Would that be right?" Stan looked baffled, so the native tried again. "We drop in when we want to, and listen or otherwise take part in the play as we like. There's nothing written down. We just. . . . I really don't know how to say it because I've never had to before. We take part in it when we like and drop out when we like. It's great fun."

"Fun!" said Stan. "It's confusing! How do you know where the play begins or ends or is going?"

"What a strange view," mused the native. "What ever begins or ends, or knows where it is going? . . . . Although I suppose that one could see things that way if one took a very limited view. But how unrealistic."

"Unrealistic!" said Stan, out of great confidence that he knew what realism is. "Why, you're just *drifting*!" But his own very recent life came into his mind then, and he wasn't so certain. Still, he couldn't quite yield, so he said magnanimously, "That's just in your plays, of course."

"Well, no. As a matter of fact, our playing partly serves to keep us in touch with reality. I don't mean that is why we do it. We enjoy the play, and that's reason enough. But also we carry over some of the spirit of reality into our work, and this keeps us from becoming too serious about what is, after all, very transient and limited."

Stan turned this over in his mind. It took a good bit of turning. "Are all your plays like this?" he asked. "No hard-working actors giving their lives to their profession?"

This time, the native looked confused. "Why on earth," he said at last, "should anyone give his life to a *profession*?"

"To make things better," said Stan.

"And did it? I think that you must be from *then*," said the native. "A most tragic era—all misunderstanding."

"What did we misunderstand?" asked Stan with eagerness. The native said nothing. "Don't tell me that 'If you gotta ask, you'll never get to know' " Stan cried.

"No," said the native, "I could, but I won't. But tell me, how did you get here?" and he moved away without waiting for an answer. He looked back at Stan as though inviting him to follow, but Stan did not notice. His mind was a massive ache from ideas that seemed to be standing on their heads. Then they went into a tumbling act in which everything moved so fast that he couldn't tell which was upside down and which right side up. Anne was suddenly his only possible anchor in chaos. He started walking rapidly down the street. If he could just find her! Then he slowed. That's what he must get out of his mind—finding Anne. He felt a twinge as he realized that if she had passed him just then she would have recognized where he was—or wasn't—and would have gone by without speaking to him. He restrained himself from turning to see if she were behind him, and brought himself into the *now* of all his senses so that he was noticing everything in the instant in which he lived. Then, he noticed that he was hungry. What could he do about that, when his money couldn't be used here? What about numismatists? There were phone booths around so he went into one. The directory seemed awfully small. He looked in the front for instructions and happily discovered that all he had to do was dial Numismatists for the information he wanted. A screen in the wall lighted up, and there were all the numismatists listed. Continuing to follow instructions, he took a piece of paper from a peculiar pad beside the telephone and held it in front of the screen. In an instant, the information was transferred, and he left the booth with the paper in his hand. A thought struck him, and he went back into the phone booth and dialed "coin dealers." The same list appeared on the screen. Now *that* was intelligent.

All the dealers were on the same street, so all he had to do was find the street. The first man he asked said courteously, pointing with his hand, "Go two blocks down, and ask again." When he asked again, the man pointed in another direction and said, "One block down, and ask again." At the next stop when he asked, the man pointed down a street and said, "Lane on the right side, halfway down the block."

It was so blessedly simple!

He walked into the first store that appealed to him, since he didn't know anything about any of them anyway. The man behind the counter looked at the money Stan gave him and handed it back, saying, "Third store to the right. He'll give you a better price than I can."

Stan looked at him in astonishment. "Why?"

"He has a customer who'll pay more."

"But don't you want business for yourself?"

"Certainly," said the man, "but that's no reason you shouldn't get all you can for this."

Stan went out of the store a little unbelieving. There was a woman ahead of him in the next store, and he noticed that she was offering the same kind of money that he had. He'd probably get less for his, now, if he got anything at all. There didn't seem to be any bargaining going on. The woman and the clerk were both admiring the money, and then the clerk put her money in a box under the counter, opened another box and counted out some other money into the woman's hand. She took it and walked toward the door. As she passed him, Stan noticed her eyes. They reminded him of someone a little, but not entirely. Maybe the eyes were the same and the hair was different, which made the eyes look different. Anyway, he didn't know anyone here. He went to the counter, and the clerk took the money and said happily, "Two in one day! Sometimes we have to wait for years! I can give you a little more for this than I gave Mrs. Chumley because Mr. Sringo will be so happy that he doesn't have to postpone his journey any longer. He has enough now to make the trip."

"But where can he use *this* money?" Stan asked.

"In the twentieth century, of course. You people who come from the past are all right because old money is real, but when we go into the past, our money is phony."

Stan took the new money the clerk held out, and walked toward the door. As he passed the spot where he had noticed the woman's eyes, several things clicked together at once. "Anne!" he thought. But no, that wasn't right; this woman was much older than Anne. He was putting two and two together and making twenty-two. Still, there was a nagging at the back of his neck, insisting that he was at least a *little* right. He went back to the clerk. "Do you have Mrs. Chumley's address?"

163

"No more than I have yours."

Stan started toward the door again, and the clerk called after him, "She did say something once about 'the children' in a way that made me think she might be a teacher."

There weren't any conspicuous signs of restaurants along the streets, but here and there on what looked like a private house there was a discreet sign saying "Diners welcome." He walked into one of them and found himself in a small hall, from which he could see a room with one large round table in it, at which a number of people were seated. The food on the table looked and smelled awfully good, and made him want to walk right in and take a vacant chair, but the people were all chatting like old friends. That made him want to join them too, but on the other hand. . . . He hesitated, standing there in the hall, but the sign *had* said "Diners welcome," and he couldn't see anything else to do but walk in and sit down. So he did.

"Hello there!" said one of the men, in a friendly but quite unbumptious way. "We were just talking about. . . ." cueing him in on the conversation. Food was passed to him. The talk was about affairs strange to him, but as it went on, he began to feel at home in it. As some people finished eating, they left, leaving some money at their plate. A maid came in and took their dishes and the money, glanced over the table to see which serving dishes needed to be refilled. Other people came in and sat down, and the conversation rolled right along, covering a most astonishing lot of ground. And as he got his bearings, he began to say something now and then, for it was possible sometimes to point out a fallacy even though he didn't really know what they were talking about. He had noticed that as a child, but then no one would listen to him. Here, they did, and laughed when he showed up a mistake. Correcting the mistake, they took up from there, and went on. There were pauses, too, when no one was talking, which seemed to be the times when they were listening most of all. He got something from these pauses. It was as though his mind cleared and information came into it in a nice uncluttered way. When Stan went out into the sun, he felt refreshed and free and living in a larger world than he had known before.

164

Mrs. Chumley left the store where she had exchanged her money and went back to school, humming. She'd done it again. There must be a time in the past when her luck would run out, but it hadn't yet, so she was enjoying it.

The children greeted her with joy. They were special children, but no one knew that but themselves and Mrs. Chumley. They were listed at the School Board as exceptional children, a term carried over from the mid-twentieth century when "exceptional" was first used for children who were not. She took out the money and put it on the desk, and the children came up and each one of them put some of it in their pockets. Then they went outside and scattered, each in a different direction, and each one of them bought something insignificant—just usual things that any parent might send his child out to buy, parts to fix a copter or a house conditioner or a speedplane.

When they returned to school, they all got together in a room that already had something in it partly made, and went to work, adding the new parts in places which would have astonished the people who knew all about copters and house conditioners and speedplanes. Mrs. Chumley watched. She enjoyed the children at work, intent on what they were doing. When she first started working with them, she had pretended to be baffled. It was good for them. For some time now, she hadn't had to pretend.

When the doorbell rang, Mrs. Chumley wondered who on earth that might be. She got up to go to the door, while the children left their work and scattered around the room and picked up books and began reading. They were all arranged in small groups, with older ones pointing things out to younger ones, the way that any good school was run. There was The Machine, yes, but Mrs. Chumley had begun with usual machines, and explained that she was using them to teach the children, and when they got more complicated it would have taken an expert or a simpleton to notice that they were different.

"Mrs. Chumley!" said Stan. "I'm so happy to find you!" And he looked so happy that Mrs. Chumley was happy too. Besides, this seemed to be something different, and there was only one possible thing for Mrs. Chumley to say to something different, and she said it: "Do come in!" As she led him to the classroom she said, "I'd rather hoped that someone else would find me, my granddaughter, but I guess she's not as bright as I thought she was. Sometimes I've thought I should have brought her with me, but then she never would have found her own way." She sighed. "I guess she didn't, anyway."

Stan looked at Mrs. Chumley more intently, particularly at her eyes. "Anne?" he asked.

"Yes," said Mrs. Chumley, "that's my name. Ohhh! You mean *Anne*!"

"I think I do," said Stan. "I wouldn't be here if it hadn't been for her."

"I'm so glad!" said Mrs. Chumley, sinking into a chair. "I thought I'd given her enough to go on, but it *is* difficult to hold your own back there, so sometimes I wondered if I had been wrong. But as long as she's got started, she's all right, even if she hasn't arrived. Who has, after all? Tell me about it." And Stan did. That is, he started to, but then he became aware of the children listening. Mrs. Chumley waved to him to continue. "We have no secrets," she said. "That is, I don't have any from them."

When Stan had finished, Mrs. Chumley explained about the children and herself.

"I thought this was an enlightened world!" Stan exclaimed.

"Oh, it is," said Mrs. Chumley, "but they've got so used to it they've forgotten that it could be *more* enlightened."

"So you're getting things out of a rut, I suppose."

"Well, I suppose I am," said Mrs. Chumley, "but that's not *why* I'm doing it."

Stan walked over to the machine, and the children gathered around him, with expressions on their faces that he was trying to understand. He tried to look intelligent as he asked, "And what is this to be used for?"

"It already has been," said one of the older boys. He looked around at the other children. "Has everyone got it?" They all nodded their heads or said yes, and he checked them over one by one to see that no one was left out. Then, "Okay!" he said, and the children began taking the machine apart, stacking the pieces in neat rows on the floor.

Mrs. Chumley watched, delight on her face. "They've really got it!" she said.

"What?" asked Stan.

"I don't really know," said Mrs. Chumley, "but they haven't tried anything with interstellar travel, so that might be it."

"You said they'd got it," protested Stan, "so surely you must know what it is."

"They've got the basic idea," said Mrs. Chumley. "It's sort of like doing arithmetic problems on paper so you can then do them in your head. After that, you don't need paper. Sometimes I thought they never *would* work it out."

"Why didn't you tell them?"

"Because then they would have been able to make use of it only in a limited way. They'd never get *beyond* it if they didn't figure it out for themselves."

Stan looked bewildered. Mrs. Chumley looked sad. "You *could* understand," she said, "if you'd just let go of what you think you know. Everything you can do outside, you can do inside—that's where it came from. Most people stop at outside. That's why 1970 still has telephone wires and stuff.

"It seems to me," said Stan, "like a mental moebius strip."

"You've got it!" she said.

"Oh, no, I haven't," he corrected.

"But you have—you couldn't have said it outside if you hadn't had it inside, and now all you have to do is get it back in." She turned to the children. "I'm going home, now. I assume you're not. Tell me about it when you get back."

"Don't they even thank you for all you've done for them?" asked Stan.

"Why should they?" asked Mrs. Chumley. "Do you know, at this moment I haven't the faintest idea what I'll be doing next?"

Stan was beginning to get the feeling of it as he held the door open for her, then walked beside her to the street. How wonderful that he had arrived just when she was about to start on something else! What fun to go along!

But at the corner she left him, saying "Goodbye" as casually as if she would see him tomorrow.

"But about Anne!" he called after her, trying to hold her. "I'm sure she's on her way!"

"I'm so glad," Mrs. Chumley's voice wafted over her shoulder.

"But where shall she find you?"

"How do I know, when I don't know where to find myself until I'm there?" And she was gone.

All the adventure went out of him again. He rushed back to the school and asked the children, "Where does Mrs. Chumley live?"

"Wherever she feels like," they told him.

"I've got to find her!"

The children looked at him curiously, as though he were a person who had got pushed out of shape. Then a trace of compassion appeared on the face of one of the girls, and she said gently, "How did you find her the first time?"

At the store! . . . But she might never go there again. He was missing some piece that was there but he wasn't seeing it.

"Let go of it," the girl said, "and it will come to you."

And then the missing piece came into his mind: he had been taking care of the need of the moment when he ran across Mrs. Chumley. But it might be so long before their paths crossed again.

"When there's no other way," the girl said, "that's the only way there is."

Stan felt humble before this child. She knew so surely, so completely, what he only glimpsed at times and then lost. "Thank you," he said, and left.

He had a lot to think about, and he wished he knew what it was. It began to come into his mind that with both Annes he was just riding along with them, like an old man trying to recapture his youth through the youth of someone else. When they left him, he was old again. But he *had* recaptured it in and by himself for awhile. How had he done it?

He wandered the streets, not knowing where he was going or what was around him, until he came to a basking place. There was a long wall, facing the sun, and there were benches against the wall, all of the same material that caught the warmth and held it. He sat down on one of the benches, then stretched out on it, letting the warmth from beneath and above seep into him so that his muscles relaxed, and in letting go of his body he also released his mind.

Why was it so difficult for him to be *on his own*? It seemed so easy for Anne and her grandmother, and when he was with them, he. . . . No, when he was with them, he went along with them, but he wasn't *free* as they were.

Someone came and sat quietly at the end of the long bench. He didn't open his eyes. But he let go of his thoughts for awhile, and listened. He heard little crunching, crackling sounds, and then the wings of birds as they came fluttering down, then their feet on the pavement, and their beaks pecking, their little jumps as they bumped into each other and then stepped back, only to move forward again. "They do everything so easily," he thought. "Why shouldn't that be true for people?" People had to work for a living and raise children, to be sure, but why was it so *difficult*? Shouldn't it be as easy for humans in their way as it was for the birds in theirs?

Why were people so stupid? he asked, as he let roll into his mind all the things that he had been keeping out of it. Graduate School, he suddenly realized, was probably not the isolated, special group that he had thought it. Probably everywhere else was the same, with its enshrined incompetents of which he had been one. Oh, he had recognized the others. The one he had failed to recognize was himself. He hadn't started out that way. He was never going to be like his professors.

He groaned as he remembered a graduate student, bright but rebellious (Stan winced now, at that "but"), who had designed and used a seal that had on it an opened book and a lighted candle, with the words: Help Stamp Out Graduate School. Stan had talked to the student about "professional dignity." The student had said, "I don't like that word 'dignity.' " Stan realized now that the "dignity" that he had recommended was nothing but pretentiousness. The student had told him so, but he hadn't heard. Not at the time. The student had said, "You're just being *nice*, and *polite*. Can't you be *human*?" And Stan had said, so reasonably (so smugly, it seemed to him now), "You'll see things in a different way, later on."

"I hope not!" the student had said, as most students did not. "What I don't understand," he went on, "is why you won't let people *think*. When anyone does, you clip his wings and think you've tamed him—if he stays. But what you've taken *out* of him is how to fly."

"The requirements of research—"

"I don't want to do *re*search," the student had interrupted. "I want to *search*. But it's submit or get out, so I'm getting out."

Again Stan shuddered in the sun. What *was* man? When he was young, he had been trying to find out. Then he had accepted a role, had become an actor on a stage with an assigned part to play. Assigned *by whom*? When he was young, he had seen another destiny for himself. And as he reunited with that youth now and let it sweep over him, he ached with a new and different kind of pain. He sat up and blew his nose because otherwise there would be tears in his eyes, and men don't cry.

Putting his handkerchief back where it belonged, he sat leaning forward, with his hands clasped between his knees, remembering things he didn't want to remember. For what he had taught was courage, but what he had *lived* was bowing to "the rules." Once he had heard one student say to another, "And another stone idol topples into the steaming jungle," and they both had turned away.

How had he got into this mess? At first he had submitted to the rules to get through grad school, so that he would have a degree and people would listen to what he had to say. But when he got his Ph.D., he saw that he would have to get into the upper brackets: *then* people would listen. But when he had got a name, by sacrificing most of himself for twenty years, people listened only when he said what they expected him to say. Any deviation was dismissed as brought on by age or overwork. The holidays when he met Anne were the only time he could remember when he had truly spoken from himself—out of his *own* knowledge.

He sobbed. Let anyone think what they wanted to think, or thought that they should think. What mattered was what he knew in himself. The more he sobbed, the clearer it became, like a child who cries his way out of confusion and into sunlight again.

He began to be aware of things around him, of passing feet, of the pigeons still fluttering around him. A pigeon flew onto his shoulder, and he turned his head slowly toward it, feeling no difference between himself and the pigeon. Then, "Mrs. Chumley!" he exclaimed to the woman sitting at the end of the bench.

"It isn't miraculous," she said. "I went back to school for a book and the children said you looked as though you'd stop at the first basking place."

"You walked away from me, before."

"Wasn't that a good thing, too?"

He burst out laughing with the glory of a child, a cosmic laughter that embraced so much more than words could say that he made no attempt to say them. "I feel so small and so big," he said, a little later.

"When you feel small and big in the right places," said Mrs. Chumley, "you're just where you belong. I'm hungry."

At dinner, people were making the most wonderful sense and fun until someone mentioned the children who said they'd been to the stars when they'd only been gone for awhile between school and supper. Mrs. Chumley put her hand reassuringly on Stan's thigh. "Don't be bothered," she said. "The children knew what to expect. Probably they told the truth to find out if I knew what I was talking about. Now they'll believe everything I told them. I hope I was careful."

"I thought it was *better* here!" Stan said quietly.

"It is. It won't take them long to discover their mistake and they'll laugh and zoom ahead."

Anne had skated into town earlier, and it had been easy to guess who the "teacher" was that the children said had shown them the way to the stars. She went to the school and got the feel of Grandma and wandered around until she got a whiff of her through an open window. That is, she heard Grandma's voice. Walking in, she joined

Stan and Grandma at the table saying, "And how do you do, Mrs. Chumley? Where did you pick up that name, by the way?"

"From an Englishman," said Grandma. "He said he would be proud to give me his name, so I took it. Sit down and eat. There's something I want to talk over with Stan." And to Stan she said, "You're going back?"

"Of course," he told her. "I've got to clean up a mess I made. I thought I would begin by rounding up all the students who wouldn't listen to me."

Mrs. Chumley shook her head. "They'll have fallen for the same thing somewhere else where it looked different. You'll be just an old man, now, who's out of his mind. When you sell yourself down the river, you have to like the river. Then you like spinach even though you hate the stuff. There's going to have to be a new school, and everyone's tired of 'new schools' and getting nostalgic for Emerson, so you might call it Heisenberg College—he's sort of bringing Emerson up to date. It will take money. There's a reasonably young man—never even got a Master's—who's now president of one of the big foundations. . . ."

"What do you know about *now*?" asked Anne. "I mean, now *then*?"

"I haven't stayed here *all* the time," said Grandma, "and even if I had, I'd know more about now *then* than is known there now. There's a lot of nonsense in the history books, but some things do come through later which weren't seen at the time. You could see the same thing in your own life if you'd look," she rebuked Anne. "I've been back several times. I worked for Schraffts, and they cater to the big foundations—luncheons and stuff. I've been in on *lots* of luncheon meetings, and had trouble holding my tongue, too.

"This man's more open than the others," she told Stan. "I'll give you a list of people who've been writing—all saying the same thing but in so many different ways that people haven't got them together yet. You get them together, scoop the cream from what they have to say, and present it to this man. . . ."

"Grandma!" protested Anne. "You're tampering with the past!"

"Tampering!" snorted Grandma. "That's the word people use when they mean 'Don't grease the wheels, we might get somewhere.' Besides, it's already happened, so how can I be tampering?"

She turned back to Stan, and began scribbling names on a piece of paper. Stan looked over the names and registered mild shock. "*Those* men!" he protested. "They don't give credit to the men whose shoulders they stand on!"

Anne, with a forkful of salad on the way to her mouth, stopped her hand in midair. "Maybe you mean whose umbrellas they got out from under?"

"I'm sorry. How long does it take to get over being a professor?"

"You've changed!" said Anne with delight. "Oh, Stan!"

"You can talk to him later," said Grandma. "Now what you do, Stan, is . . . and I'm not telling any secrets or pushing you around, because you could read this part for yourself if you went to the library. There's still a lot you have to work out on your own because history is also full of the way things didn't happen." She went on scribbling names, and he was surprised how many of them there were. He knew the work of most of them but had dismissed it for one "reason" or another, like not citing sources, going against established authority, too mystic, in some cases they didn't even have a doctorate. Now, their work was rearranging itself in his mind, and he could see what the founders of religions had been trying to get at appearing in another form, a form much more comprehensible to the twentieth century. And it was coming through in so many different places! He looked again at Grandma's continuing list, and put out a hand to stop her writing. "Those people write science fiction!" he said. "They're escapists!"

Grandma sat back and laughed. Anne took out a cigarette, made a pass with her hand over the tip of it, and the tip burst into a glow. "It's a trick," she said, "that I learned in the future."

Stan's laughter burst over theirs. "All right, Grandma. Go on."

"That's all, really. The rest you have to figure out for yourself." Then she turned to Anne: "Have you started working on the mental hospitals yet?"

"That was to be my surprise!"

"It will surprise Stan," said Grandma, "and I'm interested too, because no one seems to know just how it started."

"I worked in several of them before I found the right one to get things moving," Anne told them, "but it's going well now. Some patients have got themselves transferred to other hospitals and are beginning to work things out there. It was quite simple, really. It always is, when you find the place to begin. We just expand everything a little more, and a little more, so nobody notices, so they don't pay any attention to the *direction* of the expansion. The head men are too busy writing papers, anyway. By the time they notice what's happened, they'll think they did it themselves. Probably they still won't notice that it's a school—no degrees, no credits, no teachers, everybody just learning from each other and from everything else, and not *for* anything but the people in it.

"The 'patients' come from all kinds of jobs, so when they go back to work, everything changes a little. They're changing the work. . . . I mean. . . . Oh," she said with annoyance, "what does it matter what's changing what? It's *changing*."

"But how do people from your hospitals manage to work in the places that are filled with the old ideas?" Stan asked. "I should think they'd crack up."

"Some of them do," said Anne, "but they get sent back to us then and in a sane society they're all right, and as soon as they're strong enough they go out again. And sometimes, it's easy. They're train—Won't we *ever* get over using the wrong words?" she asked herself crossly. "They're given a chance to become themselves, and that's what a lot of other people want to be too. One woman went to work in a place just before Christmas, and she found that for thirty years everyone had been giving everyone in the place Christmas presents. She thought she would go crazy if she got into that, so she went around telling everyone, 'I'm not going to give you anything for Christmas, so don't you give me anything for Christmas or I'll be embarrassed.' She wasn't trying to change anything. She was just speaking for herself. And pretty soon everyone was going around saying to everyone else, 'I'm not going to give you anything so don't you. . . .' They said it was the *nicest* Christmas they'd had in years. They were happy clear through January."

"Everyone?"

"Well, no. There was one old biddy who did a lot of hiring and firing, and she was the one who told new employees about the custom, so they thought they had to follow it. She's still upset—other things aren't going her way either—and I hear she's developing cancer. I mean, she really is, and probably won't live very long, but that's better than *everybody else* developing cancer."

"It's going to be fun, going back," said Stan.

"Sometimes you won't think so," Grandma told him. "You'll think that none of these things are happening at all, that you built it all up to make life endurable, that it's all imagination. You'll doubt yourself and your own sanity. Maybe you'd better take along some of those cigarettes Anne has found, so you can wave your hand over one of them and know it's real."

"Couldn't I use you, instead?" Stan asked. "You're the most reassuring thing I know."

Grandma said nothing.

Anne said, half-miserable, half-enchanted, "You aren't coming back with us?"

"There's *nothing* in the history books about me," said Grandma. "I'm completely free."

"And. . . . ?" Stan was trying hard to guess but was fairly sure he couldn't.

"There's a blank space somewhere ahead. I've been farther than that, so I know. Nobody knows what happened."

"So you're going there, to find out. Isn't that risky?"

"I hope so," said Grandma.

I like putting in that story. Maybe I'll put in another one, later on. . . . I notice my pleasure in "stories." Wanting to write fiction again is a recurrent surge that I don't do anything about. Maybe it hasn't yet reached the point of surging strongly enough in relation to what I *am* doing, to push it over.

Fritz revitalized the place Monday evening and the suburban effect is mostly gone. He called a halt to the funfun and required more earnestness. "Sure, therapy can be fun, but not at the beginning." I wish he'd do that more often. I've been leading a group with Hal as co-leader, mornings and evenings 8 to 10. Four sessions, and I'm getting back in balance again. I didn't know just what it was that I had lost in the ten days when I wasn't leading and wasn't in groups, but I knew it as surely as wobbling on a bicycle. This morning's session got me into the balanced view again. I worked with Neville and didn't get him past his stuck point. I felt that nothing had happened. Janet Lederman came in then, and I've heard her praises sung like to the savior. I like her. When she took over with Neville when I had stopped, and moved in with confidence, I thought, "She's really got it. Well, I don't want to be a therapist anyway"—which I don't. That doesn't feel funny inside me—that I am getting so much out of these groups and I don't want to be a therapist. That's the way it is, and it's okay. If I had to make up my mind, I would be in a quandary, but I don't. I never do, until at some point sometimes I do, and *then* it's no problem.

Janet didn't produce a miracle, either. I liked watching her work and enjoyed her. Neville moved into a slightly different area with her than he had before.

Harriet said she wanted to work and wasn't doing it. I left her to herself. She said she wanted to work on awareness. She did it like a drip here and a drip there. I said this to her. Fritz came in and worked with her, and she put on an engaging show as a puppeteer. She came through with more crying than she would permit herself yesterday, but not all the way. She lifted the plug a little but didn't take it all the way out. Progress. Not terrific.

Then we had the hour of advanced training with Fritz—the fifteen or so of us leaders and co-leaders who are in it. Fritz asked who was in difficulty. Ruth was. She said she wasn't all there, that there was too much going on in her. Fritz asked her to pick someone in this group with whom she had most difficulty and work with him. She picked Hal. Bill was the next one, and he picked Greta. In Greta's working (which Fritz took over), Fritz asked her to tell each one of us "I have a secret" and something about it. To me, she said, "I have a secret from you—I dislike you very much." She said it with dislike, and hard. Hot chills ran all over my shoulders and upper arms and maybe somewhere else—too fast for me to keep up with them and then they were gone, like a neon light that ripples fast and then goes seemingly around the corner. Just under the skin—no deeper. I never experienced hot chills before and I liked it. That was such a funny "secret." I've known it for months.

At the end of this session, Neville came and put his arms around me, beautifully warm the way he hasn't been—soft warm—and said that this morning's session was good, as though he had only later realized it. Clearly it *was* good.

He said this to me. Maybe he also said it to Janet and something got through to him there, too. Even if he didn't say this to her, and didn't know it was true, she still could have been a part of it.

I have set that down pretty orderly, to make the succession of events clear. Summed up, I say: It's like a life. You can't analyze it, and if you do, all you can manage is to put together some of the pieces you've seen in a way that pleases you. If you put them together in a dis-pleasing way, like tragedy or martyrdom, that way is pleasing to you or you wouldn't do it—and you won't do anything about either one unless/until at some point the pleasure becomes dis-pleasure: it doesn't support you any more.

Funny, all these antics we go through.

Father Liebler, Episcopalian priest, told me that he hated to admit it, but he had used the crucifix hanging on a chain from his belt as a conversation piece when he first went to the Navajos decades ago. Navajos asked him about the crucifix, and he told them. They were not impressed. They said, "That man is crazy. Me, I wouldn't do that!" Father Liebler told me that the Navajos have no concept of self-sacrifice.

I rode once from Boston to Washington, D.C. with several people, one of them a lively young man from India who was studying physics. We talked about beliefs. I mentioned original sin. He wanted to know what that was. I told him. He laughed at this absurd belief of the natives and said, "Me, I do not feel guilty!"

When I was living in New Mexico, a young man died. Two families were equally involved in his death, equally had loved him. One of the families was Scotch Protestant. The other family was Mexican Catholic. Almost everything that one family said, or did, or suggested, about the funeral was horrifying to the other. It was gruesome. It was also very funny.

Antics.

Conditioning fighting conditioning.

Torture.

Torture felt by people.

When all it is, is conditioning—not *people*.

In the kitchen, after the session, Greta said in a friendly voice not quite at ease—forced a little—"Barry, can I have a cigarette?" She was mostly behind me. I turned around, gave her my cigarettes and lighter, and when she gave them back, looked into her eyes, ready and willing to be with her. Her eyes were like a house at night with no lights on and the doors closed. I don't know what's in Greta but now that she has got as far as saying her dislike of me instead of just showing it, and with this advanced group to work through with me in (I like that awkwardness, and the accuracy of it) maybe we'll get together. If I were trying to please Greta, I would go nuts, because whatever I do is wrong, usually. I didn't feel that way with her the day we were in the apple orchard on a farm, and it was nice—no dislike, just Greta. For a few moments.

Yesterday, in the advanced group, I worked with Fritz. I offered myself as patient, and picked Ray and Hal as my co-therapists. . . .

I felt sleepy then, and went to sleep. Now I feel sluggish. And hungry. Oh so hungry. I shouldn't feel hungry. (Not yet suppertime.)

I *do* feel hungry. . . . Now I notice that my "hunger" is from indigestion—green peppers in the chicken at noon—and I remember that I had the trots early this morning. That was a surprise.

I've given my stomach cornmeal muffin and butter. I still don't want to write about working with Fritz, so I'll write something else and see how I feel then.

Last night in community meeting, I said I'd like two hours without talking on this place. Fritz: "With all these beginners!? They'd be fantasying the whole time!"

I don't know if he thought that I meant sitting in silence, which I didn't. I meant working on jobs around the place—the usual routines but carried on nonverbally. He suggested that tonight at supper, we have no talking, "and maybe everyone will pay more attention to eating." (to chewing, tasting, what's going on in the mouth, and so on)

This morning—No, it just feels that way. Yesterday morning. . . . thinking *this* morning makes it easier for me to get into—and what's this accuracy-about-what-doesn't-matter bit?

I was shaking some, and let that develop. If I shake myself (make myself shake) it's either in one pattern or I change it to another pattern. When it's organismic shaking, it's never twice the same—moving, developing, changing, and even the subsiding is different. At first, I am aware of the room and of people around me, of my body in the chair, and so on—at least in a diffuse sort of way—even when I close my eyes. Then I become shakiness. Nothing exists but shakiness and I am shakiness. Today, this happened with breathing, too—after the shakiness had subsided. Ray asked me "What's going on?" and I answered "Breathing."

Last summer, I had been in the House with Fritz. Walking back to my cabin, I knew that I was angry at/with him. I knew that I didn't have to belt him with my anger to clear me, though I had no idea how to go about it otherwise. In my cabin, I let me *feel* my anger, feel it totally. I *became* anger. Standing still, no gestures, no voice, I *was* anger. Nothing else existed but anger. When I tried, then, to latch onto who or what I was angry at or with, I couldn't. It was like pushing through a fog to reach something that isn't there. "At" or "with" seemed irrelevant. Silly. (Like some silly concept of the natives.)

Anger.

Nothing but anger.

I felt good.

That passed. I wasn't angry any more. All washed away. I couldn't get back my anger at Fritz even when I tried to. It was like something wanted years ago that I don't want any more and can't even get back the memory of wanting it.

I had taken the hot seat (unexpectedly) with "fear" and "dark" in mind. I know my fears in the dark and they don't make any sense to me. They never have. Everything I can say about them has exceptions. Reduced to "fear" and "dark" is the only accuracy. "I love the dark and I am afraid of the dark" is true mainly, but with exceptions.

Fritz said he would like to try a shortcut. He asked me to be in my mother's womb. I had to put my hands over my eyes for that, to make it dark. (This suggested itself to me, insistently—not something I decided on.) I only partly got into it. What did happen interested me—the dropping of my head and curling of my back. Was I making myself do this, out of pictures I have seen? It didn't feel so. I was skeptical, just the same. Then my feet, which were a little stretched out in front of me and on the floor, began to move back. I was skeptical of that, too, and thought I might just hold them where they were. My legs became unbearably uncomfortable, and this was relieved when I let them move on their own, bending at the knees.

I liked it in the dark, but sharp sounds like a hard cough, chair legs scratching on the floor were very painful to me—like cutting into my eardrums. Soft sounds were all right—like Fritz' soft cough which was more like water flowing over me.

When I took one hand away from my closed eyes, to use it to show the angles of the sharp sounds coming to me, the light was almost unbearably painful—harsh. I shut it out again as quickly as I could.

Tonight we had a no-speak dinner-and-after time. I enjoyed the food so much, and at the same time—it was like swimming in the ocean. So much awareness and sensing, and so much *space*. I enjoyed the sounds I heard—enjoyed hearing, instead of being tortured by hearing.

I didn't know about anyone else. I was so happy in the community meeting this evening that many wanted more, and Fritz suggested that each dinner time be without speaking. Some people had jazzed it up (not in the room I was eating in) by making motions of milking a cow to ask for milk, and laughing. The ego trip. Thinking, not sensing. One girl said that she had said "one word" and two people jumped on her (silently). She didn't mention that the word was "Shitass!" and that she said it with a snarl. But clearly, she did have difficulty. Fritz suggested some modification of the no-speak, so that a few of the more essential words could be said. Most people really liked it, and some hoped that the "few words" would be said quietly. Glenn said that it was like being in another world. It surely was.

This is so much more than I hoped for, which was just a couple of hours of not speaking. Dinners with no-speak!

Each person said something different. Tom said that he usually is quiet throughout dinner and is banging himself on the head all the time because he ought to say something. Now he can no-speak without banging himself on the head.

I ate in the living room, with only one other person there. Twice I had the thought (sic) "I should say something," and it took a swallow to get rid of that, to get it out of my throat. All the rest was heaven-ly, and the washing of the dishes was more quiet, too, so that I enjoyed the sounds. When I came back to my cabin, I noticed the quiet in me, and that in washing day-before's dishes which were in the sink, I did it slowly and quietly. I swept the floor in the same easy way. Things got done that haven't been done, with happiness.

One woman said that even after she had left the house and went to her cabin, she had no fantasies. A couple of people said they chewed their food more—and ate less.

I am astonished.

In the session when I was getting back into my mother's womb, I mentioned to Fritz that I fantasy from sounds in the dark when I am alone, and I don't do this when it is light. Fritz' recommendation was that I try listening to the sounds and see if I can hear them as voices (or something like that). This makes some kind of sense to me—a lot more than fear-love dark does. It feels right somehow, like my spine saying "yes," although I don't know what voices or words I may be able to hear. I wanted to work on it last night, and I want to work on it now, but I may have to be somewhere more alone to do it. Or maybe I can fantasy that no one is next door, and let myself fear, and listen to the sounds and let them become voices.

When I was sick and sorting myself out, one of the things I did was take the words "I don't like pink" (which I had often said) and let the words somehow pick up something from the past and see where they came from, because they certainly didn't fit *me*. What I had in mind was very different from what happened. (*Now*, I would be very skeptical if anything came out the way I thought it would. I do get my answer, but the way I get it and what I get is so different from what I expect it to be.) I heard "a voice" in my ears, saying Idon'tlikepinkIdon'tlikepink over and over and over, rapidly. I listened. That's all, just listened. The "voice" became three voices, then clearly all three became female voices, and then they came through as my mother's voice, my sister's voice, and my Aunt Alice's voice. It doesn't matter here what I learned from that. I saw a whole configuration and "I don't like pink" was totally clear to me. Someone *else* doesn't like pink.

I feel a little sad that I can't work more on the love/fear/dark now. When I was writing about it earlier, some of the sensations were coming back to me, and I thought they might develop. Then there was a long distance phone call. Then. Then. Then. Maybe this weekend.

When I came out of the womb bit and was with the people again, Fritz told me to close my eyes again. (I wasn't fully with the people.) He said something about "depersonalization." I don't know what that means. I didn't feel de-personalized. I was me and each other person was him or her. I felt me. Anyway, I did it. I saw upside-down lips. Then they turned right side up and moved toward

182

my mouth and disappeared at my mouth. I had two clamps on my shoulders—one on each shoulder—that were like the clamps men used to put on their trousers when riding a bicycle, so the pants near the ankle wouldn't get caught in the wheel. They were white. As soon as I said they were like bicycle clamps, they turned dark, almost black. Then the one on my left shoulder was white and mostly disappearing, until there was just a little thing like a knuckle bone. I would like to know what that's about, but pursuing it won't find me the answer. If I pursued it and got an answer, it would be one that I made up myself. Either the answer will come, or it won't.

I miss "my friend" who is me.

But I'm learning more to let myself alone.

In the small group this evening, Hal said he was sleepy, and bothered by his responsibility as a therapist when he couldn't respond. Someone wanted some of the awareness work. Hal went through it first, "Now I am aware of—" inside and outside his skin. When he stopped, I asked, "Are you sleepy?" Hal: "No."

Me, now: Yes, and I am excited (not *over*-excited) about what may happen when I lie down and close my eyes.

When I went into the big group room at ten tonight, it was like a theatre with so many people, each different, such beautiful colors, and a kind of flowing movement of the people with each other, and I was both the observer and a part of all this.

When I went to bed, I pushed the river instead of letting it flow by itself. Not at first. But then I liked what was happening, and instead of just flowing with the stream, I got greedy and pushed—and lost the happening-of-itself. Trying to change what I love, and killing it.

Trying to make *more so* acts in the same way as trying to make *less so*.

I can't have done that a great deal last night, because this morning there is only a wisp of sadness, and my body is more free this morning—much more free. My spine feels flowing. My shoulders move easily. The miserable stiffness that I had "from the rainy weather," "from the bum mattress I'm sleeping on" (those were my thoughts, sometimes) simply isn't present. The air is still damp. The mattress is still a bum mattress. *I* have changed.

Fritz is right about my belly muscles: they are mostly dead.

This morning. This morning. What the devil was it about this morning.

Oh! In the advanced training group this morning Fritz said, "I am sure about the phenomenon. I am not sure about projections. Stay with the phenomenon and deal with projections in any way that comes to you."

Cheers. I feel cheery—cheer-y. I never did learn all that projection stuff—how to deal with projections. I didn't feel sure of that myself. As a group leader and to some degree a trainer in Gestalt here, I felt that I should know all this. I didn't feel that way about my own working with people; I did if I were to convey Gestalt to somebody else. When Hal and I started together, I told him I hoped he was strong in what I was weak in. This morning I told him it was projections that I mostly had in mind. In the advanced group, when Fritz asked us to state our difficulties as leaders, Hal spoke of his inadequacy in projections, or something like that, and Fritz said what I have quoted at the top.

Freedom!

Which I had all the time, and didn't take. No. I took it, but thought at the same time that I was inadequate in taking this freedom—like something missing. And of course there *was* something missing. This kind of mix-up is very confusing. There was something missing, I knew that I was "missing" the projection stuff. My noticing of "missing" focussed on the projection stuff. In *fact*, any thinking about what I'm not doing (or doing) takes my attention from awareness of phenomena, and I miss in my awareness of what is happening, in me or in someone else. It's like my being convinced, through my husband, that I was crazy—and I *was* crazy, but not in the ways I thought I was. The way that I *was* crazy couldn't get through or emerge when I was focussing on the crazy that I *thought* I was and trying to decide whether I was or not.

The organism does not *make decisions*.

Decision is a man-made institution.

The organism works always on the basis of
preference.—Fritz.

I am letting myself happen more than I did. Not a whole lot, but a little. This morning I let happen (a few minutes late) my annoyance with Harriet for manipulating Hal, and with Hal for going along with the manipulation. This precipitated a set-to between Harriet and Hal. They had worked for some time and were sliding into a lull (which they had got into before, then out of again) when Fritz came in. Harriet stopped. I wanted Hal to say or do something to get them going again, because (dirty word) *he* was being the therapist. (quotes) He didn't, so I did. Harriet and Hal got moving again. After awhile, Fritz moved in. Altogether, it was a good session for Harriet, in what she got in touch with. After lunch, Harriet came to me and thanked me for bringing her back in, when she wasn't going to go on with it (with Fritz' entry making her even less inclined to continue).

In the advanced group, Fritz wanted a match. He isn't smoking *nearly* as much as he used to. I was about to throw him a book of matches, thought, "I'll never make it anywhere near him—it will go wild"—and threw the matchbook anyway, quickly, in one sweep of my hand from where it was (right hand near left hip)—not getting into position and throwing it the way something "should" be thrown. It didn't go where I wanted it to, but it went within range and Fritz moved and caught it easily—beautifully. What functioning.

I am much less inclined to seek out someone I want to work with, as "patient" or as co-"therapist," or even be with. More willing to take whoever comes and work from there. I've got the wobbles again, with Hal as co-therapist (new factor), but I'm beginning to get back my balance again.

Fritz' smoking has gone 'way down. Most often, now, when I look at him, he isn't smoking. That used to be the other way around. After working with Fritz in August on my smoking (and some other things) I got so much released—crying, writhing, sobbing for an hour or more—and after that when I smoked a cigarette, it tasted really exquisite. For a day and a half, I noticed when it would feel that way and smoked a cigarette. When it wasn't going to taste good, I didn't smoke—or started to, then put it out. My smoking went 'way down. Then I got into a push about "getting things done" before leaving here, and going on the trip with very unrelaxed Helen and fussy baby—negative Helen, really; expressing so much dislike, disgust—and I couldn't smoke (in the car) when I wanted to, and when we stopped, I got out and smoked, and I was all bollixed up again.

Fritz is almost always a very warm and gentle old gentleman, now. He spends more time chatting with people than he used to. He's much more patient.

I am wanting very much to be more with the rest of nature, and doing other things than groups—painting, cooking, other kinds of *doing* things. But I don't want to leave here, now. I prefer two hours a day of groups to four hours. But this is the way it is—and maybe two hours isn't what I want. I get a lot out of four hours, and this is one way of letting more of me come through. I want more time for other ways. But *I don't know* if the squeeze, and this way, will help the other ways rather than be a hindrance. When I *know* I don't know, it's much easier to accept what is, than when I *think* that something else would (certainly) be nicer.

I checked with Neville and Hal this evening on what Fritz said. Boiled down: Projection is a theory. Phenomena are reality.

I go along with that. A theory is a way of looking at something so that I can do something with it. A theory is never reality.

Fritz looked tired tonight. He said in the community meeting that the groups were too much like encounter groups. I think so, too. A few weeks ago, I was leading the group in the Gestalt way. Then he said to let other people come in—not just the co-therapist, "like the other groups are doing." It seemed to me that this got us into the encounter stuff. I don't think this has been as bad in my group as in some others, from what I've heard. I know that it's more than I want, and that *I* get into it, too. When Neville comes in, he's great. Some of the others aren't willing to learn before talking.

Let me get back to *I*, and see how that comes out. I am annoyed by some of the interruptions. *I* think that I am "supposed to" let them speak—that they've been suppressed and they must be permitted to speak. *I* feel resentful that I am "supposed to" (*my* supposed to) turn the babies loose and let them grow.

I get confused by what they say. *I* get into the same mode of thinking/talking. *I* let them go on when I don't think they're getting anywhere.

Turning the babies loose is okay in some circumstances. Here, to me—The hell with that.

I like to learn a lot by listening and *then* come in, and *I* want others to do the same thing.

All that is a lot of non-sense, too. Throw it out and start over.

Be on the ball, kid. That's all it takes. Blaming anyone else is mewling.

That's not just a statement. I'm very aware of everything involved in it. Whoops! All that just went out in a wider ripple, including some other stuff. Now I wish we were going to meet tomorrow so I could do it, instead of waiting for Monday.

The only "preparation" I can make is to be more on the ball (not "clever") in everything—more aware, including aware of what's going on in me, and *say it*, in the groups especially.

If I don't do that, I am flunking out.

I've just seen another circle of ripple, including more. Everything in this ripple is me—my own non-sense—non-sensing. Going by what I thought (sick) were the rules. I don't even know if they were the rules other than my setting them up myself. (My interpretation of what Fritz said.) In any case, going by rules when this doesn't work out is the biggest non-sense, and letting Fritz be the authority instead of my own authority is the biggest non-sense of all. I think he would agree on that. He might even say, "About time." Time that I saw it.

Stay with the phenomena. That I really go along with. The phenomena of the other person and of myself. Ever changing. Moving with the changes.

I just saw another circle ripple, including still more territory. Jesus God am I dumb! I say with recognition. A big spotlight showing what is.

No mewling, now.

I am back to "Everything is okay." It's okay that tomorrow is tomorrow and Monday is Monday and that Saturday and Sunday come in between. I have no notion what happens in any of them and that's okay too. I don't have to make anything happen, either. Just let me happen with what happens.

No monkey on my back.

No analysis.

No generalizations.

No thinking about.

A rose is a rose is a rose.

I feel like putting a story in, here, so here is another story, one that I wrote several years ago. It's slower than "Window to the Whirled" and is different in other ways, too. When I read it quickly, I think it's a crummy story. When I slow down with it, I like it, and feel good with what it says.

Here and There

When they told me I had been selected, I was happy all over and scared inside, but I was more happy than scared, so this held me together. When I pushed the button, happy and scared were about even, so I was still all right. When I got there, it was another matter: I was *altogether* scared that I might not be able to get back. I should have known better. My mother had told me often enough, "Be careful what you set your heart upon, for someday it shall be yours." That had a way of happening, too. But still, as soon as I arrived, it seemed to me the most important thing in the world was to get back.

I'd been primed in every possible way—prepared for anything and everything I might find on my arrival in the future. I was braced—for I didn't know what. And then, the moment I arrived, there was nothing—just me and a semi-tropical night. Maybe that sounds easy, but it wasn't. I couldn't believe it. I didn't dare let go. It's like waiting for something too long, so long that when it comes, it's empty.

We had picked Hawaii for a bunch of reasons. The climate was mild. Whatever clothes I arrived in, I could probably switch them around to something appropriate. Shelter would be no immediate problem, nor food, and I could wash in the sea. The people in Hawaii were so racially mixed that if my appearance was odd in 2164, I probably wouldn't be really conspicuous. With so many different tongues and accents, mine would pass, even if the years had smoothed out that a lot. The islands are small and it would be easy to get my bearings in them. At the same time, they're in touch with the rest of the world and I could pick up news which would be helpful to me. And so on. The computer had been fed sloughs of stuff. We knew things might not work out the way we thought they would, but we had to go on our own thinking and chance the rest, just the way you have to live your life anyway. Except that usually you live one year after another, not jumping 194 of them. I had picked a time the same distance from us that we were from the Declaration of Independence. That seemed as much change as I could take in one gulp.

189

When I appeared in 2164 I was in Kaneohe, on the windward side of Oahu. That is, I was in half of it. Something had happened to the other half, and I couldn't figure out what. It just looked as though it wasn't there. It was night, but the moonlight was bright. The clover-leaf in the road at the foot of the Pali was gone. I could see some traces of where it had been, even by moonlight, by a difference in the vegetation—a sort of outline—but the jungly growth had pretty well wiped it out. So it looked as though things had gone backwards. So did the little old dirt road over the Pali. I thought I saw a car moving, up near the top, but if so, it didn't have any lights, so maybe I was wrong. It was certainly *still* everywhere. I had forgotten that anywhere could be that quiet.

Nighttime seemed a good time to go over the Pali road to the other side of the mountain, and come down on Honolulu by degrees toward morning, feeling my way. I didn't fear any viciousness because that wasn't in the air somehow, but viciousness isn't the only thing that can hurt you. I wasn't supposed to announce myself until I had sounded things out—if then. It would be easy to announce myself simply by doing or saying the "wrong" things.

I headed toward the Pali, with the moon-flowers blooming the way they do, only more profusely. I hoped this was a good sign. It really leaves you in nowhere when you can't count on anything. *Maybe* it's okay, *but—*

I stumbled on something and when I had picked myself up I was facing in a slightly different direction, and right before me was a little house I hadn't noticed, in the shadowy spot under a monkeypod tree. It wasn't much of a house. I crept up on it feeling like a peeping Tom and peered through a branch of hibiscus so I could look through an open window. There was almost nothing in this house, but on one wall there was the most beautiful color television screen I had ever seen—the whole wall. So then I laughed to myself. Things were just the same: people living in shacks with television sets. That was the kind of nonsense I was at home with.

But just then a child cried in the house, and the woman on the screen walked straight out of it into the room, and went out of my range of vision. I heard soothing words for awhile. The child stopped crying. And the woman came back and walked back into the screen and went on with what she was doing!

Then I noticed there was no one in the room watching television. That rocked me. I had to remember how George Washington would feel if he walked up to a 1969 house and looked through the window. Even a window of the White House.

I'd go crazy standing there alone in the moonlight, trying to figure it out. I had to get more facts.

It was hard walking up the winding Pali road, with the mountain rising sheer on the left and dropping off precipitously to the right, but my feet could get a good grip on the dirt road, and I found that I liked it. It was easier walking than when it had been paved, even though it must be rugged riding over it in a car, if anyone did. But of course they did! There were tire tracks on the road. Well, if a car came I would hear it, even if it didn't have lights to warn me.

But I didn't. There wasn't any danger because it moved so slowly, but I didn't really hear the car at all, just soft crunching of the gravelly dirt as something moved over it. I stepped to one side to let it pass, but it slowed down even more, and a man's voice called out, "You got pork?" If I said Yes, I might get into trouble because I couldn't prove it, so I said No, and waited for what came next. "Catch!" the man said, and he leaned toward me a little, but I couldn't quite see his face. Something was thrown at me, and I didn't know whether to catch it or duck. The voice sounded friendly, though—which may be why I caught it, and I found myself standing there with a piece of raw pork in my hands while the car moved slowly, quietly, on. I could see it go around another curve, then disappear, then appear dimly as it went around the next curve. An arm showed briefly in the moonlight and seemed to toss something over the cliff.

Click! This was the spot where, the old Hawaiians believed, Pele's dog hung out in a cave under the road, and there was something about if you passed over that spot at night, you had to throw out a piece of pork or Pele's dog would come out and bite you—no! That wasn't right. It was *if* you had pork in the car, you had to share it for your own protection. The mythology must have

191

got all mixed up. Well, that had happened before. I didn't believe in it, either way. I took a small plastic bag out of my hip pocket and put the pork in it. I could roast it and eat it before going in to town.

What a world! TV beyond my understanding, cars which were silent crawlers, and people who believe in the bite of the non-existent dog of a non-existent goddess. I guess it's no crazier than that we can go around the moon and still we have four-year colleges because England had four-year colleges in the 17th Century when our colleges began, and England had four-year colleges because back in the 12th Century the wealthy people of England sent their children to the Continent to broaden their education and they decided that four years was long enough for the kids to be away from home.

When I reached the top of the Pali, I just sat there for awhile, looking out over what I could see of Kaneohe from there. I could see that there were no lights at Mokapu, where the Naval Air Station used to be. It was like the blackout during the war. Involuntarily I shuddered. Not again!

I had to have more facts. So I hauled myself up and started down through Nuuanu Valley toward Honolulu. If Honolulu was still there.

The Valley had changed. There had always been a lot of stuff growing, some wild, some barbered. The barbered part was all gone, now. No estates. Just jungle. The dirt road was all muddy and yet somehow I liked it. I hadn't been off a paved road in years.

I kept watching for landmarks which weren't there. It made the walk seem endless. Even the big Nuuanu cemetery which used to be on both sides of the road was gone. Just jungle. It had really taken over. If it hadn't been for the shack, and the car, and the pork man, I would have thought maybe I was the only person on the island.

I was tired after the walk over the mountain. I flopped on the ground and slept. When I woke up, the sun was high in the sky. It scattered down on me through the leaves of the most beautiful jacaranda trees I have ever seen. The colors were the same, but you can't imagine the difference. The brightness of them was brighter, glowing, and the shadowy parts were deeper. You could drown yourself in both. I did. I just lay there, watching the lacy leaves moving against the background of the sky, with a feeling of all eternity, and of myself united with the earth, the stones, the grass, the growing things and those which never grow, as though all of us were unlimitedly alive.

Maybe that's why I didn't hear the people until they were almost on top of me. I heard their voices, and wished I could read it out of a book, instead. It was English, all right, but the accent had changed, and the written word doesn't change as rapidly as speech. I had a struggle to understand them. Their voices were pleasant—soft, lilting, rising, falling—a most wonderful variety, more like a song.

When they saw me, they came over and sat near me in the shade. No greeting. And after that, they sort of included me and ignored me, both at once. I didn't know whether I was "in" or "out."

They were simply dressed and the colors were nice. Think of your own favorite colors, and that's what they were. There wasn't much difference between the clothes of the men and women. Each time I picked on something which was different in a man's outfit. I would notice the same thing on a woman's—but not on all of the women's. I gave up.

After awhile, we said a few words to each other now and then, and it became clear that it was like all unhurried places where they give you time to think before you reply, even if all you say is Yes. It was a sort of nothing-talk, more for the music and the friendliness than for what was said. Then one of them asked me where I was going.

"To pay my taxes," I said, thinking that was a safe bet anywhere, any time. They burst out laughing! They got up, then, as though they had been intruding on me and I had just made this clear, and walked off along the road. I didn't know what went on. Ask a stupid question and you get a stupid answer? Anyway, they weren't offended. Just from being with them that while, I wondered if anything *could* offend them.

I was hungry. I cooked the piece of pork and ate it with some Jamaica raspberries that were growing all around. Then I noticed the clothes that *I* wore, to which they had paid no attention at all. They *should* have. It was foolish of me not to have rearranged them into something less conspicuous, but since I hadn't, they should have been surprised or curious or uneasy. Then I realized that just as their speech was strange to me, mine must have been to them, and they hadn't paid any attention to that, either. Was I invisible or something? No. It hadn't felt that way when they were with me. I had felt very much me the whole time—me the way that I seldom knew myself.

Well, I knew a little more about people, clothes, and stuff like that anyway, and that I'd better not mention taxes unless I wanted to work up a reputation as a comedian. Maybe that would be a good part to play. It covers a lot of blunders.

Stop thinking! It's a trap. Suppose these people don't like clowns?

It was hard to get a good look at the houses without being nosey, so I wandered along little paths and small roads. Some of the roads were so narrow they were just one-way for even a small car. I saw some people at work in gardens and others who were singing, or playing something that was a cross between a guitar and a cello. The big thing was the good feeling everywhere. Suddenly I laughed, as I thought of all the preparations for caution, when none was needed. All I had to do was go up and talk to these people, maybe even ask for breakfast.

So I went up to a house, and a Norse goddess of a woman with long blonde hair and grey-green eyes came to the door and asked, "Would you like a shower?"

Boof! Here I was, moving right into things, I thought, and then this woman—well, it was like skipping today and leaping into tomorrow, and then you find someone's already in the day after tomorrow. And at the same time—what I wanted right then more than anything else was a bath, and it was offered to me before I'd even noticed it myself. I guess the word for my feeling is "surprised," but we've used it so much to say nothing that it doesn't say anything any more.

The house was just bare boards on the outside, weathered so they blended with the rest of the scenery, and the inside on the whole was simple, but the shower was immense. I stepped into it, took off my clothes and dumped them into a corner, turned a knob—and from the whole ceiling the water came down like rain. I scampered around in it like a naked child in a storm. It had never occurred to me that our shower cubicles cramped me and a person couldn't have much fun in them, but I really loved this freedom.

Then I let out a howl, because I had left my clothes on the floor in what I thought was a safe corner, but there weren't any safe corners and my clothes were soaked. I turned off the shower, and was about to think what to do, when the door opened a crack and a small boy with blue almond eyes and a serene little face—a diminutive Buddha if ever I saw one—put in his head and his hand, holding out some folded material, saying, "You want it?" It shook out into a robe that was a sort of modified kimono. I brushed back my wet hair with my hands, put on the kimono, and stepped out of the shower room. There was a little hall, and beyond it was a long room with windows almost to the ground, looking out into the garden. The scent of ginger came into the room—the almost bare room—just matting on the floor and heaps of pillows. I walked over to them to arrange some for sitting on the floor and leaning against the wall. It was like a dream in which you know what you're supposed to do although you've never done it before.

A little black girl with African hair came in holding a large plate of food. She was like polished jet, sparkling all over. She couldn't have been more than four, and she was beaming with accomplishment as she brought me the plate. I took it from her hands and she sat down beside me. She looked at me gravely for what seemed to me like a long time, then said, "You're different."

"Oh?" I said. I could learn something from this. "How?"

Still gravely, she said, "Different."

"Different from you?" I asked.

She shook her head.

"Different from your family and friends?"

She shook her head.

I was feeling that way myself, and liking it, but who or what was I different *from*? Just then she got up, turned a cartwheel, gurgled over her shoulder at me, and ran away. She came back soon with a tall glass of iced fruit juices in a blend I'd never had before. Then she ran away and I saw her playing outside. As a woman working in the garden came near to her, the little girl said, "He's different." I held my breath, waiting for the reply, but all the woman said was "Oh?" and went on working in the earth.

When I had had my breakfast, I looked at the empty plate in astonishment. I had enjoyed the flavor of each separate food, and the texture, and color, and the combination of all of them, without once thinking about what it was that I had eaten. And now that it was gone, I couldn't guess. All that remained was a feeling of comfort and pleasure. I took the dishes and the silver and looked for a kitchen, where I washed them and put them in a rack to dry. There were no towels. As soon as I had put them all in the rack, a blower came on and dried them. When I came from, that gadget was used only for drying hands in public restrooms, where I didn't like it very much. For dishes, it worked fine.

I went out back to sit on the steps but remembered my wet clothes in the shower, and started to go back for them—only I saw them hanging on a line in the sun, all clean and bright. But I didn't like them. They seemed absurdly shaped, grotesque, like something worn by a scarecrow. My body didn't want any of them. I sat down on the step, with the tradewinds blowing through the bushes and across my face, and felt as though I could sit there forever. I'd better not hang around in this placetime too long, or—but what did it matter, really? From where I was now, most of the activity that had seemed so important to me *there* was like rats running around in a maze. I looked back on me as one of those rats. The only thing to be said for it was that a part of that time had been used to get me where I was now.

No one paid any attention to me, and was *that* nice. The work went on around me. I supposed it was work. It was like what we call work. But there was a sort of play about it. It was as though everyone was doing something that needed to be done, but without taking it seriously. You could almost think it was a game, except for *what* was being done.

One child called to another, "I'll slow you to the nearest tree!" and they lined up side by side, and started moving so slowly you could hardly be sure they weren't standing still, but when you watched their feet, one bare foot crawled ever so slowly along the grass, just barely ahead of the other foot, and then the second foot crawled forward. It was an eerie thing—almost like time wasn't, any more. "You stopped!" one child said to another. "We have to start over!" she called, and they ran back to begin again.

A girl who looked Hawaiian and about twenty came toward the steps carrying an apronful of vegetables. I looked straight at her and asked, "What am I different from?" She said, in an of-course kind of way, "Different from yourself," and went into the house. The scent of the vegetables wafted over me as she passed, and they smelled so good that even if they were turnips, I wanted to eat them. Not right now. I was still enjoying breakfast. But I didn't want to miss them for lunch.

Suddenly I thought of the dish dryer. I thought of it because I had just noticed there weren't any wires leading to the house and I hadn't been hearing the hum of an electric motor, either.

The girl came out of the house and sat beside me on the steps as naturally as though she were my sister.

"Where do you get your electric power?" I asked, my thought coming out in words abruptly as it had before, without social preamble, the way I hadn't intended them to. I was going to get acquainted first. But somehow I couldn't go through the motions the way I used to. It seemed a waste of life.

"Where does electricity come from?" she asked.

And I sat there. It comes from generators, I thought, but *she* is thinking of something else and what is *that*? But a little pig came up to the steps, sniffing, and the girl leaned over and rubbed its ears, and I forgot my question. As it slid away from me, "lotus land" floated through my mind, then that was gone too. I was just living—living in every cell of my body as I couldn't remember ever having lived before. Everything around me was taking place and I—was taking place too.

The rest of that day was like a dream—the kind in which you do

197

everything without effort. I cut down bananas and helped load them into one of the silent crawlers. I dug a ditch to divert some water. Whatever anyone else was doing, I wanted to do it too. Like a child, I thought, only now I had the skill to be helpful. When we all sat down to supper on the grass, I wasn't tired. And neither did I have that irritating restlessness, the need to go somewhere or do something.

> Last night I dreamed I was a butterfly, and now
> I do not know whether I am a man who dreamed
> he was a butterfly, or a butterfly who now
> dreams that he is a man.

It was a struggle to get my mind back to the reason for my being here. I should be gathering information, trying to understand what went on. But try as I would, I couldn't find any form or order to the way that things were gone about. No pattern, routine, or rules. Yet everything went smoothly and refreshingly, as though it had never been done quite this way before. An occasional collision or mishap was provocative of spontaneous laughter, nothing more, and that, too, never came out in the same way twice. Nobody tried to hold onto it, to make something out of it. Like a bird flying over my shoulder, it came—it was gone. These "mistakes" seemed to be a part of the whole, which would be incomplete without them.

After supper and some singing and light-hearted foolery that has its joy in the spontaneous moment, and for that reason can never be repeated, an old mother said, "The Governor will be here."

And right away I got the creeps. In spite of the friendliness, I began suspecting that everything was not what it seemed, after all. Why was the Governor coming? I rebuked myself for having forgotten why I was here, and the necessity of being cautious. I had been trained so well, and I had thrown it all away, in a matter of *hours*. Like some kid who drops his work and goes for a swim. I couldn't understand myself. My carefulness was a factor in my being chosen. I had shed it like a coat when the weather turns warm. I had been trained never to be caught off-base, to be one jump ahead of the other fellow—and I had a strong suspicion that these people were at least two jumps ahead of me.

"Why is he coming here?" I burst out nervously, not because of anything present, but because of the suspicious world from which I came, which I had brought here with me—in myself.

"He comes," said the woman, mildly. The vegetable girl leaned over and patted my arm. I felt that she did it as you would to a child or a dog who was scared about nothing. But was this to allay my fears—or my suspicions?

The little girl who had brought my breakfast was playing near me. Going on with her play, she said, "Different."

A battered silent crawler drove up, and a lean, tall man got out of it, legs very much first, with the rest of him following. As he walked toward us, a pleasant sort of melony smell came with him. Suddenly I realized that each person had a faint smell of something about him—not perfume, his *own* smell—and that the vegetable girl's own smell—faint, elusive—was walnuts. I had thought all these little smells were just the gardens—the smells of plants and animals and birds—but it was people, too. And me? They must have spotted me instantly. And sent for the Governor? When strangers appear?

The Governor came over to us and sat on the grass, talking of the rainbows of that morning. It seemed they had been exceptionally good, and he was particularly fond of rainbows. He smiled in my direction and said, "They can't be collected, you know."

Then there was a pause, a kind of communion which swept me into it. Everyone was silent. I wanted to break through the silence with all the questions which were in my head now, but although my mouth opened, my tongue wouldn't move. Waves began washing through my mind, wiping out all the fears, the questions, until there was absolutely nothing, and this emptiness somehow contained everything there is.

It was the Governor who broke the silence, and jolted me. "You have come a long time?" he asked. That doesn't sound terrible, but do you know what it's like to have your own deepest secret, known to no one but yourself, suddenly announced in public?

I wanted to stall, but in spite of myself, and against all the instructions programmed into me, I answered "Yes."

He nodded. "You must be the first."

199

If I was the first, how could he. . .? Then I got it. "I think so," I said. "There are others here, from other times?"

"No. . . ."

"But then—"

"They went back."

"From *here*?" I burst out, incredulous.

"From *now*," he corrected me. "The people from the past don't seem to have the knack of living now."

I was still puzzling over that when the Governor leaned his back against a traveller's palm and closed his eyes. "The islands were different when you lived here," he said, startling me again. He answered my quiver as though he had heard and understood it. "All those who have come here had lived in Hawaii at one time. I've heard that Arabs come to Arabia and New Yorkers to New York."

It hit me first easily, then hard, that all our elaborate reasons, all our computering, had stemmed from this: I had suggested Hawaii because it was a place where I had felt at home. It made the whole thing so absurd. All that work, all the discussion and planning that had seemed so necessary to all of us at the time, in deciding about Hawaii! It had all come from *me*, from my own interest. It was what I wanted. How we had fooled ourselves, with all that checking. It could only have come out different if someone had wanted me to go somewhere else. Then he'd have fed different information in, and got another answer according to what *he* wanted. For a moment I had a glimpse of the simplicity of people here and understood the wisdom of it. Then it was gone. I wished the right things wouldn't always slip away so easily, and the wrong ones come in so easily—and then I got a headache again as they went into a whirl and I didn't know which was which.

"Is everywhere like this now?" I asked.

"Everywhere?" He opened his eyes to catch my meaning of that by observing me. "No. There are some others like us—small places which for various reasons have become unimportant—although of course they're different, *too*."

"How come it's like this here?"

"We like variety," said the Governor.

"Variety!" I exclaimed, out of my strong feeling of something so beautifully the same all over. But what was the same was the ease and good feeling, a common ground. What was different was—well, there were all the things that just didn't go together. "You seem so rural," I said, "with modern improvements, of course. I saw a television screen—a woman walked out of it, and—" I suddenly felt foolish. Probably I had misunderstood the whole thing.

The Governor smiled. "They're interesting, aren't they? Some people like to have them."

"But who makes them?"

"The people who like to make them."

"But suppose there aren't enough people who want to make them—I mean, suppose more people want them than make them?"

The Governor looked at me with compassion. It must have been that, for it didn't make me feel stupid or ignorant, but understood in a way that I didn't understand myself. It was reassuring—felt good—to be understood in this way. It made it seem possible that I should someday understand myself. But it didn't answer my question, and I asked it again with my eyes.

"Nobody wants to go on making the same thing over and over and over," he said. "Not in the same way. A few times, yes."

"But if many people want them?"

"They don't. If they possessed everything that they enjoyed, they would have too much. And if all—or most—people all had the same things, there would be no variety in going from home to home, and no sharing—for how can you share what you have if everyone else has it too?"

For a moment I seemed to understand it, but then it got away. I felt something very *wrong* about this place, which had seemed so right. It was *good* for everyone to have everything, the way we do, and the only wrongness is that some people still don't have it.

Then the little girl's voice echoed in my head, "You're different," and I heard the young woman's "Different from yourself." I glimpsed one aspect of the split in me—muddledly—for I wanted to run from the rightness of this place that was feeling so wrong, and wanted to run to the wrongness of the place I came from that was now feeling so right. I was knowing so keenly my loving things as they were here, and thinking them wrong—like a threat—like something I must resist, the way that I had always resisted the wayward thoughts that made me want to walk out on everything I had and start over fresh with nothing but a lemon tree. To want to do that was bad, was irresponsible, it wasn't taking your place in life and building the country and making a better world for everyone. So I cut off the pain and the joy of my knowing, my *own* knowing, and limped along in the half-life of what everyone says.

In the world I came from, everyone was different from himself. He had to be. Or thought he did, which comes to the same thing. Here, I had a chance to get together with me. My mind cleared, and I saw it—strong and firm. I came alive when I knew it, like ten years dropping off my shoulders.

I'll never go back, I thought then, suddenly. The thought had been with me before, but not so clear as now. They could recall my machine, but there was no way that they could make me get into it. That dreary, dirty world could get along without me. I told the Governor so.

"You don't feel the necessity to change us?" he asked. "Don't think that we are idling, wasting our time? Don't think that you could improve our vehicles by taking them apart and discovering why they are so quiet, and then adding this to your knowledge of how to make them go fast?"

"No," I said. Then something made me honest again. "I've had some thoughts like that," I said. "I may have them again sometimes. But they'll wash away. I don't know what's happening, but they keep seeming to be more silly—in this little time. Not just silly—strange. They don't belong to me. It may take time to get rid of them completely, but they won't cause you any trouble. I won't let them."

I was startled to see tears in the Governor's eyes. Maybe it was only a trick of the strange light that seemed to be coming from the skies.

"Hey!" I yelled suddenly, for I had seen some lights moving in the sky, so slowly that I hadn't realized at first that they weren't stars.

"Soarers," the Governor said.

"Planes? But how can they move so slowly? What are they like?"

"Birds, I suppose you could say—or maybe more like leaves floating on water."

I asked him to tell me about them in detail, but he shook his head. "I'm not unwilling, but what can I really say?"

"How are they powered?" I wanted to know, and he answered, "Could you explain a jet plane to Benjamin Franklin?"

"But I'm from the atomic age!" I pointed out. "We know so much more now—I mean *then*."

"Enough to understand everything?"

"Why, sure. I don't mean that we already know it, but we know enough to be able to interpret and extrapolate, no matter how complex. . . ."

"That's part of the difficulty," he said, and rose, then, and went to his silent crawler. What was it that I had latched onto about simplicity? Before I could begin to think about it, a light flashed from the crawler to the sky, just once, and winked out. Almost instantly the sky was filled with gigantic buds—hibiscus, tuberose, frangipani, keni-keni—bursting into flowers that bloomed and died and released new buds. Stars grew to monstrous size, then burst, scattering millions of tiny stars from hill to hill across the valley. They showered down on us, glowing, and they didn't burn. When I put out my hands to catch them, they winked out and disappeared. Out over the Pacific, rockets screamed as they streaked up to the heavens, then exploded with booms which seemed to rock the hills around us. I was vibrating all through me, shaken up, living in such excitement that, glorious as it was, I felt that I could take no more. The sky cleared in an instant. A night-blooming cereus appeared— growing, growing, until its white petals were like huge canoes, the golden center of the flower glowing. I was swamped, enveloped, lost, invaded.

Then suddenly there was silence, coming so swiftly after the noise and action. The night-blooming cereus faded away, and as it faded, through its petals began to appear what was like a reflection

203

of the island of Oahu—or was it the other way around? As the one in the sky became more real, the one that I was sitting on became less so. Which one was illusion? Then music wafted across the stillness, not as noise, more like a zephyr playing with a breeze, so lightly that I could not be sure that it was music that I heard.

I lay back on the grass, then rolled over, pillowing my head on my arms, and lost—consciousness I was about to say, but if it was consciousness that I lost, then what was it that I found?

When I became aware of people again, and of things around me, it was like being in a cloud. The figures were shadowy, the voices were murmurs barely heard. Then a faint fragrance of walnut, and I knew that the vegetable girl was here beside me. I seemed to be lying in something familiar that made me sad.

"We are sorry," she said, and I could hear her sorrow. "But without you there, we could not be. You are a part of our becoming." I saw my life in a way that I had never looked at it before. She wiped a tear from my cheek, and I didn't know whether it was hers or mine—but then, I knew that it was ours.

She took my hand and placed it where my fingers recognized the starting button. Together, we pressed.

This morning, Fritz met with the whole group. He talked first about dreams. What he said was all very clear to me and I was going to remember it. I haven't. I don't remember *anything* that he said. But I really noticed what he said, so I'm probably all right. What he said, that I accepted, has gone into the inner computer, where it is available to me as needed—appropriately. I can't tell anyone else what he said. I'd get zero on an examination. But I know it where I can use it except for examinations.

Mrs. Chumley has just come back in. Here is another story that she wrote about me.

Consider the lilies of the field
—or how to play a good game of cards

The title of this story, if it is that, could just as well be The Way of Zen, but it isn't necessary to go around by the east to get to the west. In any case, it is more immediately about Mrs. Chumley—who came back to the nineteen-seventies to visit her granddaughter Anne. Some of Anne's friends asked Mrs. Chumley how she had learned what she knew about living. This had so many answers that Mrs. Chumley had to feel her way into which one might be most acceptable to her present questioners. That didn't mean that it was *un*true, but that it was *very* true. If you think that there is only one road to Rome, you don't know Rome very well.

With these friends of Anne's, Mrs. Chumley chose to use a game of cards to explain. You can get the same information about how to live from playing any game, she told them, but I shall use solitaire so that you can try it for yourselves without having to hunt up someone else. After all, you have to live life alone. It is only then that you really come together with someone else. Another advantage of solitaire is that you can't blame someone else for how things did or didn't come out, or give them the credit for it, either. It's altogether between you and the cards.

She shuffled the deck, first in the way that is known as "scientific" and then again the amateur's way. This seemed to her the best way to mix them up completely, although sometimes she wondered whether this might not put them back where they had been. However, it never seemed to come out that way so she didn't wonder about it very much—just enough to know that she wasn't excluding anything.

Then she began laying the cards on the table, beginning with a row of eight cards, face up. She placed another row partly over but not concealing the cards in the first row, and continued this pattern until all 52 cards were showing their faces—the tops of them, anyway—on the table. There were only four cards in the last row, of course.

That's one of the rules, Mrs. Chumley said—the way that you lay down the cards. If you don't follow it, you're not playing this game but something else. There aren't many *rules* for any game. In this one, aces—when you can get at them—are played at the top of the board the way they are in most games of solitaire, and you build up on them by suit and sequence in the usual way. At the bottom, you imagine four parking places for cards. You can move any exposed card into one of them temporarily to get it out of the way until you can put it somewhere else.

Mrs. Chumley's nose began to get moist as it did sometimes when she and the old-model germs of the twentieth century got together. Her handkerchief whisked out of her open purse that was on the other side of the room, and into her hand. She sent it back quickly, saying to her granddaughter, "Anne, would you bring me my handkerchief? I forgot when I am."

The deck as it is laid out, she continued, is chaos. Your job is to make order out of it by getting the cards into the four piles at the top. Only one card may be moved at a time unless it is in a sequence: then, you have to move the whole sequence or none at all—unless you want to put the cards in the parking places for awhile, which has to be done one by one.

You see, there really aren't many rules, and these are necessary because without *any* rules there's no way out of chaos. Without *any* rules—which are only limitations—you wouldn't even recognize chaos. If you don't have them, you have to invent them. They don't restrict you—they make it possible to play.

Conventions are another matter. People who hope to find *The Way* set up conventions to make it possible to play without thinking, by using still another set of rules. That makes it work instead of play. This is the wrong kind of no-thinking, and I'll get to the right kind later. Conventions are probabilities, and when you limit yourself to them you miss the possibilities. This is monotonous. Besides, in a game with more than one player, conventions work only if everyone abides by them. When even two people with different conventions come together it can literally be murder, although as a rule the dying is slow. That doesn't really make it any better.

207

When one side goes by conventions and the other doesn't, the conventional side loses. A six-year-old beat me at chess once because he knew the rules of the game but not the conventions. He tossed in his queen as though she were a pawn, which caught me off guard because I had been playing with conventional people. I lost. I couldn't get mad at him, although for a moment I did, because at that time I was playing with the knights and would chuck in everything else to save them. My partners were furious when *they* lost, because conventions had become rules to them and they got in a bind when I broke what seemed to be a rule and yet they couldn't accuse me of it because it wasn't. You know—like a cop who can't put you in jail for what he thought he could, because you haven't broken a law the way he thought you did. You've only broken a convention. Of course if you "think" like the cops (you could hear Mrs. Chumley put the word in quotes) you meekly go to jail and serve your sentence for something you never did, to expiate a guilt that is just fantasy.

After I had played with the knights until I got bored because there wasn't much else to learn about them, I went on to the bishops, then the rooks, and so on. I got to the point where I could really do a razzle-dazzle with the pawns. When I'd been through all of them, whichever piece was appropriate got used in its own best possible way. That's why I don't play chess much any more. My partners desert me because they get mad, which is silly. You see, they go on trying to beat me in what they think of as their way, which is everybody's way, instead of responding to my way in their way—which makes chess very interesting and exciting when people do it. It's the same with bridge or tennis.

The person who taught me this game of solitaire taught me some conventions as though they were rules. The person who taught *him* the rules had taught him those conventions at the same time, and neither one of them had made any distinction between the two. "Lay the cards down in eight rows" and "Never fill all four parking places at once" were taught at the same time and placed in the same category. But while the first is a certainty, the latter is only a probability. Sometimes probabilities just won't get you out of the fix you're in, and then you have to look for the possibilities—which of course you can't do if you think they are impossible. So you stay stuck. Then you think that the world is against you, which in a way is true, but it is only the fictitious world of conventions that is against you. When you try to get out of it, people yell, "You can't do that!" and they're so certain that you can't that you're likely to become afraid. So then you stay in it. And this proves to everybody that there is no way out, because nobody has tried to get out.

When someone breaks a convention and gets away with it, people say that he was lucky. But he was being accurate—acting in accord with the reality of the time. To act on the basis of anything else is illusion. How can I play *this* game on the basis of the way the cards were in time past or might be in the future? Past and future have no real existence because the only time that you can act is now. You can think about the past or think about the future, but that isn't *living* because you're only *thinking about* them—you can't *do* anything in either of them.

Mrs. Chumley suddenly realized her present when-abouts and added, Unless you're there—but then of course you're here, the space equivalent of time now.

And here, she said, looking at the cards on the table, is this game. It's the only one we can play at this time. Unlike most card games, you can see where each card is. This is more like life. You always have all the relevant information to act here-now. It's when we become mixed up with the future and the past and other places that we don't know what to do. But we don't need to worry about all the other times and places. And anyway, the past is over, and the future grows out of the present, so if we make the right move now, the future comes out all right too.

Mrs. Chumley looked at the cards again and explained, If there are any exposed aces, you play them up on top, and then any exposed cards that will play on the aces, and so on. This isn't a requirement, to do this immediately, but it's sort of like doing the dishes: no possible harm in it. It gets a certain number of cards out of the way, which leaves things clear for something else.

After that, if you see some card that can be moved onto

another card, delay it. You haven't yet taken in the whole field. That's trying to solve a problem without including all the relevant information that is available. You get in a mess.

How does this particular game look to you, by the way? she asked the half dozen people around her.

"Hopeless," said one.

"Impossible," said another.

Another said, more cautiously, "It doesn't look to me very possible."

It looks the same way to me, said Mrs. Chumley. It isn't one of the deals that looks easy—not that all those that look easy, are. But if I thought about it, I'd certainly chuck in this game and start over. So, I stop thinking.

One of the young men moved away from the table with a snort. So did an older man, although without a snort because he liked Mrs. Chumley. A younger girl also moved away, with a snort, because she liked the young man.

When I stop thinking, Mrs. Chumley went on, I don't have any opinion. That makes a lot of things possible. When I have no opinion, I don't feel the need to do anything—either throw out the game or tussle with it. I'm just interested in looking it over—you know, like a small child who has never seen you before. He examines you, before deciding what he'll do about you. Another word for it is scanning.

I begin at random, noting a card, say this seven of spades. It has to go on an eight of spades or have a six of spades go on it. So I look over the board and spot the eight and the six. *Spot* it—that's all. Don't try to hang onto it because you'll be doing the same with all the other cards, and the part of your mind that you do this with can't remember them all. So I just spot them, and it gets registered somewhere in the back of my head. When they're all there, it tells me what to do.

"Hey!" said the young man who had wandered away, coming back to the table, "She's programming herself!" The young girl came back to the table and stood beside him. He thought how wonderful she was, always moving in concert with him. The older man stayed where he was, with his back to the others, but he was listening.

Mrs. Chumley went on spotting the cards until she had covered almost every card in the deck, and a few that hadn't been spotted directly had come in indirectly. Now, she said, the whole board is in my head even though I don't know where it is, and then I know what to do although I don't know anything about it. It doesn't always make sense to me as I move the cards. Sometimes I feel like a fool, and sometimes I feel very rash and heading for disaster. But the impulse comes so surely from the *inner* computer that I *have* to do it. Without the discipline first, though, the impulse comes from another place. Then everything may feel altogether wonderful, but it winds up in a mess.

The cards moved in her hands so rapidly that no one could keep track of all the moves, but none of the people present, who were watching closely, could catch her in an error, either. And suddenly the whole board was obviously clear and ready to run up into the four piles at the top.

"Even if she cheated, she couldn't do it!" said the young man who was interested in programming. "Would you do that again?"

Mrs. Chumley shuffled the cards and laid them out again. It's this part at the beginning that is tiresome, she said when the cards were all in place on the table. I mean, it is until you get used to it and can do it instantly. You want to *do* something. You're so used to doing something that you feel guilty when you aren't doing anything. Something's wrong. You feel that you should start yourself up. But if you are really in touch with yourself, you know that it isn't true, and that what you're really afraid of is that if you don't start yourself up, someone else will. Most of us fear that man left unprodded will do nothing. It may come from the mechanistic explanations in science—a machine is not self-regulating and self-perpetuating: it has to be stimulated by external forces, or otherwise it will run down. And when living creatures are conceived in the mechanistic framework then we feel obliged to keep them running, and bring pressure to bear to see that they keep running, or restart them if they seem to have stopped.

You needn't be at all afraid to stop. Your heart keeps beating and your lungs keep breathing. Still, when you do what you think of as stopping, it's so different from what you have been doing that it feels wrong—like the little girl who had been crippled for so long that when the doctor straightened her out she complained to him, "You made me crooked!"

Of course there's a wrong do-nothing same as there's a wrong think-nothing. That's what makes things so confusing. You can make yourself do nothing by putting pressure on yourself, and that's wrong. In the right way, you remove yourself from all pressures, including from yourself. It feels rather like backing up, but it's only slowing down. If you walk slowly on a street while other people rush past you, it feels as though you're walking backward—if you've been accustomed to rushing, yourself.

While still talking, Mrs. Chumley had begun to put a finger on this card and that, indicating that she was spotting them with her eyes. Then she began to move the cards, sometimes in ways that made sense to those watching, and other times not. Then the cards were all in order, either in the four piles at the top on the aces or in columns on the board all cleared and ready to move to the top.

"Does it never fail?" asked a woman who hadn't said anything before.

Yes, it does, admitted Mrs. Chumley who had no difficulty admitting anything. Then I'm never sure whether the game was impossible or whether I slipped—or whether I slipped so as to lose a few games because I was tired of winning.

"Tired of winning!" said the shadow of a voice.

The easiest way to win is not to care, said Mrs. Chumley. Each of you must have noticed this in your own experience at some time or other. You don't care, so you say what you think, and things work out the way that you thought they wouldn't if you said what you thought. When you say what you think when you *do* care, this may be good, or at least better than not saying it, but it doesn't come out the same way, or it takes longer to arrive at the same place. It's the same with *doing*.

There's beginner's luck, too. When you know that you don't know anything, don't have any reputation to sustain, aren't trying to impress anybody, not even yourself—you just take a crack at it and zing! You've got it. Only then you try to repeat it, and *trying* doesn't make things happen from the same place. The first time, you didn't have any picture in your mind of what would happen. You just acted all together and it happened and surprised you. The second time, you try to produce what happened the first time by trying to make your body act in the same way. All of this takes place in a part of your head that isn't very good at it. If you work hard enough, you may be successful, but you wear yourself out, too, because you're using one part of you to force another part of you, instead of letting the whole thing happen through all of you.

When you do something through simple attraction, it isn't really trying. All of you moves together according to the design of yourself. You're not interfering with yourself. When you *try*, you figure things out in your head, or you "pull yourself together" to do it. When you succeed in this way, you succeed in spite of, not because of, and wear yourself out in the process. It's like running a machine without oil. You get stiff and creaky.

I think it has something to do with our two nervous systems, she said. She couldn't say that she knew, because then she would have to explain what she knew, and the words and concepts that could be used to explain it properly were still in the future, here. So she had to speak about it crudely, without precision.

Our two nervous systems are really one system, she said, because they work together. Trying to separate them is like the pound of flesh and Christian or any other blood. One of them beats our heart and breathes our lungs whether we want it to or not. It acts by itself, like the internal computer. Fritz uses "computer" for the plotter or planner mind which I can easily become aware of if I'm not; the one called "thinking," the I-computer, the one that *I* can use. That's the *other* one, the one that acts or overacts pretty much in accordance with our intentions. Some people use it for random painting or random cake-baking. They don't see the absurdity of being *intentionally* "spontaneous." Absurdity? It's *impossible*. So is "I'm being spontaneous."

When it overacts it interferes with the other one, instead of the two of them functioning properly together in the way that they

213

know how to do and I don't. When I "take myself out of it" or "have no desires" I don't do that *entirely*. I'm still interested. But not *over*-interested. And all of me functions in the way that I was built to do. Then, one system keeps me in touch with time and the conscious and the other with the timeless and unconscious and I'm right where I belong—everywhere at once. Harmony and accuracy together. Making distinctions between business and the arts is *silly*, she said. It all depends on *how* it's done.

And then she sighed, which she didn't do very often, but these two young people standing beside her thought that they knew what love is and they were drowning in it, the world forgotten and all that.

LISTEN! she said, so abruptly that she startled everyone except Anne, who understood. Each one but Anne searched the sounds that he heard for something that he should be listening to or for, and missed the symphony of sound, of birdcalls, motors, breathing, rustling, scratching, murmuring, with an occasional honk or clank—and missed too the silence that lay behind it. But the silence of Mrs. Chumley and Anne continued, first surrounding the others, then pervading them until they became the silence itself, while continuing to be themselves. They were and knew themselves to be simultaneously the whirling atoms with vast space between, and the persons who could be touched and felt and bumped into. And then, the symphony was heard. There was love in the room, love without boundaries or dimensions or limitations, each person unexpectedly and beautifully himself.

The young man's eyes were a bit damp as he said to the girl, "I thought I knew. . . ."

And she answered, "I know. . . . I thought that I did, too."

The older man said softly, "And one clock stopped. . . . and knew the meaning of time."

214

Now I want to put in some other stories, written by other people.

No! says the censor. Your stories are running closer and closer together. They should be spread out.

Who says that? Who is this dictator who is full of rules which he rules with by swinging the ruler in his hand to show he is the ruler?

I am! I am the ruler. I am the rules and I have the ruler.

Unh-uh. You're just a bunch of words that think they're thoughts. Phony.

I AM POWER-FULL.

Unh-uh. Your power rests in me. You have it only so long as I let you have it.

I feel like putting in another story, and here it is. The copyrights must have run out on Tolstoy by now, so I'll just put it in. I wonder if anyone has done *that* before. I haven't, and I enjoy my surprise that I'm doing it.

Three Questions
by Leo Tolstoy

It once occurred to a certain king, that if he always knew the right time to begin everything; if he knew who were the right people to listen to and whom to avoid; and, above all, if he always knew what was the most important thing to do, he would never fail in anything he might undertake.

And this thought having occurred to him, he had it proclaimed throughout his kingdom that he would give a great reward to any one who would teach him what was the right time for every action, and who were the most necessary people, and how he might know what was the most important thing to do.

And learned men came to the King, but they all answered his questions differently.

In reply to the first question, some said that to know the right time for every action one must draw up in advance a table of days, months, and years, and must live strictly according to it. Only thus, said they, could everything be done at its proper time. Others declared that it was impossible to decide beforehand the right time for every action; but that, not letting oneself be absorbed in idle pastimes, one should always attend to all that was going on and then do what was most needful. Others, again, said that however attentive the King might be to what was going on, it was impossible for one man to decide correctly the right time for every action, but that he should have a council of wise men who would help him to fix the proper time for everything.

But then again others said there were some things which could not wait to be laid before a council, but about which one had at once to decide whether to undertake them or not. But in order to decide that, one must know beforehand what was going to happen. It is only magicians who know that; and, therefore, in order to know the right time for every action, one must consult magicians.

Equally various were the answers to the second question. Some said, the people the King most needed were his councillors; others, the priests; others, the doctors; while some said the warriors were the most necessary.

To the third question, as to what was the most important occupation: some replied that the most important thing in the world was science. Others said it was skill in warfare; and others, again, that it was religious worship.

All the answers being different, the King agreed with none of them, and gave the reward to none. But still wishing to find the right answers to his questions, he decided to consult a hermit widely renowned for his wisdom.

The hermit lived in a wood which he never quitted, and he received none but common folk. So the King put on simple clothes, and before reaching the hermit's cell dismounted from his horse, and, leaving his bodyguard behind, went on alone.

When the King approached, the hermit was digging the ground in front of his hut. Seeing the King, he greeted him and went on digging. The hermit was frail and weak, and each time he stuck his spade into the ground and turned a little earth, he breathed heavily.

The King went up to him and said: "I have come to you, wise hermit, to ask you to answer three questions: How can I learn to do the right thing at the right time? Who are the people I most need, and to whom should I, therefore, pay more attention than to the rest? And, what affairs are the most important, and need my first attention?"

The hermit listened to the King, but answered nothing. He just spat on his hand and recommenced digging.

"You are tired," said the King, "let me take the spade and work awhile for you."

"Thanks!" said the hermit, and, giving the spade to the King, he sat down on the ground.

When he had dug two beds, the King stopped and repeated his questions. The hermit again gave no answer, but rose, stretched out his hand for the spade and said:

"Now rest awhile—and let me work a bit."

But the King did not give him the spade, and continued to dig. One hour passed, and another. The sun began to sink behind the

217

trees, and the King at last stuck the spade into the ground, and said:

"I came to you, wise man, for an answer to my questions. If you can give me none, tell me so I will return home."

"Here comes someone running," said the hermit, "let us see who it is."

The King turned round, and saw a bearded man come running out of the wood. The man held his hands pressed against his stomach, and blood was flowing from under them. When he reached the King, he fell fainting on the ground, moaning feebly. The King and the hermit unfastened the man's clothing. There was a large wound in his stomach. The King washed it as best he could, and bandaged it with his handkerchief and with a towel the hermit had. But the blood would not stop flowing, and the King again and again removed the bandage soaked with warm blood, and washed and rebandaged the wound. When at last the blood ceased flowing, the man revived and asked for something to drink. The King brought fresh water and gave it to him. Meanwhile the sun had set, and it had become cool. So the King, with the hermit's help, carried the wounded man into the hut and laid him on the bed. Lying on the bed the man closed his eyes and was quiet; but the King was so tired with his walk and with the work he had done, that he crouched down on the threshold, and also fell asleep—so soundly that he slept all through the short summer night. When he awoke in the morning, it was long before he could remember where he was or who was the strange bearded man lying on the bed and gazing intently at him with shining eyes.

"Forgive me!" said the bearded man in a weak voice, when he saw that the King was awake and was looking at him.

"I do not know you, and have nothing to forgive you for," said the King.

"You do not know me, but I know you. I am that enemy of yours who swore to revenge himself on you, because you executed his brother and seized his property. I knew you had gone alone to see the hermit, and I resolved to kill you on your way back. But the day passed and you did not return. So I came out from my ambush to find you, and I came upon your bodyguard and they recognized me and wounded me. I escaped from them, but should have bled to death had you not dressed my wounds. I wished to kill you, and you have saved my life. Now, if I live, and if you wish it, I will serve you as your most faithful slave and will bid my sons do the same. Forgive me!"

The King was very glad to have made peace with his enemy so easily, and to have gained him for a friend, and he not only forgave him, but said he would send his servants and his own physician to attend him, and promised to restore his property.

Having taken leave of the wounded man, the King went out onto the porch and looked around for the hermit. Before going away he wished once more to beg an answer to the questions he had put. The hermit was outside, on his knees, sowing seeds in the beds that had been dug the day before.

The King approached him, and said: "For the last time, I pray you to answer my questions, wise man."

"You have already been answered!" said the hermit, still crouching on his thin legs, and looking up at the King, who stood before him.

"How answered? What do you mean?" asked the King.

"Do you not see," replied the hermit. "If you had not pitied my weakness yesterday and had not dug these beds for me, but had gone your way, that man would have attacked you and you would have repented of not having stayed with me. So the most important time was when you were digging the beds; and I was the most important man; and to do me good was your most important business. Afterwards, when that man ran to us, the most important time was when you were attending to him, for if you had not bound up his wounds he would have died without having made peace with you. So he was the most important man, and what you did for him was your most important business. Remember then: there is only one time that is important—*Now!* It is the most important time because it is the only time when we have any power."

219

Dick's eyes are wobbling and jumping. What he sees is wobbling and jumping. At this point, he has as much trouble *with* his glasses (which he has been wearing since age seven) as he does without them. He wants to make an appointment for new glasses, and he wants to get along without glasses. He came to me for some Bates-Huxley exercises. One of them is: Imagine a soft ball held between the thumb and middle finger. With your eyes closed, move your fingers together as though you were squeezing the ball, and imagine the ball slowly changing from a circle to an oval, as you squeeze it. Then let it out again, slowly. When Dick did this, his fingers went crooked and rigid. (Dick always looks as though he is hanging loose.) He noticed this, and his straining. "For the first time, I am connecting I-strain and eyestrain!" Fritz had told him that there is a connection between the eyeballs and the balls. Dick was willing to admit this as a possibility, but he couldn't feel it. Now that he's been able to connect straining in his hands and his eyes—I wonder.

Fritz talks a good deal about confluence as "bad," which of course it is if you stay there all the time, and also a therapist will be a lousy therapist if he gets into confluence with his client, patient—the person who comes to him. If you don't get lost in it, it's nice—especially if this is with the rest of nature rather than with another person which is more likely to lead to complications. I like this description by Kenneth L. Patton:

> Words, our own or another's, can never be more
> than a commentary upon living experience.
> Reading can never be substituted for living.
> What do I understand about a tree? I have
> climbed into the branches and felt the trunk
> sway in the winds, and I have hidden among the
> leaves like an apple. I have lain among the
> branches and ridden them like another bough,
> and I have torn the skin of my hands and the
> cloth of my trousers climbing up and down the
> harsh bark. I have peeled away the skin of the
> willow and fondled the white sweet wood, and

my ax has bitten through the pure fibers, and my saw laid bare the yearly rings and the heart-wood. Through the microscope I have copied out the traceries of the cells, and I have shaken out the rootlets like hair upon my hand; and I have chewed the gum and curled my tongue around the syrup, and shredded the wood fibers with my teeth. I have lain among the autumn leaves and my nostrils drank the smoke of their sacrifice. I have planed the yellow lumber and driven in the nails, and polished the smooth driftwood with my palm.

Within me now there is a grainyness, a leafiness, a confluence of roots and branches, forests above and afar off, and a light soil made of a thousand years of their decay, and this whisper, this memory of fingers and nostrils, the fragile leaf-budding shivering within my eyes. What is my understanding of trees if it is not this reality lying behind these poor names? So do the lips, the tongue, the ears and eyes and fingers gather their voices and speak inwardly to the understanding. If I am wise I do not try to take another into that strange, placeless place of my thoughts, but I lead him to the forest and lose him among the trees, until he finds the trees within himself, and finds himself within the trees.

How can we be free to look and learn when our minds from the moment we are born to the moment we die are shaped by a particular culture in the narrow pattern of the "me." For centuries we have been conditioned by nationality, caste, class, tradition, religion, language, education, literature, art, custom, convention, propaganda of all kinds, economic pressure, the food we eat, the climate we live in, our family, our friends, our experiences—every influence one can think of—and therefore our responses to every problem are conditioned.

Are you aware that you are conditioned? That is the first thing to ask yourself, not how to be free of your conditioning. You may never be free of it, and if you say, "I must be free of it," you may fall into another trap of another form of conditioning. So are you aware that you are conditioned? Do you know that even when you look at a tree and say, "This is an oak tree," or "That is a banyan tree," the naming of the tree, which is botanical knowledge, has so conditioned your mind that the word comes between you and actually seeing the tree? To come in contact with the tree you have to put your hand on it and the word will not help you to touch it.*

*From *Freedom from the Known*, by J. Krishnamurti, Harper & Row, New York 1969, p. 25. Reprinted by permission of the Krishnamurti Foundation.

I am cleaning house nicely, putting in all these things which I have been carrying around with me. It's like having them all in one small convenient suitcase. But that's not why I did it. The secondary thought is about the convenience. The primary attraction was wanting them in here, as they emerged into my world—came out of the file case where they haven't been even remembered for a long time—and into this book. When the first one emerged, I didn't know that any others would follow. Now I feel like looking into that file case and seeing what else is there. *This* is primary. What happens after is secondary.

The Listener by John Berry has come in without my going into the file case to look. Now, I look. I've got it. I see the twilight sky with clouds that mostly look as though they had been swept into streaks and shadows, and a light place of sky swirled around with dark grey clouds, the trees on the hills looking still like a painting, the lake waters rippling in places, swirling in others, moving like a stream in others, the dry maple leaves carpeting the shore, and I say, "Yes. This is true."

The Listener*
by John Berry

Once there was a puny little Czech concert violinist named
Rudolf, who lived in Sweden. Some of his friends thought he was not
the best of musicians because he was restless; others thought he was
restless because he was not the best of musicians. At any rate, he hit
upon a way of making a living, with no competitors. Whether by
choice or necessity, he used to sail about Scandinavia in his small
boat, all alone, giving concerts in little seaport towns. If he found
accompanists, well and good; if not, he played works for
unaccompanied violin; and it happened once or twice that he wanted
a piano so badly that he imagined one, and then he played whole
sonatas for violin and piano, with no piano in sight.

One year Rudolf sailed all the way out to Iceland and began
working his way around that rocky coast from one town to another.
It was a hard, stubborn land; but people in those difficult places do
not forget the law of hospitality to the stranger—for their God may
decree that they too shall become strangers on the face of the earth.
The audiences were small, and even if Rudolf had been really
first-rate, they would not have been very demonstrative. From
ancient times their energy had gone, first of all, into earnest toil.
Sometimes they were collected by the local schoolteacher, who
reminded them of their duty to the names of Beethoven and Bach
and Mozart and one or two others whose music perhaps was not
much heard in those parts. Too often people sat stolidly watching
the noisy little fiddler, and went home feeling gravely edified. But
they paid.

As Rudolf was sailing from one town to the next along a
sparsely settled shore, the northeast turned black and menacing. A
storm was bearing down upon Iceland. Rudolf was rounding a bleak,
dangerous cape, and his map told him that the nearest harbor was
half a day's journey away. He was starting to worry when he saw, less
than a mile off shore, a lighthouse on a tiny rock island. At the base

*Reprinted by permission of the author. First published in New World Writing #16 (1960).

of the lighthouse was a deep narrow cove, protected by cliffs. With some difficulty, in the rising seas, he put in there and moored to an iron ring that hung from the cliff. A flight of stairs, hewn out of the rock, led up to the lighthouse. On top of the cliff, outlined against the scudding clouds, stood a man.

"You are welcome!" the voice boomed over the sound of the waves that were already beginning to break over the island.

Darkness fell quickly. The lighthouse keeper led his guest up the spiral stairs to the living room on the third floor, then busied himself in preparation for the storm. Above all, he had to attend to the great lamp in the tower, that dominated the whole region. It was a continuous light, intensified by reflectors, and eclipsed by shutters at regular intervals. The duration of light was equal to that of darkness.

The lighthouse keeper was a huge old man with a grizzled beard that came down over his chest. Slow, deliberate, bearlike, he moved without wasted motion about the limited world of which he was the master. He spoke little, as if words had not much importance compared to the other forces that comprised his life. Yet he was equable, as those elements were not.

After the supper of black bread and boiled potatoes, herring, cheese and hot tea, which they took in the kitchen above the living room, the two men sat and contemplated each other's presence. Above them was the maintenance room, and above that the great lamp spoke majestic, silent messages of light to the ships at sea. The storm hammered like a battering ram on the walls of the lighthouse. Rudolf offered tobacco, feeling suddenly immature as he did so. The old man smiled a little as he declined it by a slight movement of the head; it was as if he knew well the uses of tobacco and the need for offering it, and affirmed it all, yet—here he, too, was halfway apologetic—was self-contained and without need of anything that was not already within his power or to which he did not relinquish his power. And he sat there, gentle and reflective, his great workman hands resting on outspread thighs.

It seemed to Rudolf that the lighthouse keeper was entirely aware of all the sounds of the storm and of its violent impact upon the lighthouse, but he knew them so well that he did not have to think about them; they were like the involuntary movements of his own heart and blood. In the same way, beneath the simple courtesy that made him speak and listen to his guest in specific ways, he was already calmly and mysteriously a part of him, as surely as the mainland was connected with the little island, and all the islands with one another, so commodiously, under the ocean.

Gradually Rudolf drew forth the sparse data of the old man's life: He had been born in this very lighthouse eighty-three years before, when his father was the lighthouse keeper. His mother—the only woman he had ever known—had taught him to read the Bible, and he read it daily. He had no other books.

As a musician, Rudolf had not had time to read much either—but then, he had lived in cities. He reached down and took his beloved violin out of its case.

"What do you make with that, sir?" the old man asked.

For a second Rudolf thought his host might be joking; but the serenity of the other's expression reassured him. There was not even curiosity about the instrument, but rather a whole interest in him, the person, that included his "work." In most circumstances Rudolf would have found it hard to believe that there could exist someone who did not know what a violin was; yet now he had no inclination to laugh. He felt small and inadequate.

"I make—music with it," he stammered in a low voice.

"Music," the old man said ponderously. "I have heard of it. But I have never seen music."

"One does not see music. One hears it."

"Ah, yes," the lighthouse keeper consented, as it were with humility. This too was in the nature of things wherein all works were wonders, and all things were known eternally and were poignant in their transiency. His wide gray eyes rested upon the little fiddler and conferred upon him all the importance of which any individual is capable.

Then something in the storm and the lighthouse and the old man exalted Rudolf, filled him with compassion, and love and a spaciousness infinitely beyond himself. He wanted to strike a work of fire and stars into being for the old man. And, with the storm as his accompanist, he stood and began to play—the Kreutzer Sonata of Beethoven.

The moments passed, moments that were days in the creation of that world of fire and stars; abysses and heights of passionate struggle, the idea of order, and the resolution of these in the greatness of the human spirit. Never before had Rudolf played with such mastery—or with such an accompanist. Waves and wind beat the tower with giant hands. Steadily above them the beacon blazed in its sure cycles of darkness and light. The last note ceased and Rudolf dropped his head on his chest, breathing hard. The ocean seethed over the island with a roar as of many voices.

The old man had sat unmoving through the work, his broad gnarled hands resting on his thighs, his head bowed, listening massively. For some time he continued to sit in silence. Then he looked up, lifted those hands calmly, judiciously, and nodded his head.

"Yes," he said. "That is true."

Dear Fritz. I invited him to have hot chocolate with me this evening. Soon after he came in, he said, "I am thinking that eventually I will. . . ." Seventy-six years old.

"For the first time in my life, I am at peace. Not fighting the world," he said. When I think what that means. . . . I have got confused, in trouble, and there have been times when I was at war with the world, but that is not the way that I would describe my life. . . . In a way, I have been at war with the world all my life, but the degree was different. For long periods it was more of an undercurrent, not strong enough to be an undertow, and there was a lot of swimming on the surface with sunlight sparkling on the water and myself sparkling in the sun.

It is beautiful to be with Fritz arrived at peace.

"Isn't it wonderful that at our age we can. . . ." It surely is. . . .

Lasha is so dear—and also so intelligent. She is also so intellectual, so reasonable, so out of touch with *feeling*, and confused. Fritz said tonight that he taught her how to kiss, that she blushed, and then said something like "Why shouldn't I feel this way?" Whatever nasty old man he may have been (I don't know how much of that is legend, or how much boasting), that's not what he was with Lasha. I can easily imagine doing that myself.

Fritz shook my hand when he was leaving. I felt kissed.

Having arrived on my own last night at going my own way as a group leader and to some degree teacher—in the learning/teacher way, Fritz said this evening "I've got to find some way to teach it." (Gestalt) I felt free to do my own exploring. gestalt, I know. Gestalt is a means of helping people to arrive at some experience of gestalt and how to go on working on their own. This is my definition of "therapy" that I wanted to re-define and didn't know how to do it when this book began. I can best learn "how to teach it" by working on myself and at the same time working with others and noticing what happens.

The problem is the same that it has always been—with Jesus, Buddha (sanctified by centuries)—the problem which Zen strove to get beyond by not saying anything that could be grasped intellectually. The "tree of knowledge" problem.

• • •

• • •

• • •

The nine dot problem is to connect the nine dots with four lines which may cross, but must never go back over themselves, without lifting the pencil from the paper. You have to go outside the dots (which seem to be the limits) to do this. With the nine dots as Intellect, you have to go beyond it, when intellect *seems to be* the only way to solve the problem. So you go 'round and 'round and 'round and don't come out *here*.

Now I am looking for something that wants to come in here—a page from *In and Out the Garbage Pail* done in Gothic script. I can't find it. I wonder if I gave it back to Fritz. I remember putting it away carefully. In that case, I may as well forget it.

Anyway, I found some stuff I wrote last year that can be thrown out. Heave ho! I do like throwing out.

Here it is.

It is obvious that an eagle's potential will actualize itself in roaming the sky, diving down on smaller animals for food, and in building nests.

It is obvious that an elephant's potential will actualize itself in size, power, and clumsiness.

No eagle will want to be an elephant, no elephant to be an eagle. They "accept" themselves, they accept them "selves," they don't even accept themselves, for this would have the background of possible rejection. They take themselves for granted. No, they don't even take themselves for granted, for this would imply a possibility of otherness. They just are. They are what they are what they are.

How absurd it would be if they, like humans, had fantasies, dissatisfactions and self-deceptions! How absurd would it be if the elephant, tired of walking the earth, wanted to fly, eat rabbits and lay eggs. And the eagle wanted to have strength and thick skin of the beast.

Leave this to the human: to be something they are not: to have ideals that can not be reached, to be cursed with perfectionism so as to be safe from criticism and to open the road to unending mental torture.

I've found a cartoon. It's dittoed. I know who gave it to me. I don't know who drew it. I want to give it to Fritz, put it on the bulletin board, and send it to Russ Youngreen to do a better one, in black ink, to use here. The last emerges as my preference. I'll do that, when this sheet comes out of the typewriter.

Now my bed emerges, cozy and warm. Tempting. Attracting me away from the cold floor. I yield to my sleepiness, out of which the image of my bed appeared.

My mood is different this morning. I don't know what it is.

The lake is sort of dull-mystic now. Am I dull-mystic this morning?

A seagull flies past—squawking.

It is more important (to me) (now) to bring someone to life than to be moral.

I am now in confusion.

Two ducks fly past. Or are they geese?

But of course a person must know what he's doing.

He mustn't seek his own life through someone else and think he is doing it for them.

So who knows what he's doing, and how often do I know only *after* I have done it?

Recognize. Recognize "I am doing this for me."

Beware! says almost everyone, especially parents to children. Beware! Don't make mistakes or terrible something will happen. Your life will be ruined. You'll never be accepted by society. You won't get anywhere in life.

You won't be accepted. You won't get anywhere.

Beware. Be-aware, it meant originally.

Be-aware—really aware—and you don't need to worry about anything. No fear. That's where no-fear is. Not beware! (Be cautious.) Just be aware.

Deke said the people here would have taken two weeks to get out of the follies that were going on, which Fritz stopped—or very much modified, to the point where something else is happening—by saying a few things and making a few changes, in a few minutes.

Which is "better"?

Does anyone know? *Can* anyone know?

Out of a four-week workshop, with one week in confusion already, two weeks to discover and change is too much.

Too much.

Too much for me.

I can never know how anything would have gone if I had done it some other way. I can never go back and prove it. I discovered that when I was sick, when the doctor and I both wanted to begin again, to see what would happen if we had gone about it in another way. This wasn't possible. Everything that happened the way that we *did* go had produced changes. We could not go back to where we were. We could only work things out from now.

"You never step into the same river twice."

The folly of "proof." Of proving something by doing it over. The folly of words, like "doing it over." I can never "do it over." Something has changed.

I am loving this fat squat little dictionary this morning. My hands really feel it. My eyes really see it. I feel affection when I look at it, when I pick it up, when I put it down.

"Prove" comes from a word meaning "test."

I look up "test." Surprise! It comes from a word meaning "earthen pot." "tile, jug, shell, etc." *That* kind of testing. Like putting starch and iodine together.

I can't put my finger in water in a jug today and find out how it was yesterday—or a few minutes ago. I can only know how it is *now*.

I can't know how *I* was yesterday. I can only abstract something from me-yesterday. When I abstract from my yesterday and you abstract from your yesterday, and I abstract from my yesterday experience of you and you abstract from your yesterday experience of me, and all this gets fighting. . . .

A young woman was angry, hurt, pushing, beating with words, "You wanted to leave right away and I pushed myself (and worked so hard) to get everything ready so that we could, and now you don't want to leave for a few days." "I've done all this *for you*" was in everything she said. Her husband started to say, "*Who* wanted to leave right away" (when vacation began), then waved his hand and said "Skip that." In a neutral voice he asked, "What do you want now?" She didn't say anything. It wasn't necessary. Her face revealed that she wanted to leave right away, that she always had, and that she had been pushing herself and him to get what she wanted.

Yesterday evening I told Fritz that I would like to fix his breakfast this morning. Expression of willingness. No groups today. No early rising. He said a few words which I don't remember. They didn't make a sentence but they made sense. He is enjoying fixing his own breakfast.

Clouds on mountains.

A seagull is sitting on one of the big upended logs that hold the dock in place. Another bird is flying. How many birds are flying, all over the world?

Sadness. Water in my eyes. Hands very light and gentle on typewriter. My nature still is, in spite of all attempts to destroy it. Soft, soft the words. Tenderness. I feel dissolving in my shoulders. Dissolve. Dissolve the armor. Sharp, almost painful, very good, exquisite, delicious feeling, like before orgasm. My genitals are jumping. Pumping. Dissolve. Dissolve. My bare heels are hard and cold on the floor. Dissolve them. Do this myself (phony) until the dissolving—happens by itself. Then let it alone. Don't touch it. Not even lightly with my mind. My feet are coming alive, like moving from numbness to tingling. b b b b I see the letter with my eyes closed. Something wants to come next to it, another letter that keeps getting mixed up with the b and I can't see it very well. It happened of itself. I move it to make the separation. e that's it. e be, no b e. My eyes are still closed. I noticed I didn't make the space (ting goes the bell, and I move the carriage back(I'm not sure about those parentheses, if I hit the right keys. b e. Intellect comes in and says yes! be. The fashionable word these days. Let me see if something more comes. here forms itself. now there is xxing out of something else that followed. I can't read it through the x's. it leaped out in my vision, seeing it written as if with a new typewriter ribbon. Now, no words. Luminous lavender light, tinged with rose. (eyes open) For a long time, I kept looking, and nothing formed. Just a beautiful lavender light, tinged with rose.

I have just noticed that those pre-orgasm sensation-al fireworks stopped. I don't know when. Now, it is as though they had diffused all through me, like life/joy flesh, which hadn't seemed to me dead before, but now, looking back on it, it stinks. Like it wouldn't even bleed. Where I am now is not the end. . . . A few more genital jumpings, now, like saying "yes"—and I feel my forehead coming alive, my back, my shoulders, and my breasts. To push it would be insanity. Let it come and go. "It" means the organismic, which knows so much more than I do . . . My shoulders. What is happening in my shoulders. Like strong hands placed on them, moving them around. Like massage. That's what it feels like. But what a massage!

Like a giant's hands working on my shoulders—strong, gentle, and huge—huge in relation to human hands, exactly right to fit my shoulders. Now those hands, without leaving my shoulders, are working my chest. I *think*, "But what about my belly muscles. They need it most." I am content to let my organism—*me*, move as it wills. *Me* needs no directions—least of all from *I*. . . Water comes into my lower eyelids, not enough to overflow. With my blinking, my eyeballs feel bathed.

Now those hands seem to be simply holding my shoulders in place—strongly. No one else is doing that. My shoulders are doing that. How strong I feel. How strong I am. My neck and head are becoming stronger. Strength is coming into my chest—my hips, my thighs, my legs below the knees, my ankles, my feet. I stand up and stretch. My right hand and arm wobble madly. I let them shake with big shaking movements. I stop typing, doing it again, letting the whole right side of my body get involved. I notice that my left side, down to the sole of my foot, felt strong—weakness in the right side. I still don't match, but something is going on in my right side that I don't remember having happened before. Movement. Inside movement. Something going on.

That's enough of that for now. Don't push the river, it flows by itself. At this point, I would be pushing, wanting more. I withdraw, and leave the prescription to *me*.

I have come back to the typewriter. When I left it, I started walking to the bathroom. me stopped, and began weaving from side to side, with little sighs, some reaching out of the arms with an up-and-down flowing movement in rhythm with the weaving.

My neck is feeling great! My neck is feeling.

I left the typewriter again, and when I had taken the same few steps, my belly started pushing forward, then my hips back. My feet stayed in the same place as I bent in the middle, forward and back, arms hanging loose and going any way they did. Never twice the same. If I had started doing the same thing, I would know that *I* was doing that. Organismic me is infinite variety, moving with the changes, never the same river, always surprising me.

For two days, I haven't wanted to be a Gestalt therapist and I haven't *been* a Gestalt therapist. This morning, Fritz worked with Lasha, then Tom. Lasha—for more than three months so tough with herself, not letting go, not permitting herself to be female—let go of herself and cried and loved and was so beautiful. I've loved Lasha from the day she came. Every honest, immediate response I made to her was rejected—by stiffness when I put a hand on her shoulder, by words when I said "I feel so good to see you again." ("Are you being sarcastic?") (Me: "If you heard sarcasm, you must have crazy ears.") When her shell broke this morning and she was so tender, I was afraid (thinking) to go to her as I wanted to. Suppose *my* going to her cut her off, shut her up again. I could bear to be shut out, as I have been: I couldn't bear to have Lasha shut herself out again. I tusseled quite awhile (longer *seeming*, I'm sure, than it was) then let myself, my love, come through, and went to Lasha. She hesitated a moment— hesitation was in her eyes—then let me in. I put my arms around her and, bless Lasha, part of her putting her arms around me was holding my head like a cradling, like a caress, as if she were holding a baby. *Real* Lasha. Water comes in my eyes now, and sunlight seems to dance in those few tears, one of which is now dribbling down the outside of my nose, while others are dripping down inside my nose. And now, I'm crying. Not sentimental tears. No thoughts about. Just crying, and crying too, is good.

A seagull is walking on a log boom. Reflected in the water, he is walking upside down. He hopped from one log boom to the next—eight or ten inches—both upside down and rightside up. . . . He did it again. This time he was a bird on top and a shadow in the water. It is raining now and the water has changed—not reflecting very much as it is all pocked with raindrops.

Here is such a great place to live with change, to live more now. People are changing too. A man who says one day that he is here entirely and only to learn what he can use when he goes back to his patients, may any day discover that he is also here for himself. Maybe he already has. To go on meeting anyone where he *has been* is to miss where he is now. I have to meet people now or I don't meet them anywhere. If I meet them in memory, I don't meet *them*, and *I* am not meeting. Memory is meeting, and memory is not *me, now*.

I feel that I am slugging today and think my writing must be dull. But right now I've *got* to slug, and slugging is okay and dullness is okay. . . . I really felt that as I said it, and *dullness* developed sparkles all around! What happened to dullness?

The lake is *reflecting* everything now—in color.

Glenn: To please Fritz, you have to do what you can't.

Shawn: To please Fritz, you have to do what you *think* you can't. And you have to not give a shit whether you're pleasing Fritz or not.

I know what I have to do to please Fritz. That is, it will please Fritz when I do it. In other ways, pleasing is already present. But I have to do it to please me, not Fritz, out of my own sensing, my own wanting. Until I've done it, it is only fantasy. And now, I'd better not think about it any more or I won't do it. Thinking about it can go on forever, filling in more and more details of what never happened, what *can't* happen when I am thinking about it.

The First Principle*

When one goes to Obaku temple in Kyoto he sees carved over the gate the words "The First Principle." The letters are unusually large, and those who appreciate calligraphy always admire them as being a masterpiece. They were drawn by Kosen two hundred years ago.

When the master drew them he did so on paper, from which workmen made the larger carving in wood. As Kosen sketched the letters a bold pupil was with him who had made several gallons of ink for the calligraphy and who never failed to criticize his master's work.

"That is not good," he told Kosen after the first effort.

"How is that one?"

*From *Zen Flesh, Zen Bones* by Paul Reps. Charles E. Tuttle Co., Inc., Tokyo.

237

"Poor. Worse than before," pronounced the pupil.

Kosen patiently wrote one sheet after another until eighty-four First Principles had accumulated, still without the approval of the pupil.

Then, when the young man stepped outside for a few moments, Kosen thought: "Now is my chance to escape his keen eye," and he wrote hurriedly, with a mind free from distraction: "The First Principle."

"A masterpiece," pronounced the pupil.

Sludge, sludge, sludge. I feel like a muffled mallet. Like trudging down the road with a heavy burden on my back. I've lost touch, and don't know if I am trudging or putting in the stairs. A flight to the second story is easy and I can feel good about being there, but I still have to go back and build the stairs. Without—

I'm thinking about! I'm thinking. Inventing my own labor. Sludge, trudge. OUT!

Let emerge whatever does.

I love Van. I phoned him last spring and said, "I'm calling for George who doesn't know what to do with his mother. "Shoot her," said Van amiably—without knowing George or his mother.

Where did Lasha's work this morning begin? To assign a beginning is to go back to the beginning of time—which I suppose is when the first organism—of whatever kind—became aware of time. Arbitrarily, I pick when Fritz made a zzzz-ing noise in imitation of her voice, and asked her to do that to some people. She did, then started brushing mosquitoes off her—how she experienced the sound. Then she was to be a mosquito to various people, which she did, to perhaps eight people before she came to Deke. Out of what happened then, Fritz asked her to be therapist to Deke. Then he asked her to return to the hot seat and to the therapist she had chosen at the beginning. I remember that she said to him, "You're always so nice. When are you going to start demanding?" I don't remember words after that—just that they were soft and low, and ended with Lasha's coming through real.

When I see something like that, I think, "Quit now. You haven't got enough years left to learn." But I know that it's not just years as a therapist: it's where I am, in me. Get to work on myself, and the rest will take care of itself. As long as I keep blocking, awareness keeps being interrupted. A hundred years as a therapist won't do me as much good as unblocking me right now. The variety in Fritz' work as a therapist arises from his awareness. What he *knows*, through years—a lifetime—as a therapist probably gets in his way as often as it is helpful. Cancels out. Fritz says he tries as far as possible not to think. *During* therapy, he is like Carl Rogers—same conclusion: Carl says that *during* therapy, any theories only get in the therapist's way.

When I shut myself up, I start thinking. That seems to me the way the trouble begins—as children. This morning, I got out of thinking after shutting myself up, by going into my body and letting things happen there. I felt much more strong after that, and I was here without thinking—and appreciating Hal's work with Bob. I was very much present. But I still don't feel entirely that I've got a mouth.

Q: Are you proud of yourself?

Fritz: No, I am not proud of myself but I no longer despise myself.

Pat: Fritz, I'm afraid of you. I can't count on you.

Fritz: You can count on my love. You cannot count on my support.

This morning, I fell flat on my face again in the advanced training group. Karl took the hot seat and asked Romily and me to be co-therapists. He started off in the past tense. Instead of telling him that I was impatient with him for not getting with it, I tried to be patient and point out to him what he was doing. I got all shook up—and did the same thing again when he continued in the present tense but was still telling a story, not being in the dream, and I got shook up again. From there on, I was doubtful of everything I noticed. Romily was beautifully changed. I noticed, and felt good about that. I noticed how beautifully Karl came through, when Fritz took over, and felt good about that. But I was *still* holding onto my mistake—and made another one. When Karl was through, I told him I was phony at the beginning. The past is *talking about*. I know that. I got all con—no, that's words. I didn't feel confused. . . . I felt clear, and at the same time not seeing something. Like if I am looking at the lake and someone else sees a hydroplane on the water and I don't see it. . . . Fritz told me I was talking about. I recognized that, and didn't know what to do with it. He gave me a clue in saying "I am—I was." Stay in the now. I was trying to find some way to say the past (which wasn't present any more) in the present tense. I couldn't find some way to do that. I was still holding onto the past which wasn't present in me. Whatever I did *now* feel was blotted out by my hanging onto the past (memory) which was not present in me except by my keeping it there. Fantasy.

I don't remember what Fritz told me to say to each person. It was something like "I lose the moment by—" to which I added: I lose the moment by trying to be something I'm not. I lose the moment by holding back. I lose the moment by thinking about, and some others. When I came to Glenn, I didn't say it so strong, because with him I am more in the moment. It was "opportunity"—maybe "I miss the opportunity."

The only thing I have to say for myself is that I stayed with it—didn't qualify, modify and so on. I stayed with it *really*. Only later did I realize that I hadn't said, "I don't do this with" "I don't do this all the time" "I didn't do it this morning" "I didn't do it last night," didn't say "Fritz, you know that last night when you said that I was not comfortable with some of my physiology, referring to 'going to the bathroom,' I said, loud and clear, 'I *LIKE* GOING TO THE BATHROOM.' "

I was with now close enough so that I didn't think any of those things at the time. I still held back, delayed saying what came into my mind. Wasted all those moments. Same as I did when Ray asked what my hands were doing on the chair arms: I noticed, and *held* the noticing (to be sure of it) before letting myself be expressed—my experiencing. Same as I did so often in the awareness week in June: I am to let out my voice, let whatever I'm feeling sing: it took only an instant to notice the feeling—moments (that felt like five minutes though I think they weren't) to let that feeling come out in voice. (I didn't say either, in going around the group this morning, what I have just now remembered, "I was doing *fine* and happy with my doing until you gave me Hal as co-therapist." It's a good thing I didn't! Or a bad one. For of course that's something for me to work out with Hal. The problem of doing it has got me bollixed up for some time. I make a program to say something. At least (I pat myself up a little) I don't spend much time on it. Then, next session, I am primed—and everyone comes in all fussed up about Don's leaving and the manner of his leaving, and *I* go into *that*—don't even pick up on what is bothering me in Hal's voice as he joins in on the gossip. I'm in my gabble zone. I've lost touch with me me me me me ME ME ME MEEEEEEEEE.

I have put up three signs.
DON'T THINK
BE UN-REASON-ABLE
LET MISTAKES GO—THEY WEREN'T WORTH ANYTHING IN THE FIRST PLACE
Fritz said they are programs. He seemed to like the last one although that is a program too.

I've lost touch with my knowing that mistakes don't matter.

If I hadn't made the first one, I wouldn't have made the second one. If I hadn't made the second one, what followed wouldn't have happened, which has got me (right now) tied in knots and with a headache, and at the same time—I am delaying getting to work on the headache. Postponing. Putting off. But the headache is what *emerges*.

I paid attention to the headache. What emerged then is what I couldn't remember before: Fritz telling me to say—I've lost it again, except the expression of *both*—like I did last night with Pat when I told her, "I want to ask a question, and I'm putting it down because

241

I don't want you to answer it, just ask it"—and gave her the question. Now the headache is emerging again. . . . Express both what I want to say *and* what I am doing with it.

Liberate. Don't *de*liberate.

When we were breaking up, and Fritz had already turned to leave, I said "Hey!" I got that much out fast. Then I paused while the words were stuck in my throat—holding them back (something like) "I don't like your bringing in that bathroom bit (which he had, again) when what brought this on happened later." He turned around and said "thank you" as though he wasn't feeling that, but maybe he did, later. Image: Fritz finding the silver lining! Those words seem so funny.

Hell. I *know*. I know that living with what I know is important. Authentic. Real. And I know it's only the ego that gets clobbered, that "hurts." He really means "thank you" even if he is hurting at the time. I've had that feeling about Jesus and the cross. My own knowing—I'm just beginning to be in touch with it. Ego-I is screwing me up, giving me a headache, and I want ego to *die*. . . . I got up and choked a pillow. As I did, "ego" looked as silly as that wobbling end of the pillow above my hands. Stuffing with cloth around it. Cloth with stuffing in it. Stuffing with cloth around it with stuffing in it.

Tsu! comes like a hiss through my teeth.

Only ego. What I want to get rid of. The only "person" I want to die, that I want to choke and kill, is ego, not ego choke me. The only way I can do that. . . . fighting ego keeps ego alive, because fighting itself is ego—is to be submissive. . . . What I thought would come next, didn't. Instead, when I became submissive—to ego's choking—both ego and choking disappeared. Not to what ego *says*, but to what ego *does*. When I submit to what ego *says* I'm still ego. When I submit to what ego *does*—pain—the pain leaves, and so does ego.

So thank you, Fritz, for the pain.

Thank you, Barry, for the pain.

Even while I hurt, I thank you, Fritz.

Which sure sounds like the Christian religion—the part that I loathe. d. I'm not loathing it now that I understand it. I still think we'd do better to throw out the Bible and start over.

Throw out everything and start over.

That feels right, really right, but I'm still hurting, some—still not accepting pain. . . . I stay with it—not hold it—just let myself feel it, doing nothing, and it dis-appears. While I stay with it, I have no thoughts about it.

Gestalt Institute of Canada—a Christian Jewish Buddhist Hindu school. I notice I put myself first. (I am a Christian in the same way that Fritz is a Jew. We're classified that way. We grew with it in our environment. We don't go to church or temple and we don't *believe*.) Well, good. My voice-friend isn't so strong as before, but there's a sort of whisper, "High time." Maybe he's feeling a bit strangled right now—or unstrangled and recovering, still hasn't got much voice. I've been missing him.

Last week and this week, in "my" group (all that means is that when Fritz asks the group leaders to stand up, I stand up) I have more looked forward to the end of this workshop than to its continuing. Now, I'm glad it's continuing. All this time, I have felt as though buried under a couple of feet of earth—burrowing my way up a little, *very* slowly. Now, I'm closer to the surface—beginning to see light.

Fritz! You don't *know* how I've come out *some*. You don't *know* what I discovered yesterday, and it worked out fine. You don't *know* the progress I've made. (I'm giving myself a headache again.)

Fritz (*my* Fritz): So? You want to stop there?

I sit here knowing the answer and not saying it.

No! Until I've stopped de-liberating, I want to go on.

Fritz, you've slipped back yourself, lately. Thinking, analyzing. You've lost your peace. Last night you mentioned a *should* of yours. *Your* shoulds are ridiculous to me. Only ego could have a should like that.

Fritz (*my* Fritz): So yours are immaculate conception?

Fritz is waiting for the *Garbage Pail* to come out. His friends like it. He is impatient to know what his enemies will say about it—which means him. How much time he spends this way, I don't know—only when it emerges to me—as it did again just now when I met him as I was going up to the House. "Any mail?" meaning "Any word from" (I run into difficulty here, stop and think, so I'll move on—) "Any word about the *Garbage Pail*?"

All I do know is, it's *thinking about*—the intermediate zone (Fritz), the gabble zone (me) and *I* can't be in that gabble zone with only *one* foul-up. When I'm in it, I'm in it, and any other junk in there can get at me, too.

Usually, when Fritz comes toward me, even if I want to touch him, I wait for him to make the first move. This time, I moved to him, put my hands on his shoulders, and we kissed. When he looks happy, he looks *happy*. Beauty-full. I don't feel a lot stronger, but a little.

It sure wasn't a mistake to make a mistake.

When I went to the advanced group this morning. . . . I don't like "advanced." The ten o'clock group. The tennergroup. . . . I took with me a bandana to blindfold my eyes. If I had done that—blindfolded my eyes—everything would have come out different. In what way different, I don't know. The possibilities are all the possibilities there are within this situation. They don't include Russia, Mexico, and Lake Cowichan. Within that room—*all* the possibilities—with sixteen or seventeen people—are beyond my ability to imagine. Blindfolding my eyes, within those limitations could have produced anything. I didn't do it. I wanted to, and I didn't. I was waiting. Waiting for the "right time." I suspect in this case it means, "When no one's attention is on me." Anyway, it was a fine example of waiting for the right time that never comes.

Crazy, crazy. I was all set to tackle Hal at the first op. No op. I wasn't holding anything back. I felt comfortable.

Jerry Rothstein arrived today from San Francisco almost dancing with excitement at coming here, at being here. He's going to have a group working with myopia on Friday. Glenn said that Karl wouldn't be in it—that he didn't believe eyes themselves could be changed. I told Glenn that was yesterday. He said, "Oh no, this morning." I said he's got the Bates book now (he got it from me last night) and he's going to get Huxley's *The Art of Seeing*. Glenn: "But just *this morning*... oh no, that was *yesterday* morning. *This* morning he was talking about elongation of the eyeballs." (from Bates)

That's one of the greatest things about this place: you don't know where anyone *is* unless you're with them. Other than that, it's likely to be *was*, which of course it is, only here this becomes so clear that it's inescapable. It sure makes nonsense of gossip when you know that by the time you say it, maybe it isn't true any more.

Fritz clobbered Melissa yesterday in the tennergroup and again this morning in my cabin group, clobbered her ways of attempting to control him, her word plays that reduced everything he said to nothing. Sometimes she cried, sometimes she fought. When she switched from one to the other, he said, "That's your other way." Not accepting any single bit of her manipulations. This evening in the cabin he asked her (like inquiry, not solicitous) how she is and she said, "Different." She sounded different, too.

From my own life I know that when my old ways don't work, I have to change. I don't think I can ever clobber anyone the way he sometimes does, and I can't see it wrong for him. Besides, the people who come to him choose him—choose *him*—and they are responsible for their own choices, just as I am. Melissa knew when she came here that she wanted to bust out of her pre-planned lifescript, and she chose Fritz to do this with. I'm sure she didn't want what she got yesterday and today. Out of that, today she is for the first time getting something of what she wanted.

Bob D. is so likable, so very likable. And he is so compliant. I have no idea what to do about that and it wouldn't be any good if I did. . . . I'm beginning to see the uses of frustration, getting people in a fix where they can't be compliant. I like Carl Rogers' way of frustrating—by not giving answers, *along with* something else. . . . I see too where Bob D. is *not* compliant, which I was missing for

245

awhile. I'm feeling a little bit sharper than I was, at seeing what is.

Fritz mentioned my predicament: spontaneity vs. deliberation. There is *no* question which I want, which I trust.

I am going to bed without deliberation.

Sometime yesterday I really wanted to go on with the groups. Maybe sometimes. Other time, I didn't even want to stay here. Right now this morning when the lake and hills are in—they are in—what words which words. Look here. It's seven a.m. Pacific standard time and close enough to north so that. . . .

Try again.

There is some light in the sky, not much.

Right now I feel good about being here now which I'm not and when I think about an hour from now I begin disagreeing with me.

Something is happening in my shoulders and feet which is not pain and I don't know what the devil it is and I like it.

My face skin feels burning like sunburn. This keeps happening, past ten days or so.

What is happening in my shoulders and feet which is not pain is movement. Fairly large movement. Like pushing wet sand with your hand.

This place is crazy, you know? Two and a half acres of land with small buildings and people mostly indoors and thirty-four of them going up/down thisside/thatside and you never know where anybody is inside or outside whether speaking of outside their skin or inside their skin, except Fritz who notices so much more than any of the rest of us and spends some time after community meeting playing chess or poring over his stamp collection. Does he? All I know is I see him sometimes through the window sitting at his desk where some of his big stamp books are and I have no notion what goes on inside him any more than other people had about me when I played solitaire. Why do we need to know? Why do we need to pretend that we think we know? Why do we need to judge whether what is going on is good or bad?

What can I say about a place where each person's view/experi-

246

ence is different and keeps changing and good becomes bad and bad becomes good and don't like becomes like and like becomes don't like and right now right now right now is gone before I can say it.

Mrs. McGillicuddy has gone to Alberta to visit her sister. The President has gone to play golf. Mrs. McGillicuddy is talking to her sister. The President is talking to whoever he plays golf with. My grandmother went to London. Did she, whadidshebuy? The President wore a blue suit. Mrs. Mac wore a flowered dress. Is a Zendo more or less efficacious than a Gestalt institute and if so why which nobody knows or can know. There is no way to find out. Different people go to them in the first place and in the second place the people who go to one and then the other to prove something are not the same people they were in the first place. That is something that I am seeing, not something I am thinking about. Is this school better is that school better and if this school is worse that may turn out to be good. Nothing matters except. . . . Nothing matters. Not really. At the same time it does. Don't ask me to tell you, find out for yourself, you bum.

I am the source of all wisdom.

Man is not a source of information. He is a sink.

What information do I have *really*?

It's a little over a mile from here to Lake Cowichan.

Do I like the groups?

Sometimes.

Do I not like the groups?

Sometimes.

Have I been here too long?

It is a mile and a half to Lake Cowichan.

Dear Larry:

Dear Sir:

Dear Mr. President, I would like you not take the goddam world so seriously you gotta do something with it.

Dear Barry, I would like you not take the goddam world so seriously you gotta do something.

I would like you not take yourself so seriously you gotta do something. That sounds like my friend the voice. The voice got into the words as they wrote. You can't hear that voice in which the words were written. When you read them, you read my words with your voice and tell me what I said. It's your own voice so *listen*, don't tell me.

Each time I latch onto something and feel bright, everything that I've written before seems like slobber. I don't feel like throwing it out for that. *I* am starting now, from where I am. Without everything that preceded this, how could I be where I am?

Fritz told us this morning to write an essay on "shouldism." I'm sure he didn't say "essay." I did. Now I have two meanings of "essay" in my head and one I like and one I don't: one is the kind of trying that is effortless, letting things roll so I can find out what they are; the other is a literary composition, arranged in a certain form and chiseled in a certain style.

Let me try the first one:

Shouldism comes from couldism. It could have been different. I could have been different. You could have done something else. The weather could have been nice. I could have been born to different parents. My child could have had a career and made a big name and lots of money for himself (and me). You could have been on time. I could have not made that mistake. (How could I, when until I'd done it, it didn't look like a mistake?) "You could have, I could have" leads right into "You should have" and "I should have."

A general semanticist named Harrington whose first name I have forgotten said that he knew an Indian who was fluent in his tribal language and also in ours. Harrington asked the Indian if there were such words (meanings) as "could" and "should" in his Indian language. The Indian was quiet for awhile, then shook his head. "No," he said. "Things just are."

I think there must be this lack in some other Indian languages (concepts) because I sure have seen Indians look baffled when white folks told them it could have been different, they could have behaved in another way, or they should have done something else. I've also seen the bafflement of white folks when Indians went on doing something after they'd been told they shouldn't, and the bafflement of Indians when the white folks became baffled at the Indians' bafflement.

Fritz said if anyone had a way out of this shouldism. . . . I doubt there is *one* way, but one of the ways we might try is to notice our "coulds"—not only our shoulds. I don't like that one. I'd rather drop could and should out of our language and see what happens. Not "bad." Just "I don't want to use those words any more." I think everyone would agree to this in terms of the *other* dropping them, and most would find it more difficult to drop his own. But if we did this, we might begin to lose the concepts, and if one person did it, he would certainly not accept coulds and shoulds from the other. Words do drop out of languages, usually not deliberately, but if people find this liberating, a lot of them (us) would do it.

I am fed up with that talking about.

We need a change in language (concepts) if we're to get beyond them. There I go again.

In the large group this morning, one thing led to another and I wound up with Bart who expressed his dislike of my softness. A few moments later, I felt strong and my body stood straight—that's all. Bart jerked back—his shoulders jerked back quite a way. Bart said it was "the sudden transition." I said, "Okay. I'm standing here. I'm going to stand straight." I stood straight. Bart: "It's hard to stand up to you." I didn't have a motive when I said/did it. The thought came to me and I was interested to find out what happened. I was very surprised. How much was learned by both of us in that couple of moments, just by *doing* something instead of talking about. Doing something in a different way. What happened to Bart surprised me. What went on in me surprised me. Bart had *his* surprise. *I feel different*, like something awakened in me.

We were supposed to choose someone we *dis*liked, for whatever it was that we were doing. I don't dislike anyone totally. I went looking around for someone on the loose and saw Bart standing alone and went to him. I don't know if Bart thinks I picked him because I dislike him very much. Anyway, this came of it, and it seems to me that if instead of choosing from the group the person I dislike most (or whatever I am supposed to do) I shut my eyes and moved around and grabbed someone, something would happen that way too.

Twelve hours of sleep just ended. Sun bright, reflection from water dazzling. Shoulders tight. Tight? My flesh around the shoulders and down the back feels as if it is kneading itself.

At least, I have got rid of "I have to." How did I get rid of "have to." By noticing each time I thought "I have to" and recognizing what I didn't have to, only *thought* I had to—and when I threw out (didn't do) the have to's, what was left was the want to's. Clearly the want to's—not mixed up any more with the have to's.

This morning I am confused. On Thursday in group, with Fritz, I expressed in the same voice (loud and clear). . . . the heck with that. I get into trouble as soon as I start writing it. Confusion. Nothing clear. Everything soft and fuzzy and dissolving into nothing. I feel no should about bringing it back.

Fritz, you're not noticing the steps I've taken, those hazardous steps I've taken which aren't hazardous and I see that but they *feel* hazardous so they are. I feel you pushing me for more. Don't push the river, it flows by itself. I don't want you to tell me how well I'm doing. Just leave me alone. I've started. Let me move at my own pace. Notice that I *am* moving now, in a new way, timidly, but I'm doing it, and I wasn't doing that before. Let me take my timid steps, noticing how good they are and gaining confidence through my own experiencing. Don't give a ghost of a grunt when I say I'm working through the problem of the very small groups—*my* problem in the very small groups, let the others have theirs. I really don't give a damn about them except as they reinforce my statement about *my* difficulty. Those problems are somewhere else, not here, not mine.

How impatient am I with the same kind of timid steps taken by others?

I'm not. I notice, and like them. Both Bobs took some of those timid steps and I like them, like small tender sproutings. I don't want to push them. I think I should. Not that I have to, but I should. In this Gestalt Institute with Fritz as head. He wants me to. Maybe he does want me to. Maybe he doesn't want me to. I don't *know* that; I *think* that. What I can *know* is me. I don't want to. How wide my chest is when I say that. I am astonished, not expecting to feel so strong and good.

I have been sometimes pushing (in my terms) whether I wanted to or not, sometimes going along with me. Like stutters. Phony/real/phony/real. Not saying what I am doing, even to me. Not being clear, in me or with anyone else. With Fred so much dead this week, I have thought that I should take over and do something and sometimes I did. I didn't want to.

So I switch my "should" and the meaning of the word comes out different. Gets wiped out, in fact: it isn't here in me any more. I "should" do what I want to do? Silly! (Sensing of absurdity, not "reasonable" decision or way of looking at it.) *I want to.* That's all I have to and all I should.

I want to.

I don't want to.

Noticing.

And no damn explanations.

(Eric Berne says we only need three words—yes, no, and *wow.*)

Like that letter to Jordan I've made three tries at writing. The first part—seven lines—answering three questions in two letters from him. The second part attempts to answer one question. It runs on, each time, for about twenty-five lines and I don't like what I've written and know that I haven't answered his question, so I throw it out and try again. I don't *want* to answer that question, beyond saying "I'm here and I like it." I think I *should* convey more information about this place, and my enthusiasm for it. When I write letters full of my enthusiasm for this place, that *happens.* I don't make myself do it. It flows. With this letter to Jordan, I am making myself do it, and it comes out lousy. Going on making myself do it, it gets worse each time, I get more frustrated.

Sneeze sneeze sneeze sneeze sneeze—I don't know how many of them. A stream of them. Sunlight coming through windowpane. I notice I am hot and sticky, wearing a flannel nightgown. In my own cabin, alone, and no one outside even, I have my nightgown on. I take it off and feel good. "I want to" is so easy.

I don't "should" write Jordan about this place. . . not only don't "should" but when I'm not with it, I'm not with it, and whatever I write comes out sounding like a blurb, not the spontaneous enthusiasm that I feel when I feel it.

One "should" out of the way. The letter to Jordan will go easily now, in eight lines, and get on its way instead of sitting on my desk, stuck.

Whether Fritz is or is not pushing me is something I can't *know* even if he tells me: It's whether I believe him or not—when I am where I am now. Sometimes, it is *sensing*: then I know. No interference from my thinking.

Whether Fritz has been pushing me is irrelevant. *I* have been pushing me. When I get rid of my own pushing of me, anyone else's pushing doesn't push me—and then I don't feel pushed. I am not "resisting." I just am. Like the Navajos when they do not let our pushing get into them and do not push themselves.

I feel my body—"from inside" to distinguish from feeling me by putting my hands on me. But "from inside" seems silly. I am my body, and my body (I). . . . I am alive. *Agito ergo sum.*

What a lousy grammar we have, to express real, to express what *is.* In expressing myself, I am trapped by language. The lake is not "out there." I feel it flowing in me. The hills and trees are not "out there." I feel their stillness in me. The sky is not "out there." I feel the same vastness and lightness in me. The floor is not "out there." I am in touch with the floor. The chair I sit on—hmm. . . . When it comes to the chair, I see I've been trapped in language again, or still. This chair and I. I feel flowing between us *and* contact (touching).

Either/or—the intellectual split which formed our language, or out of which our language was formed. I can use it to say "The typewriter is on the desk" and "I am sitting on the chair" and "I am typing" but *not* to express what goes on in me among us.

Hmmm. *My* experience is not *yours*, and except for the language trap, there is no reason for me to express mine. In fact, I *do* express it, through my body which is me. Eyes, skin color, posture . . . *all* these expressions and their changes are obvious. I don't need to say a word. But, living so much trapped by language as I do, *I* am out of touch with what I experience. In attempting to describe what *is*, I am exploring the trap. What our language *says* is "going on" distorts reality, and when I use the words and grammar,

I distort me. In my struggling, I become more aware of the distortion, of the mis-fit of my words and me.

Marcia came in just now. I saw her coming and had a slight thought/movement of leaving my chair and getting a kimono. I let it go.

The sun is warm. I am warm. I am warmed by the sun. The sun is warming me. On this first day of November in Canada where I have never been before on the first day of November, I am warm verging on hot.

I have a thought—I think that I have left many unfinished situations in my writing. I don't care. Where I began the previous paragraph was not where I ended. Unfinished situations are all over the place, all over the world. Only the ones that I hang onto need to be "finished," so that I let go of them, let them be "past." Where I began that paragraph is: The sun is warm. I am warm. I am warmed by the sun. The sun is warming me. . . . I was going to go on with grammar, then something else emerged.

Sun. Me warm. Says the whole thing, and leaves much more time for enjoying "Me warm. Sun."

When Rick was unwilling to give up Shakespeare for *being*, I thought he was nuts. I discover my own reluctance to give up the flow of words for pidgin English. Be 'ware. When I stop the flow of words—just did, then—I am so *much* more aware. My sensing becomes so heightened beyond my usual that I feel somewhat *painful* delight. . . . and now I am reluctant to come back to words.

"But they might be helpful to someone else."

Let them find their own way.

"But you have used books. . ."

Some more argument runs on through my head in fantasy. I don't hang onto it. It isn't there any more.

Children playing with the water.

Children and water playing.

Fill in the rest with whatever you want. You do that anyway. Who takes, from *Person to Person*, anything he doesn't want?

Children and water playing.

That much is real. Whatever I go on with is fantasy. Go on with your own.

What does my real of "children and water playing" do for you?

In the Honolulu public library one day, I saw a stoutish woman with an umbrella under her arm—

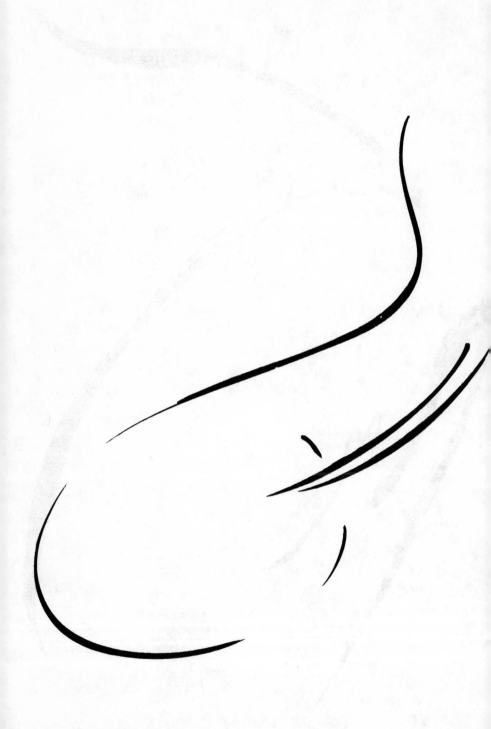

Stone

I really thought I had ended the book on that last page. It was only a glossal stop.

One thing remains the same: Each Sunday, I wish there were another day of weekend.

Yesterday Jerry said he wanted to come back as soon as possible (he's gone, now) because he wanted to be with me and with Fritz and we'll both be leaving. I said maybe this writing wouldn't be done, and I'd stay longer. He said that put him in trouble because he wanted me to stay and he wanted me to finish the book.

I've just been through the same thing with my son, and it's like when I used to say "I wish it would stop raining" and people would say "Oh, don't wish that! We need the rain for the crops." What difference did it make—the rain would stop or go on, regardless. If people can make rain, this ability does not come from the place my wishing comes from.

I know why this book often feels like sludge to me. It is sludge. When I finished *Person to Person*, I said, "Now I've got to go out and live it, as far as possible." That is not easy. At the end of *Person to Person* I saw the Christmas tree. Now I am swatting through the brush to get to it. I can't *make myself* arrive at mystic experience.

No doubt drugs could do that. I haven't tried drugs. The mystic experience is not my goal. I have given up on that. Truly. I'm not suppressing it. The wish is not here. I don't have a goal—beyond sometimes a fairly immediate one. In this sense, I am flowing with the river, not trying to push it. In other ways, I still am learning to let me happen, and this is tricky. The trickiness shows itself to me now mostly in connection with those genital jumpings that I mentioned. During the day, they don't usually happen. When I lie down at night, most often they do. When they don't, I notice that I am rehearsing, which I want to give up. This rehearsing is usually not strong: it disappears when I look into my body. One night recently, I couldn't get out of rehearsing. I went on and on doing this, getting more and more tired. Spontaneous image: a black oblong like the erasers used on school blackboards moved back and forth across my forehead. This was dreamlike, in that my forehead wasn't really there. The eraser erased my thoughts. I felt ease. Then the thoughts came back again. Just now, it seems to me that I might try (experiment) being the observer of these rehearsals.

When I was sick, one of the things that happened was that the whole world—all of it—was full of friendly people being friendly, and I was at ease and happy with this. Then flick! like the click of a camera shutter, the whole world was entirely populated by people doing each other in, and I was afraid, revolted, and couldn't live in this world. All those words take time and do not match the experience which went flick/click/flick/click/flick/click/flick/click/flick/click so rapidly, so many times. I felt tied up in knots, jerked or yanked out of that into bliss, then yanked out of that into knots. Joy/despair/joy/despair, and so on. Powerful emotions, both of them, and a jolt in switching from each one to the other. I *had* to do something. I made myself the observer of what was going on, watched what was happening as if it were happening "out there."

The typewriter stopped. Lights went out. I took a shower and the water soon trickled. So I did what I could, that didn't require electricity or water, got interested in that, and lost interest in writing. Now I am feeling like writing again. I also feel that I'm taking off from another landing—without knowing what the other one was or this one is.

A young Japanese who didn't want to take the hot seat, and who said very little, took the floor (on his back) instead and worked a lot of trouble out of his body by letting what wanted to happen happen. I am always impressed by the outcomes of the experiments in *Gestalt Therapy*. I haven't done all of them. Getting at them as they're written in the book is like picking a bunch of pieces out of mud and then trying to put them together while they're still wet. I feel like re-writing them. I think this is something like trying to write a foolproof cookbook. But I'm not trying to make them foolproof—just readable.

I don't feel like going on with that. Who do I think I'm helping by putting the Gestalt experiments into simple English or something? "The moment you think you are 'helping,' you undo the whole thing." (Swami Vivekananda.)

Cockeyed morning session. Last night was cockeyed too but in a different way. At the end, I couldn't remember any of it but had a strong feeling that the whole thing was *crazy*, like *mad*. I learned a lot and I don't know what it is. No matter. It's part of my experience, and that's what I learn from.

This morning "nobody wanted to do anything" in the language of the groups. I suggested something, Stella vetoed it, nobody else said anything. Fritz came in. David started something on Fritz' suggestion and didn't get very far. I don't think that *nothing* ever happens. I *know* that something always happens. "Nothing happened" means that nothing spectacular happened or that I haven't noticed what is happening.

A few people in the group started cocktail party talk. I said I was bored. When I said it, I heard in my voice that I was *irritated*. That *is* boredom—what boredom is.

I tried reversing things—*anything*—and everything stayed stuck. *I* was stuck. I said so. Neville got one of my prisms to turn things upside down for me. I got fascinated, like looking into another world. When I looked at people through the prism, they were interesting in a pure sense—without any kind of opinion, judgment, evaluation or demand. I just enjoyed them.

I realized one thing I could do myself: I was sitting ("what people do" in groups). I got up and walked across the floor and back. This simple movement felt good. I began to wander around and do things—like emptying some coffee cups into the sink, putting together some letters to be answered which had been strewn across my desk. I went to the bathroom, on the way back noticed a Cowichan Indian necklace, thought "Natalie would like that" and gave it to her. Threw out a few things and gave a few more away.

I was aware of what the others were doing in a peripheral sort of way. Not interested. Not bored. Interested—but not intent—on what I was doing.

A lot of other things happened in me that I don't remember now. They were like opening a small window and seeing a larger window, opening that and seeing a larger window and opening that.

All of a sudden—LIGHT.

Not one thing after another, but everything at once. No "order of events." I have to put them down in order because there is no other way to do it, but for you to receive them that way is not my experience, so mix them up any old way—it doesn't matter how—and this is it:

I no longer felt "bound" by the group, by having to behave in a certain way.

I was doing things I felt like doing in my cabin. Everything in my cabin was available to everyone else. They could do what they liked with it. Paints, brushes, paper, felt pens, a bed to go to sleep on or lie on and watch the leaves outside the window, a few dishes in the sink to be washed, books to read or leaf through—and also they were free to walk out of the cabin. I couldn't tell them to be free. Then they wouldn't be: they would be "free" with my permission.

School. I have been resenting school. That's been coming

through in various ways. So what do you do when you're bored with school?

I cut. I didn't go to the supervision seminar or advanced training or whatever it is.

The extension of my weekend that I wanted!

I read the words, and they say nothing. It's all thinking, without any expression of my *feeling*. So mix it all up with light and air and sunshine and seeing and breezes blowing and feeling all this and laughter and—

Whewwww! Freedom. Right here/now in this training center called Gestalt Institute of Canada.

I haven't been *taking* my freedom, which is the only way I can give it to someone else. Then I blame the *place* for binding me. My *concept* of the place—not the reality.

My concept of the place. My concept of the role. My concept of the "groups" and what "should" happen in them. What I "should" "do for others." What I "should" make happen.

Just yesterday I said to Tom, "How can I be spontaneous going to groups from 8-11 a.m. and 8-10 p.m.?" Yaaaaah. I didn't *have* to go to them. . . . I should have seen that: I thought of some other people, "Well, you didn't *have* to come." But *I* "had to" be here, and behave in a certain way.

I've thought of the places where I was more spontaneous than I am here, longed for them, and knew that I wanted to work this out *here*. But how the devil could I do that? Yaaaaaahhhhhhhhhh.

Somehow, in the course of my doing what I wanted to this morning, within the possibilities of this cabin which were available to everyone else—and what a lot of stuff there is in this place to do with if anyone felt like doing it—not enough for days and days, for all of us—now, I'm not sure of that—but for seven people for two hours, I'm sure of *that*.

Somehow, in the course of my doing and saying and whatever was going on in Deke, he realized (expressed, sounding as though this were new to him) what a "school" ("education" sense) would be like if it were really education, and what he said is what Fritz said about the "college" he would like to have.

I'm seeing nearly everything in a different way, now.

And now I'm sleepy.

Slept and had a dream.

Now I am knowing that this place is good for me and bad for me—which I've always known. In July, I didn't go through a hassle about cutting classes, or a hassle to arrive at cutting classes. I just cut. I noticed that I was accepting some of Fritz' concepts which do not agree with mine—they were becoming a part of me, and they were *not* my view. . . . All this crud about *whom* do you introject, and *why* do you do it? Why don't some psychologists notice what *they're* doing, and find out?

A line from the dream: Fritz, with real meanness and intense disgust—"Carl Rogers is a *liar*." Maybe it was, "I *hate* Carl Rogers because he is a *liar*." In the dream, "I" thought "No wonder Carl doesn't want to get together with Fritz." I tried hotseating it. That didn't work out.

I'll try something else from Gestalt. I'll ask "my Fritz."

Me: I thought these two men could get together. Now I see they can't. (I skip my Fritz, getting my answer without him.) They *don't* get together outside me. Neither one of them wants to. Inside me—

Not "my Fritz"—"my Barry." What shall I do about this? I have a headache. I know how I can dissolve this headache, and that I learned from Fritz. If I dissolve it, I won't know what the dream is telling me.

My Barry: So tell the dream.

Me: Dream, you bug me. I *don't* feel mean and hateful like that, and I don't feel hateful to Carl, or even mean.

Dream: Did I tell you that?

Me: No, Fritz said that, like it is *always* that way in dreams. "Every thing in the dream is some aspect of yourself."

Dream: (silence)

Me: So, you leave me to myself, to find my own answer. You gave me the clue, though, didn't you?

"Submissive" was in the dream, too. I was submissive to two guys, neither of whom I liked very well. They were two guys but really one. They went along with each other like one. They told me what to do and I did it, to please them. "To please them." Yeah. I didn't dis-like doing it: just didn't especially feel like doing it and wouldn't have done it except they wanted me to.

Still doing it—what I have always done. If I disliked doing something—*strongly* disliked it—I didn't do it. Otherwise, "they want me to and what does it matter?"

It wasn't for these guys' love. I didn't like them, except they were people and their peopleness I like.

Hmmm. I also did it "to show" that I was "free"—capable of doing it.

Like last night.

The whole thing is last night.

I did what I didn't feel like doing—though I wasn't especially set against it—to please others. But I didn't *want* to. I was submissive. Submissive to the group. Some of it, I enjoyed. I fought off some that I didn't. *Dis*-liked it to the point where I did something to keep it out of me, threw it back where it had come from, would *not* accept it. I felt good about that, that I kept it out of me. And at the same time, I didn't feel good about it because. . . . I didn't see the because. Now, I do. I wouldn't have got into it if I hadn't been submissive *to others* in the *first place*.

Hmmmm.

I let myself be put in the "hot seat"—Fritz said last night that he had noticed that we are not ready yet for the English language. The English language is *not ready yet for me*. Obviously, I put myself in the "hot seat" but that does *not* convey everything involved in this action. I did it from the wrong volition. Right volition is *me*. Right volition—the only should I should be submissive to—didn't get me off the couch where I was sitting.

I went to Lake Cowichan with Deke. We spoke of what we arrive at here and how we keep arriving at the same thing—lose it, find it again. After we got back, sitting in the kitchen finding it difficult to hang onto what I know, I realized that we keep losing it because the society in which we live is against our holding onto it. Language is against us. Etiquette is against us. Habit is against us. Conventions are against us. We need another kind of community, in which to become stronger—one with more willingness to change— with more understanding of the *basic* change (or "radical change" in Krishnamurti's language) we need to make and wanting to make it. Not a *should. I want to.*

When Deke said he was going to Lake Cowichan, I knew that I wanted to go. Then I thought "Maybe he wants to go alone." I washed that out and asked, "Do you mind having company?" Still the timid, roundabout approach. In Indian style, I could have said "I want to go to Lake Cowichan" and let Deke deal with it from there, and accepted whatever he said of himself.

I told Deke this on the way to Cowichan and we practiced it a little. This felt good, like a veil of cobwebs taken from my eyes.

That's what I want—a place to practice, and people to practice with. We were doing that more in June and July. In August when so many new people came, that got busted up. Beginning in September, I thought, "Gestalt has got watered down, so much."

In this morning's group, some people were joshing about "What kind of breakthrough did you have?" "I had a Freudian break-through." "I had a Reichian breakthrough," and so on. I said, "I had a Barry breakthrough." Natalie wanted to know what that was, and I couldn't say what it was. I could only say some things that were parts of it. Out of that expression, a few minutes later, I knew what a "Barry breakthrough" was, and held back the answer because "it wouldn't be understood." I told the group what was going on in me, washed away my censor and said it: "I used Gestalt (in working on my dream), broke the rules of Gestalt, and that is Gestalt."

No one showed any sign of comprehension and I wasn't bothered.

That's my diploma.

I haven't left the campus yet but I'm on my way—to Hornby Island for a week, staying at and looking over a place which Fritz thinks of moving to and expanding. It sounds like a possibility for what Fritz has in mind—a "satellite" system with a center in the center, and around it like petals, "movement" "therapy" "art" and so on. That's not what I want. I want a place—mine is much more difficult to talk about. His is easy to understand. That makes mine look woozy but it *isn't*. Unformed, yes. Let all these activities arise out of *us*, in their own way, whatever that is, with Gestalt contributing to the freeing. All these things grew out of us in the first place—that's how they began. I want a new beginning.

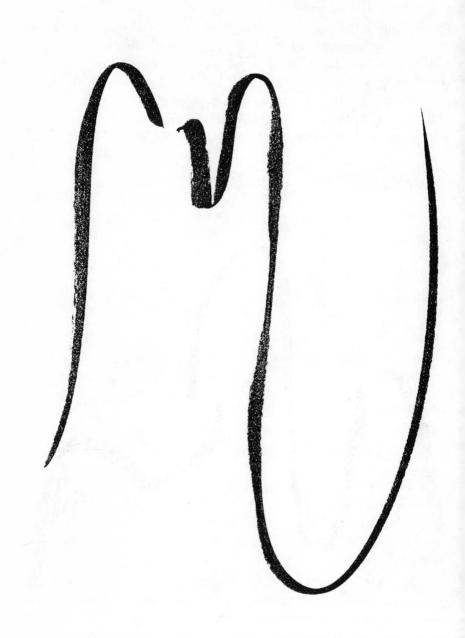

California, 1970.

Life doesn't move the way we tell or write it—or think it should—or try to make it. It goes more like this:

Fritz was concerned that most trainees didn't latch onto Gestalt. They used the gimmicks, without understanding. Good things can happen, doing this, but that is not Gestalt. It can become anti-Gestalt.

In my cabin one evening in November, Fritz said, "They are playing Gestalt games." He drank some of the hot chocolate with sweetened whipped cream, which he liked very much. "I've got to find some way to teach it," he said, meaning, to teach it in a way that this wouldn't happen.

I was bothered too, by what I called "watered-down Gestalt," which seemed to get farther and farther from Gestalt. In my gestalt community, I knew that wouldn't happen. People who came there would be committed to *really* getting the hang of it—just for themselves.

In Vancouver, a few weeks before the move to Cowichan, Fritz took me to Stan Fox's house to see rushes of some of the Aquarian films that were made of Fritz and Gestalt—instructional films. Afterward, we talked about a kibbutz, which was what he wanted.

He bought Cowichan because he loved the place on the lake, the down payment was only $12,000, and he could do something there until he could have what he wanted. There were similarities in what we wanted, and differences, too. "You are a psychotherapist and you want a training center," I told him. "I am not a therapist, don't ever want to *be* a therapist, and I want a gestalt community." I said that if I found a property large enough, he could have his training center on it. I visualized it a long way from the community, with lots of space between.

At Cowichan, I realized that a training center on the same property would louse up the community. The two were incompatible. I didn't understand this: I just knew it—in the same way that I knew that some things at Cowichan were sprouting me and others were bashing me down. Now, I understand that, too.

Sometimes, last winter, Fritz' problem in training Gestalt therapists came to my mind. I wrote to him in Berlin, "You want to find some way to teach it. How do we learn it?" That felt like a good question—one that might lead to "how to teach it."

Yesterday, a seventy-six-year-old woman from Oregon came to see me. She had heard of me—and Gestalt—through a friend of hers in Australia, whom I had met there in March. She had read *Verbatim* and wanted me to work with her on a dream which troubled her. She had previously been the patient of a psychoanalyst, and had great difficulty staying with the dream. She would start re-living the dream and almost immediately veer off into "free associations" or case history—explanations, interpretations. The young man and the forest in her dream reminded her of an experience in Bali, and she started to tell me about that. It was very difficult for her to interrupt this and get back to the dream. The young man was somewhat like Jesus, and she started to tell me what she thinks of Jesus, about her religious background, and so on. The woman coming toward her in the dream reminded her of a graphologist whom she has not met, from whom she has had a reading. She had brought the analysis for me to read.

She understood her habit and knew that she wanted to break with it, and she had the greatest difficulty doing this. We spent more time getting back to the dream than we did with the dream, in the hour she was here. She got something out of both, and went off with confidence that she can work on her own dreams now. She'll do that, too. She wasn't quite ready to accept the message that she got from the dream, which was "Stop struggling!"

How many hours could we have spent in the Bali forest, with her religious background and beliefs, and with the graphologist, without arriving at this simple, direct message from the dream—from herself to herself?

Out of the time spent with her, in some way that I do not understand, I suddenly saw that if any of the people who have lived in my gestalt community—*really* lived there—should want to become therapists, they would be first-rate Gestalt therapists, using tools they understand.

I don't want to train therapists, and I wouldn't be training therapists, and out of this would come really good therapists—of which there are damn few around.

"How to teach it" is not to teach it.

How simple life is. Live with awareness, not by rules or conditioning or thinking or shoulds or shouldn'ts. How difficult it is to see all the rules and conditioning and thinking and shoulds and shouldn'ts which come between I and Thou, and between I and me. Clearly, this is not *mankind*, for all of them vary from place to place, from time to time, from culture to culture, from subculture to subculture. And when we try to break with this, we are likely to fall into another trap. Reaction from convention is still tied to the convention. Going from one opinion to another, I am still pinioned.

Awareness that I have an opinion is awareness. If I have an opinion about that, I'm trapped again, and not aware. "The music is loud and this tires me" is not opinion. It is observation. It's odd that living with facts is lively—ever-changing—and living with illusions becomes monotonous, repetitive, and dull. We live with illusions in the hope or expectation that sometime in the future something will take us out of our boredom.

Awareness.

Happening.

Happiness.

My new beginning has already begun. I still want a ranch or farm where, with some other people, I can strengthen my beginning, and where what happens out of all of us is unknown.

> Questioner: How can I be sure that I am seeing what to do?
> Krishnamurti: You can't see what to do, you can see only what not to do. The total negation of that road is the new beginning, the other road. This other road is not on the map, nor can it ever be put on any map. Every map is a map of the wrong road, the old road.

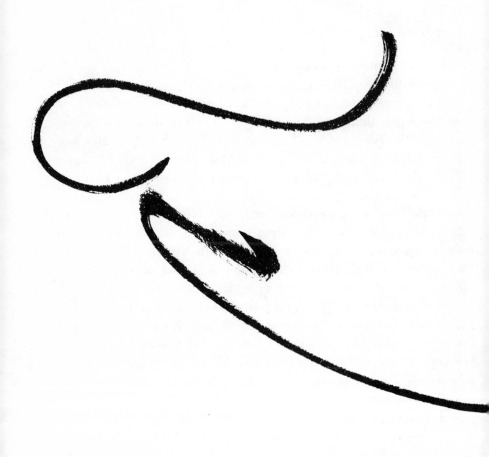

If the human episode
        now mostly self-bludgeoning
Continues to deny itself exposure
        to pure nature
It will die of rot.

And pure nature won't care.

                        — Puma Gallery
                          San Francisco